Designing *for* Print

AN IN-DEPTH GUIDE TO
PLANNING, CREATING, AND
PRODUCING SUCCESSFUL
DESIGN PROJECTS

CHARLES CONOVER

WILEY

Published by John Wiley & Sons, Inc., Hoboken, New Jersey
Published simultaneously in Canada

For general information on our other products and services or for technical support, please contact our Customer Care Department within the United States at (800) 762-2974, outside the United States at (317) 572-3993 or fax (317) 572-4002.

Wiley also publishes its books in a variety of electronic formats. Some content that appears in print may not be available in electronic books. For more information about Wiley products, visit our web site at www.wiley.com.

Library of Congress Cataloging-in-Publication Data:

Conover, Charles.
    Designing for Print: an in-depth guide to planning, creating, and producing successful design projects. Charles Conover.
        p. cm
    Includes bibliographical references and index.
    ISBN: 0-471-23723-X
Graphic Design (Typography) 2. Layout (Printing) 3. Desktop publishing. 4.
    Computer graphics. I. Title.

Z246.C57 2003
686.2′2—dc21   2003043260

Printed in the United States of America

10 9 8 7 6 5 4 3 2

Table of Contents

3 Chapter Three: Designing with Photographs

4 Chapter Four: Advanced Typography

4 **Chapter Four:** Advanced Typography

5 **Chapter Five:** Preparing Your Images

6 Chapter Six: Illustrating Effectively

7 Chapter Seven: Putting It All Together

Introduction

About The Author

Charles Conover spent fifteen years working in publishing as a designer. He spent ten years working as an Associate Art Director at *PC Magazine* in Manhattan. As a junior designer he managed the graphics department which was responsible for creating charts, graphs, and technical illustrations for the magazine. During that time he was also in charge of investigating emerging desktop publishing technologies for the art department. After that his responsibilities shifted to designing layouts for cover and feature stories. During his time at *PC Magazine* he received a DESI award for his technical illustration work and an award of design excellence from *Print Magazine* for his editorial design work.

While working as a designer, he also spent six years as an adjunct professor at Pratt Institute teaching computer painting techniques and basic animation. It was this experience that led to him teaching as a full time profession. In 1997 he became a full time professor teaching graphic design at Long Island University. He teaches a wide range of courses that cover numerous aspects of the design process including digital imaging and illustration, desktop publishing, typography, editorial design, and digital painting.

While he continues to work professionally as a freelance designer, he has also exhibited his work as a fine artist, primarily as a painter and printmaker, in New York galleries and museums.

Why I Wrote This Book

This book is directly linked and shaped by my experiences as a design professor. One of the first observations I made as a professor teaching graphic design was that students were entering the design field for different reasons than previous generations of designers had. The introduction of the computer as a design tool was largely responsible for this, causing an increasing number of students to consider design as a career path. I found that the general perception among students was that the computer made designing easier. While the computer has changed the methodology of design, the process of design essentially remains the same. Throughout this book I try to demonstrate how the traditional processes of planning and thumbnailing projects remain an essential part of the design process as well as show how accepted compositional and typographical techniques remain relevant no matter what tools are being used to design with.

Another thing I realized was that students were often confused as to how to properly integrate the software applications when they designed. I found that some students did not clearly grasp the role that each software application plays in the design process and were letting the computer limit them creatively. When they considered the many forms that a design might take, they limited themselves by thinking in terms of what the computer would allow them to do. One of the things that I stress in my courses is that the computer is simply a tool that helps designers bring their projects to fruition the way in which they envisioned them. Students need to strive to get what they want out of the computer, not let the computer dictate their designs. This ability requires both creative planning and technical expertise. This book is intended to introduce and clarify the proper ways that design applications can be used to competently design.

One method I used as a professor to help reinforce the technical demonstrations I gave in class was to develop related handouts. These handouts were designed to help guide the students through a particular task as well as serve as reference material should the technique be employed in a later project. Since my design background involved creating technical graphics that required information to be clearly explained, it was in my nature to create handouts that were attractive, concise, and clearly laid out. After a few years of creating these handouts I began to realize that I was accumulating a large set of useful handouts that might form the basis for a graphic design textbook. Much of the material found in this book originated from handouts that I designed to accompany computer demonstrations and class lectures that I conducted in college design courses.

The Objectives of this Book

This book addresses both the technical and theoretical aspects of design and how they can be applied to specific design projects. It is designed to introduce the reader to the general guidelines for successfully designing as well as provide illustrated step by step procedures for creating design elements that are commonly used. The first few chapters focus on applied design theory and cover the general design guidelines regarding proper and effective use of type, creating and using page formats and working grids to achieve interesting page compositions, and successfully combining type and imagery. The later chapters are more technical in nature and they cover advanced typographic treatments, technical illustration, and imaging techniques. The last chapter addresses how to properly format and prepare design projects for final output. The full color insert provides examples of finished designed projects that employ many of the techniques and approaches discussed within the book.

One major technical objective of this text is to show how to properly integrate the standard desktop publishing programs; *QuarkXpress*, *Illustrator*, and *Photoshop* to create well designed projects that will output accurately. To clarify this I have stressed using the right tool for the right job throughout this text. This should help the reader figure out the correct and most efficient way to solve technical design issues. While this book shows how to use certain tools as they apply to specific tasks, it also suggests alternative ways that a tool might be applied giving the reader a clear understanding of each tool's potential. Understanding the intricacies of each tool leads to discovering more complex ways of using them in conjunction with each other, and ultimately to developing personal methodologies and original techniques.

By covering the many different ways that a design can be approached I hope this book will help the reader become a versatile designer. Designers are essentially problem solvers and each design that they are faced with represents a puzzle. By being familiar with a range of compositional options and typographical and imaging techniques available to them, young designers will be better equipped to solve these problems and achieve successful design solutions. While the infographics and examples provided in this text are designed to demonstrate specific tasks they are also intended to serve as a starting point, to encourage the reader to experiment and build upon the provided techniques, so that they may develop design techniques of their own.

What This Book Is Not

This text is not meant to serve as a technical manual for any of the software programs that it covers. The text has been written with the assumption that the reader has a working knowledge of *QuarkXpress*, *Illustrator*, and *Photoshop*. The technical infographics are meant to demonstrate the proper way to approach specific design tasks but the book does not provide specific information on every tool included in these programs. It does not focus on a specific software program but rather on how to properly use the right program for the appropriate task.

How To Use This Book

The materials covered in this text apply to any advanced graphic design course that covers print media and requires students to be able to integrate the design programs successfully. While I recommend that students take the time to read the text in its entirety, the infographics are designed so that they cover their specific material completely without having to refer to previous examples. This makes the text skimable and designers can pick and choose particular techniques without having to read the entire text. Used in this way the book could also serve as a reference source for professionals.

Acknowledgements

I would thank Margaret Cummins, my editor at John Wiley & Sons, Inc., for giving me the chance to write this book and patiently guiding me through the process.

I would like to acknowledge the following people whose help along the way has directly lead to the writing of this book; Gerard Kunkel, for believing in me and providing me with my first real chance to design, Ken McAll for his collaboration and encouragement as a young artist, and to my mother, Val Conover, for raising me in a creative environment and exemplifying what a life as an artist means. I would also like to thank Thom O'Connor, David Foster, Dean Markadakis, and the Art department at *PC Magazine* for their support and generosity, and the Art Faculty at C.W. Post for showing me the academic ropes. And lastly, I want to thank my wife, Sohee Kim Conover, for her love, encouragement, impeccable clipping paths, and for always providing an honest second opinion.

Contributors

Thom O'Connor is the staff photographer at *PC Magazine*. Sohee Kim Conover is a designer and illustrator working in New York City. Alli Rufrano is a photographer and professor at Long Island University.

Chapter One
Planning Your Design

Planning a project is often the most fun and creative part of the design process. It is a time when you get to experiment and develop a range of possibilities for your design. It is also one of the most crucial times in that the decisions you make here will affect the entire project. Once you have committed to a design approach, much of the rest of the design work involves applying that approach to the elements found within the design and fine-tuning the project's overall look.

With that in mind, you need a clear understanding of a project before you begin to design, no matter what form your project takes, be it a CD cover, package design, or page layout. This will help you create a strong design that will effectively and attractively convey the project's message. In this section we look at how to initially plan and appropriately format your design so that it will be flexible and consistent. Most designers find that when the overall plan is not thoroughly thought out, the chances are greater that the final design will fall short of their expectations. Conceptualization, research, thumbnailing, and formatting are all essential parts of the design process.

Form and Function

The most obvious facet of design is its visual aspects—the typefaces, images, and layout that make up a design's look and feel. It is these aspects that are most commonly associated with graphic design. These elements are also what initially attracts the reader's attention. One sometimes overlooked aspect of design is function, the design's ability to fulfill its intended purpose. Function is the driving force in any design project. The true measure of a design's success is how well it satisfies the project's formal and functional demands. Great design is the product of strong aesthetic, conceptual, and technical skills. The first step in beginning any project is to start by conceptualizing the project to find an appropriate theme or metaphor for the design.

Conceptualizing a project is easiest when you have a clear understanding of the design's purpose. The fundamental mission of design, as with any art form, is to communicate. That communication may have different purposes: to persuade, to evoke a response, or to provide information. The designer's role is to find a way to effectively convey that message. In order for designers to do this, they must have a clear grasp of the project's intended purpose. This is achieved through clear communication between the designer and the client. These discussions should cover all aspects of the design, from conceptual issues to production and budget concerns. Understanding the breadth of a project and taking all the issues into account will help you to better visualize the form your design should take.

This chapter will introduce you to numerous ways to approach your design. Many designers find that starting a project is often the hardest part and that once they actually begin to design, the process gets easier. The hardest part for many artists is putting down the first stroke. The samples provided in this chapter should help you jump-start your own projects. There are always a number of design solutions for any given project. Understanding this will make you a more versatile designer and help you cope when a design changes, either because the design demands it or because the client does. Magazine layouts are often changed to accommodate the last-minute sale of an advertisement or a late-breaking news story. While it is always preferable not to have to rework a design, the bottom line is that those recently sold advertisements that your design must now accommodate are helping to pay your salary. Being versatile, patient, and amenable to change are helpful characteristics for a designer who works with deadlines and whose designs are subject to change.

Type, Image, and Composition
Designers have many means of getting a message across through their designs. The most common vehicles used to communicate are type and image. Using words is often the most concise way to make a point because language is the most direct form of communication. Photos also can be used, and the right image can often have more visual impact while communicating a literal meaning almost as clearly as type does. The image you choose, the way in which you use it, and how it interacts with your type are integral to the design's ability to communicate. There are

Gathering Imagery: 3D Objects

Scanning 3D objects is a great way to create original art. In essence you are using the scanner as a camera. Here's a look at some different ways to incorporate these methods into your design.

CLIPPING PATHS Compose objects on the scanner before scanning and then create paths to silhouette items. The china marker above has a drop shadow applied in Photoshop.

CONSISTENCY To gain a consistent look throughout a university Web site, different art tools were used to represent each program within the department. Background leather texture is from a scanned portfolio.

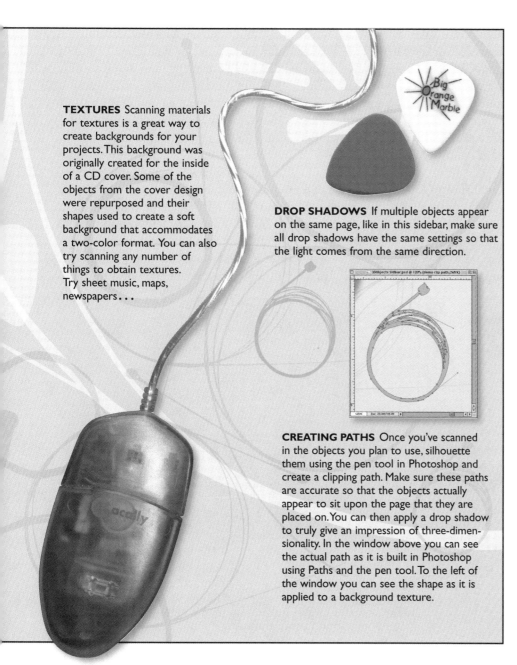

TEXTURES Scanning materials for textures is a great way to create backgrounds for your projects. This background was originally created for the inside of a CD cover. Some of the objects from the cover design were repurposed and their shapes used to create a soft background that accommodates a two-color format. You can also try scanning any number of things to obtain textures. Try sheet music, maps, newspapers...

DROP SHADOWS If multiple objects appear on the same page, like in this sidebar, make sure all drop shadows have the same settings so that the light comes from the same direction.

CREATING PATHS Once you've scanned in the objects you plan to use, silhouette them using the pen tool in Photoshop and create a clipping path. Make sure these paths are accurate so that the objects actually appear to sit upon the page that they are placed on. You can then apply a drop shadow to truly give an impression of three-dimensionality. In the window above you can see the actual path as it is built in Photoshop using Paths and the pen tool. To the left of the window you can see the shape as it is applied to a background texture.

also other subtle ways of composing a design to engage a reader's attention. By placing emphasis on appropriate elements, a designer can control the composition's focal point, and in the process help direct the reader's eye. Using these methods, a designer can also control the visual pacing of the piece. Each project forces the designer to address questions regarding the role of type, image, and composition in communicating the project's message.

A Word About Words

While designers often depend on copy writers to supply them with copy, it is not uncommon for designers to contribute to the writing of a project, as words are always directly related to visuals. Meetings between art and editorial staffs are often collaborative efforts where writers and graphic designers work together to develop their articles. In the process it is not uncommon for writers to contribute visual ideas or for graphic designers to suggest possible headlines. Having strong verbal and conceptual skills is a plus for any designer, and there are methods and aids you can use to enhance these skills.

Words often help to stimulate visual ideas, and one way to begin a project is by playing with words. Start by writing a list of words that relate to the project's focus. If a project needs a tag line, consider catchy phrases, puns, or plays on words. Popular song and movie titles are a great resource for headlines, titles, and tag lines because they are shared by the common culture and their references are widely understood. Start with the dictionary and a thesaurus. Look up words you already know. Sometimes just reading the words used to define it will spark an idea. A word's secondary definitions can also provide food for thought. Many copy writers use reference materials to help them synthesize words. There are a wide range of writing aids available: phrase finders and books of idioms, quotations, rhymes, antonyms, and synonyms can be found in the reference section of your local bookstore or at the library.

Developing Conceptual Visuals

Along with a list of associated words and phrases, create a list of visual ideas of related objects and images. Drawing analogies or making references through the use of metaphor and symbol is a common design approach. Well-known stories and shared cultural references are great vehicles for making a point. For example, magazine articles on the Kennedy administration will often use Camelot and King Arthur's Roundtable as a theme to convey the grace and ideology of the period. For example, let's say you are designing a project whose purpose is to emphasize the multiple features of a particular device. Here you might consider using an image of a juggler, an octopus, or a Swiss

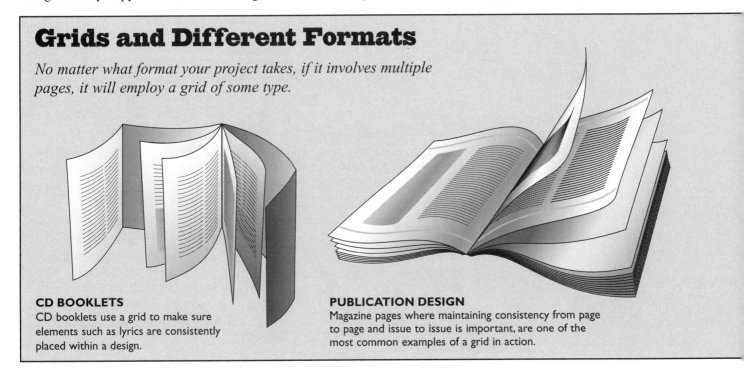

Grids and Different Formats

No matter what format your project takes, if it involves multiple pages, it will employ a grid of some type.

CD BOOKLETS
CD booklets use a grid to make sure elements such as lyrics are consistently placed within a design.

PUBLICATION DESIGN
Magazine pages where maintaining consistency from page to page and issue to issue is important, are one of the most common examples of a grid in action.

Army knife, all images that can act as a metaphor for versatility and an ability to handle many tasks.

A couple of suggestions regarding project conceptualization: Don't be afraid to include an idea that you think may be weak. You, or a collaborator, may later see it in a different light and it could spur an idea. You never know where a good idea will come from. Try making it a practice to write down your ideas when they come. Nothing is more frustrating than forgetting a

good idea, and it often is the case that ideas are fleeting. Another method of preparing a design is to look at how other designers have handled similar material. The better you understand the material, the more likely you are to successfully handle it. Approach your project from as many angles as possible before you make any concrete decisions about its final form.

Gathering Imagery

Most professional designers have a budget to contract with photographers and illustrators to create art-

work specifically for their projects. Student designers don't have the luxury of commissioning original artwork, so they need to search elsewhere for their imagery. Let's discuss a few ways of collecting resources and creating artwork for your designs.

The rise of stock photography over the last ten years has provided students with a means of designing with photographs without resorting to scanning previously printed material or using their own photographs. Most stock houses provide sample library CDs of images that students can use royalty-free. While these images contain imbedded watermarks that cannot be removed, the files are high-resolution and perfect for prototype designs. The watermarks are purposely unobtrusive, as the stock house is hoping that once you get the client's approval on a project you will then purchase the image and the rights to use it.

Along with stock photography there are collections of images in the public domain that can be used free of charge. They provide a great source for a variety of nostalgic imagery. These diverse collections might range from a series of etchings of Victorian dress to Art Nouveau motifs and borders. Dover Publications offers a wide range of

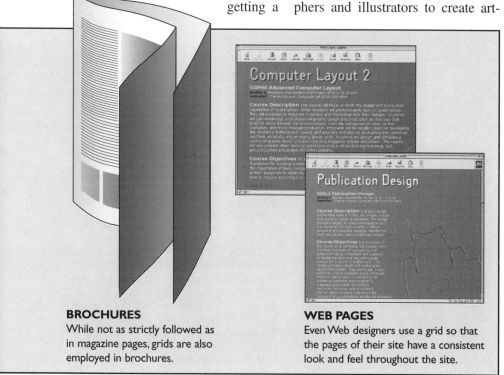

BROCHURES
While not as strictly followed as in magazine pages, grids are also employed in brochures.

WEB PAGES
Even Web designers use a grid so that the pages of their site have a consistent look and feel throughout the site.

inexpensive resource books (see index). These images are generally of a higher quality than many of the royalty-free clip art collections available. I recommend avoiding the use of electronic clip art. It can be low-quality and rarely matches the content of your project in a very specific manner.

Other methods of getting visual materials include using your own artwork or scanning resource materials. If you have strong illustrative or photographic skills, you should certainly incorporate them into your work. But there are other methods that you can employ, such as scanning in textures and three-dimensional objects. Scanning materials for textures is an effective way of creating interesting backgrounds. For a university Web site, for example, the designer scanned in a series of art tools to represent the different areas within the art department. A similar approach could be applied to a brochure design for a music school. There are numerous flat and three-dimensional objects that can be scanned and used as textures or images. Related items such as sheet music, guitar picks, and instrument strings can be placed directly on the scanner and then with some manipulation be suit-

Developing a Working Grid

An initial step in designing multiple-page projects is to create a working grid. A wide range of grids can be used for different functions.

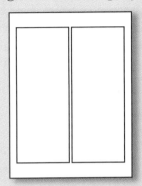

Two-Column Format

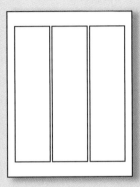

Three-Column Format

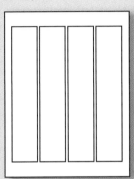

Four-Column Format

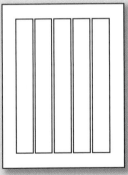

Five-Column Format

Page size helps determine the formatting of columns. Five- and six-column formats work best when used within larger pages. Generally the smaller the page size, the fewer the number of columns it will be able to accommodate. Too many columns can create overly narrow text widths and awkwardly set body copy.

system maintains a consistent look and feel from page ■ to ■ page. While it's easy to see that the similarity and consis

■ Justified alignment creates awkward spacing.

tency of color used throughout a design, what is less noticeable is the relationships of elements to each other on

Here flush left text reduces large spaces between words.

NARROW COLUMNS Column width and type size directly affect each other. Narrow columns cause text to break awkwardly, especially when it's set justified. Because it forces alignment to both right and left margins, large gaps can occur between the words. Note the even letterspacing of the text on the right. A change in alignment makes awkward, uneven type easy to read even at a thin width.

Margins and Gutters

Margins are the space between the page edge and the columns. Margins can be set equally or unevenly depending on the page orientation.

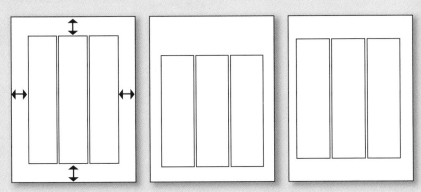

The margins are set evenly on the example at far left, unevenly on the two examples to the right. Uneven margins in the middle example allow for more white space on the page and give an openness to the design. The margins on the example at far right allow for additional space in the gutter for facing pages.

Grid Variations

Grids are not limited to equal column widths and margins. Experiment with the grid formats according to your project's needs.

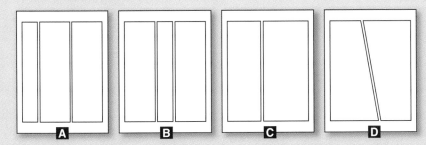

In A and B the grids include a narrower column that could accommodate support text such as a timeline or glossary.

Uneven columns in C break up the page interestingly. The diagonal direction in D is less conventional but effective.

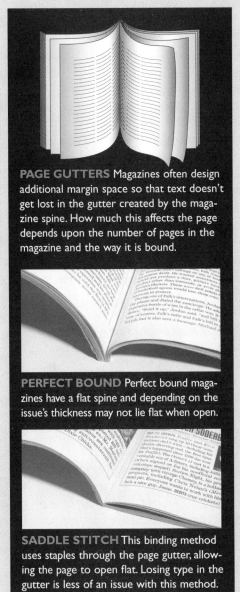

PAGE GUTTERS Magazines often design additional margin space so that text doesn't get lost in the gutter created by the magazine spine. How much this affects the page depends upon the number of pages in the magazine and the way it is bound.

PERFECT BOUND Perfect bound magazines have a flat spine and depending on the issue's thickness may not lie flat when open.

SADDLE STITCH This binding method uses staples through the page gutter, allowing the page to open flat. Losing type in the gutter is less of an issue with this method.

able to design with. When you scan three-dimensional objects in this way you are essentially using the scanner as a camera.

There are many reference materials that designers use to indirectly influence their designs, such as design books and magazines. Most designers collect books on a wide range of design schools and styles, and these are especially useful when you need to capture the feel of a particular period. For example you might consult a collection of menu designs from the 1950s for a design that required a retro feel. These kinds of books can provide a sense of the typography, color, shapes, and motifs reminiscent of a period.

As a general rule, collecting more visuals than a project requires will provide you with more options. The time to experiment with a design's possibilities is in this initial stage. If you begin with only a few images, you may be forced to make them work, which means chances are they won't. Occasionally you may find the perfect image right at the start of a project, but this is the exception, not the rule.

Creating a Game Plan

Once you have done your research and gathered appropriate reference materials, you can begin to sketch

Placing Elements Within the Grid

Single Pages

The simplest way of using a grid is to place the design elements in perfect alignment with columns, therefore letting the column format determine the object's dimensions.

Corners are a natural position for placement of design elements.

Avoid placing your elements in positions that create small blocks of text that force the reader's eye to jump around.

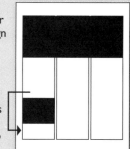

BLEEDS The image on the top left "bleeds" off the edge of the page. This helps vary the grid.

SUBDIVISION Another way to expand the grid is to subdivide it by having the object straddle the columns.

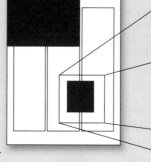

These formats include magazines, brochures, CD booklets, package design, even web pages. The ■ grid system maintains a consistent look ■ and feel ■ from page ■ to page. While it's easy to see that the similarity and consistency of color used throughout a design, what is less noticeable is the relationships of elements to each other on the page. If you consistently handle your design elements ■ in terms ■ of spacing (text runarounds, number of lines between objects, baseline grid placement (x-height, ca

awkward spacing

▲ Elements straddling columns should be placed evenly between the columns. Surrounding type should be wide enough to avoid awkward spaces in the text

Four- and five-column formats are more diverse compositionally but also have pitfalls. Thinner columns make it harder to subdivide the grid and still maintain readability.

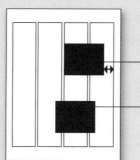

This element subdivides the format awkwardly, creating an extremely narrow column width to the right of the image.

Here the same element is placed so it straddles three columns in a way that doesn't create narrow column widths. This type of placement breaks up the grid and enhances the composition.

Facing Pages and Spreads

◄ Splitting up image and text on facing pages is common. But without elements that help to integrate the two pages, the overall effect may be of two separate pages rather than one integrated design.

◄ Running the image across four columns is one way of integrating the two pages into the design, helping the reader see the design as one composition rather than two facing pages.

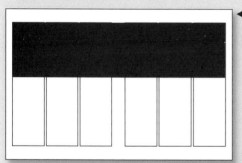

◄ Running elements across the spread can be an effective way to bring each page into the design. Note that the image's depth doesn't perfectly divide the page, creating an unequally balanced (and more interesting) composition.

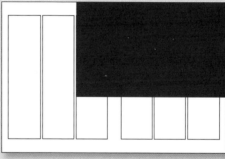

◄ Positioning the image in the upper right and having the element bleed off two edges gives the impression that the image continues outside the frame of reference, creating a sense of implied space.

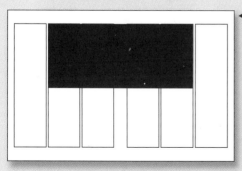

◄ The placement of the element helps draw the reader's eye into the center of the page. Images that run across the gutter should be positioned so that no pertinent information gets lost in between the pages.

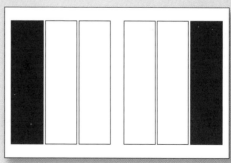

◄ The relationship of these elements creates a sense of balance. Because of this positioning the two elements seem connected by similarity in size and positioning and yet stand in opposition.

out the design. Sketching, even in a rough state, is integral to developing your layout. With the introduction of the computer to design, this initial stage is becoming increasingly overlooked. Sketching is always worth the small amount of time that it requires. Creating a small "thumbnail" sketch provides you with the opportunity to solve many of the basic challenges posed by a design before you actually begin to build it. By including all of the fundamental elements within your thumbnails, you will have a well-thought-out

plan for your design. The more complete the thumbnail is, the less likely you will be to overlook an element and then have to readjust your layout later.

Formatting the Project

Once you have come up with a working concept or theme for the project and have created a thumbnail, you can begin to build the structure of the design. If your project involves multiple pages, you will need to start by creating a page format.

Custom Page Formats

The grid is a commonly used device that acts as the underlying structure of a design. The most obvious example of a grid system is text columns. The first thing you do when you create a new QuarkXpress document is define the vertical grid of columns and the page margins. The parameters that you set here will affect your entire design, as all of the elements will be placed in relationship to these column guides and margins. Think of the grid not as a constraining limitation, but rather

Sketching out a Game Plan: Thumbnailing

Thumbnail sketches are a prerequisite for planning any design project. They help develop the overall look and form of your design.

Before you actually begin to build your layout and focus on the specific elements that make up a design, you need to create a master plan for the project. The easiest and most direct way to do this is to sketch out by hand a rough drawing or "thumbnail" of the layout. The more complete you make the plan, including as many specifics as possible, the easier it will be when you are designing the pages. This ensures that you haven't left out any integral elements before you begin.

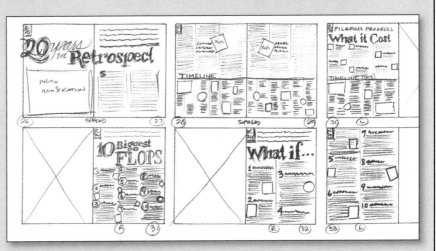

THE DRAWING BOARD This thumbnail layout for a magazine article includes all of its elements in great detail, as well as addressing page orientation. It's a great way to get a feel for an article's pacing.

as a means to make sense of and bring order to a design, a device that helps you maintain consistency throughout your project. Grid systems can take numerous forms, and designers employ them in a variety of ways to produce interesting compositions. One common method is to subdivide the grid. An example of this would be to set up a six-column grid for a page that contains three columns of text. This allows the designer to use half-column increments, thus adding versatility to the design and helping break up the rigidness of a strict grid.

Setting up the Vertical Grid

There are a few things that will determine the number of columns that can be used. The most important of these is page size. Generally, the smaller the page size, the fewer the columns that can be accommodated. For example, a standard-size magazine like *Time* can comfortably accommodate a three- or four-column format, whereas a large-format magazine like *Rolling Stone* can be designed with five or six columns. The smaller format can't accommodate five or six columns because the columns would be too narrow to properly set paragraph text. Column width is essential to type readability, and when a col-

umn gets too thin, the body copy tends to break awkwardly.

Column width and type size directly affect each other. The size of the paragraph text and the typeface used play a role in determining column width. For instance, while a one-inch column width might be fine if you are using a condensed version of Futura set at 8/9, the same column width will not accommodate text set in 13/14 Times Roman. Like type size, the alignment of the text also determines how type appears in narrow columns, especially when the type is justified. Narrow justified text doesn't work well because it forces alignment on both right and left margins, causing large gaps between words. This can be fixed by adjusting hyphenation settings, inserting soft returns, forcing word breaks, and writing to fit, but this is laborious work that might all have to be redone should any late copy editing or text changes be made. A simpler way to fix this would be to change the alignment to flush left, which will reduce awkward spacing and uneven type breaks.

Margins and Gutters

Along with setting the number of columns on your page, you will also control the positioning of these

columns by setting the margins and gutters. *Gutters* can refer to the space between the columns and also to the space between two pages when they face each other. *Margins* are the area surrounding your columns. Large margins give a sense of space and openness to a design, but they also reduce the amount of space that is allotted for columns and consequently affect how much type can fit on a page. If your design is text-intensive, your margins will need to be smaller. Margins can be set centered and evenly spaced or can be set to allow unequal space around the columns. One thing to consider when setting up margins is the page orientation. If the pages will face one another, then a gutter will form within the spine where the two pages meet. Depending on the type of binding used and the number of pages in the project, the designer may consider allotting additional space to the inside margins so that type does not get lost in the page gutter.

The Horizontal Grid: Baselines

The baseline grid is an unsung hero of multiple-page design. It quietly sits below the surface, less obvious than the column grid but equally important, as it ensures the cross alignment of body copy. The baseline grid should be used for any project that has linked columns of text running throughout its pages. The most important reason to use a baseline grid is to ensure that your column text cross-aligns. *Cross alignment* refers to the alignment of text in adjacent columns. When paragraph text does not cross-align, it has a sloppy and nervous look.

Setting up the baseline grid is essentially a three-step process. First you need to set up your text leading. Then set the increment of your baseline grid to match your leading. This can be done by adjusting the document preferences for paragraphs. The last step is to select the text and make it snap to the grid. This function can be found in the Format settings. Just as all the elements sit in relation to the column grid, all running body copy and images will align in a relationship to the baseline grid. Once you've set your margins, columns, and gutter widths and created a baseline grid, you essentially have a grid of vertical and horizontal guides that will help you place your elements in precise and consistent relationships to each other.

Maintaining Consistency
The degree to which you rely on a grid system will depend on the proj-

Layout Variations

Because these projects contain folded multiple pages, the layout must work with the 3D form. Projects such as CD booklets and brochures can take many forms.

CD Booklets

In a CD booklet design composed to fit in a standard jewel case, the page size remains constant. Construction of the booklet itself offers a wide range of variations. One pitfall of this format is its small page size. It can be a challenge to accommodate large amounts of text, such as lyrics. This set of samples incorporates combinations of folds and booklets.

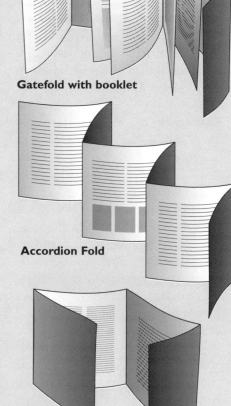

Gatefold with booklet

Single Fold

Accordion Fold

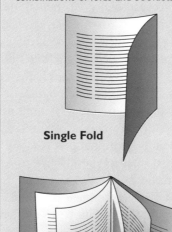

Booklet

Gatefold

Brochures

Unlike CD booklets, a brochure's page size can vary greatly. It can be folded in simple or complex ways. Remember when building your mechanical to trim inside folding pages slightly so that they fold comfortably.

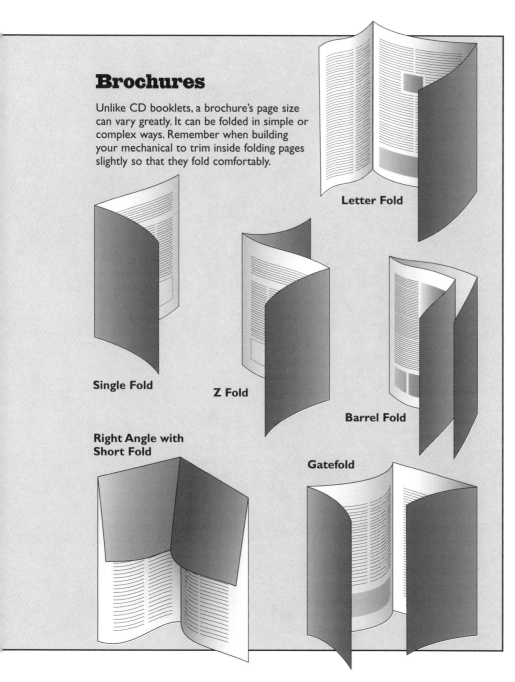

Letter Fold

Single Fold

Z Fold

Barrel Fold

Right Angle with Short Fold

Gatefold

ect. A poster design that doesn't require columns of text will depend less on a strict grid than a page from a magazine. But even in the simplest of designs there is usually some sort of measurement system in place. Objects are always placed in logical relationships to each other, no matter how few elements are included in a design.

Formats that involve multiple pages will invariably require a working grid. These formats include magazines, brochures, CD booklets, and even Web sites. The grid system maintains a consistent look and feel from page to page. While it's easy to see the similarity of color used throughout a design, the consistency in the placement of elements in relationship to each other from page to page is much more subtle. If you consistently handle your elements in terms of spacing and placement on the page, this subtlety will be conveyed and each page will feel like it belongs to an overall design. This consistency involves more than simply placing elements uniformly on the baseline grid. A strong, consistent design will handle all the smaller details, such as runaround distance, paragraph indents, and holding rules, in a similar manner.

Building Mechanicals

Once you've figured out the format your project will take, you need to build the mechanical. The mechanical needs to be built precisely and accurately so that the printer will know how to trim, fold, or perforate your design.

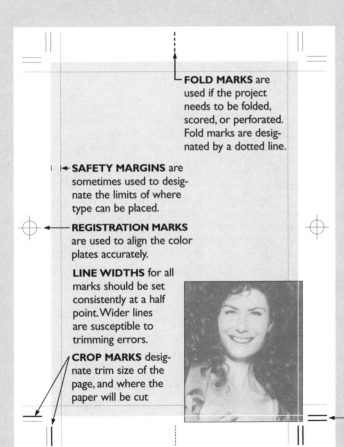

FOLD MARKS are used if the project needs to be folded, scored, or perforated. Fold marks are designated by a dotted line.

SAFETY MARGINS are sometimes used to designate the limits of where type can be placed.

REGISTRATION MARKS are used to align the color plates accurately.

LINE WIDTHS for all marks should be set consistently at a half point. Wider lines are susceptible to trimming errors.

CROP MARKS designate trim size of the page, and where the paper will be cut

DIE CUTS Die cuts are indicated on a mechanical by creating the shape to be cut. The line should be created in a spot color so that this information is output on a separate plate.

IMAGE BLEED If you have images that bleed off the page, you should allow some of the image area to run off the page edge so that when it it trimmed your image will fully bleed off the page. This leaves room for error if the page is trimmed improperly.

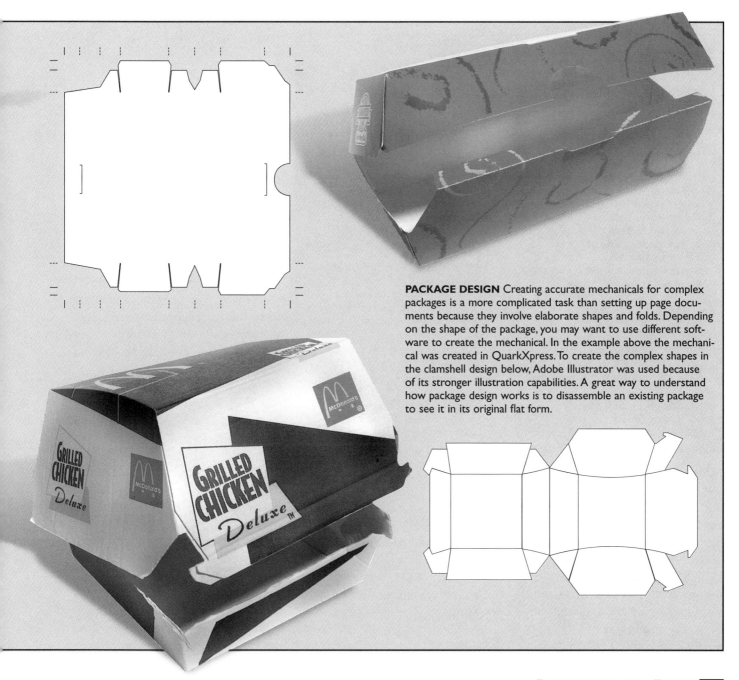

PACKAGE DESIGN Creating accurate mechanicals for complex packages is a more complicated task than setting up page documents because they involve elaborate shapes and folds. Depending on the shape of the package, you may want to use different software to create the mechanical. In the example above the mechanical was created in QuarkXpress. To create the complex shapes in the clamshell design below, Adobe Illustrator was used because of its stronger illustration capabilities. A great way to understand how package design works is to disassemble an existing package to see it in its original flat form.

A Room of One's Own

Having a good workspace is essential for any profession. While designers require the right equipment, they also need a space that is conducive to the creative process.

Since the personal makeup of graphic designers varies so much, so do the spaces that they prefer to work in. Some designers have no problems creating in cluttered offices, while others require a sense of order. Whatever your character is, every designer requires a suitable workspace. Whatever type of environment you prefer, solitude or chaos, here are a few suggestions that may help you work more efficiently and reduce frustration.

- **REST YOUR EYES** If you have a window, look out of it occasionally to allow your eyes to rest and refocus.
- **COMFORT** Your chair shouldn't cause any back discomfort. It should also have armrests, preferably adjustable ones.

- **PERSONALIZE YOUR SPACE** In the workspace above, a running list of font samples is posted on the wall for quick reference. Designers will often surround their workspaces with visual references.
- **MONITOR** A large-screen monitor is preferable for designing print projects.
- **INPUT DEVICES** Optical mice are well worth the investment when you consider how frustrating cleaning and working with mice that have dirty trackballs can be.

Master Files and Templates

All magazines rely on a style book that outlines the standard styling and placement for every element that regularly appears on the pages of the magazine. The style book includes type and color specifications as well as positioning instructions and advertisement configurations. It ensures consistency not only within a single issue of a magazine, but also from issue to issue. Another useful technique that will help you manage a project is to set up a system of master templates. These types of files can be applied to any design project and, depending on your needs, they can be set up in QuarkXpress, Illustrator, or Photoshop.

A Photoshop master file would contain all the relevant layers and paths. These files might be used when you want to make sure the position of elements is consistent throughout a design's pages. This technique is commonly used by Web designers who use Photoshop to build initial page designs. While each Web page on the site may contain different content, the positioning of fundamental elements that appear on every page, such as navigation buttons, will remain the same. Essentially the master file contains all the layers for the entire site, and it is from this file that all the separate pages originate. While there will inevitably be some pages that break standard format, this system will allow your site to have an integrated feel.

An Illustrator master page might contain a logo file that will appear within your layout. Logo files must remain consistent, and companies go to great lengths to make sure their logo, and hence their corporate image, is presented in a consistent manner. This file includes all possible size and color variations for the logo. Color variations usually consist of a one-color version and a black and white one.

Another way you might use a master Illustrator file is when you are creating a series of similar type treatments that will appear throughout a project. You would use this file each time that you need to create a headline variation, as the file already contains the type size, color, and line weight information. Like the Photoshop master file, all of your related type treatments will originate from this file.

Building Master Pages

Just as the baseline grid helps maintain consistency throughout your design, building master pages in QuarkXpress ensures that all foundational elements are placed accurately on every page. Because QuarkXpress is a page layout program, it has a unique system for building master pages, one that is powerful and easy to use. It can save a designer hours of tedious work as it seamlessly maintains consistency over the entire project. Essentially when you create a master page you are building a template that has all the formats and page elements in preset positions. These formats include margin, gutter, and column information as well as any elements that need to be positioned precisely on all pages. For instance, you do not want to manually place a page number, commonly called a foot and folio, on every page of your layout. When you manually place these elements, the margin for error is high. It is easy to incorrectly number the pages, especially if pages are added or deleted during your layout, or to inconsistently position the page numbers from page to page. By using master pages, you will never have to worry about such problems, as QuarkXpress has an autopagination feature that automatically numbers the pages and updates the numbering if the order of the pages changes.

Any element that you need to appear consistently throughout your pages can be used as a master element. They include linked column text boxes, rules between these columns, background tints, and eyebrows. Eyebrows are usually elaborate section heads that typically appear in the top outside corner of a page to define the specific section that the page appears within. When these elements are placed on the master page, they become master elements. Once you have created a master page, you can simply drag out a copy and all of the page's foundation elements will appear precisely as you positioned them. From this master page you can create other master page variations. Different versions of master pages are often created according to their page orientation. For instance, the positioning of elements may change depending on whether the page falls on the right- or left-hand side or appears as a facing page on a spread.

Master pages are a valuable time-saving device for designers. Designers working on a weekly magazine don't have time to build each page from scratch every week. Because of tight deadlines, designers depend on these features to help them create well-designed pages in a timely manner.

Along with master pages, designers also create libraries of commonly used elements that can be set up in QuarkXpress. This allows them to simply drag out prebuilt elements and then adjust them to specifically meet the requirements of their page layout. Another time-saving device that can be set up in a master file are style sheets, which enable designers to flow text into a design so that it is already styled according to the magazine's specifications. By taking advantage of all these methods, designers are free to spend their time focused on design considerations rather than page production.

Chapter Two
Designing with Type

Once you've worked out a plan for your project, one that includes an accurate mechanical, a working formatted grid, and a thumbnail sketch, you can begin to focus on the elements that comprise the design: predominantly type and imagery. In this chapter we explore working with type. Because no element is more integral to a design's ability to communicate than type, it must be sensitively handled to be effective. Type can take on numerous forms according to its intended purpose and can be styled to address a wide range of functions. Type can be used for captions, headlines, body copy, tabular material, even as a texture. In each case the type is styled differently, according to its purpose. For example, a caption contributes to a design in a much different way than a headline. While there are general guidelines for working with all type, these different functions greatly determine the form the type takes.

Being able to style type so that it is both attractive and effective starts with understanding the function that the type serves. This section covers the basic guidelines for working with type, as well as how to create attractive type treatments. Some of the areas it covers include type pairing, designing display type, formatting body copy, and selecting appropriate typefaces.

Type Basics

Generally all typefaces fall into one of two styles: serif or sans serif. Serifs are marks or flourishes that appear around the extremities of the letter form. The text that you are reading at this moment is set in a serif face. Serif faces are sometimes referred to as roman faces, as their character forms reflect the chiseled type of ancient Rome. While these serifs adorn the character, they also help with readability. The serifs give the typeface's characters a uniqueness that makes them quickly recognizable. The horizontal direction of the serifs also helps to guide the reader's eye horizontally across the page.

The more modern sans serif faces are designed without serifs. The word *sans* comes from the French word for "without". They are also referred to as grotesque or gothic faces. Most sans serif typefaces are designed with an evenness of stroke. These two styles of typefaces, serif and sans serif, have unique characteristics. Because of these differences in form, they often work well when used in combination with each other.

Display Type and Body Copy

Most type takes on one of two forms depending on its intended use: display type or body copy. Display type refers to headline or title text, usually set in a large size. The purpose of display type is to communicate the broader message of a project and to attract the reader's attention. Body copy refers to paragraph text and it provides the reader with more specific information. Body copy might consist of a single paragraph in an advertisement, or linked columns of running text in a newsletter. The typefaces used within a design are selected according to their purpose.

Most typefaces are designed to perform different tasks. Intricate and elaborate typefaces are usually best used as display type, whereas typefaces that maintain their readability at smaller sizes work well when used as as body copy. Some font designs are more versatile, especially those families with wide ranges of weight variations, and can be used as either display type or body copy.

Type Pairing

It is generally advisable to limit the number of typefaces used within a design. Too many faces can give a design a busy look. One common practice designers use in their approach to selecting typefaces is type pairing. Type pairing involves matching serif and sans serif faces to find a combination in which the two selected typefaces complement each other. Most designs require no more than a few well-chosen typefaces. Successful type pairing is a matter of selecting typefaces that work aesthetically with each other while also reflecting the feel of a project. Leaf through a well-designed magazine or notice the opening credits of a movie and chances are you will see type pairing in action.

Type pairing does not limit the designer to using only two typefaces, but rather includes the entire families of each representative

Type Fundamentals

Before you start designing with type you'll need to understand how type is set and functions, as well as be familiar with the many different terms that are associated with its usage.

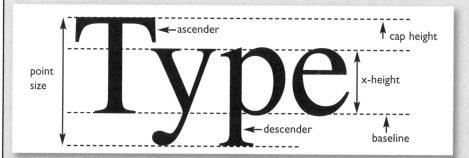

THE ELEMENTS OF TYPE All typefaces share similar elements. These are the basic type elements and reference points that designers commonly use and refer to.

Leading

Leading is the space between the lines of text, the vertical space from baseline to baseline. In the examples below, the top sample has no additional leading added to it. The lower sample has an additional 6 points of leading, which increases the vertical spacing.

16/16
While fragments of preindustrial culture persisted well into the 1900s, the influence of the period would dimin-

16/22
While fragments of preindustrial culture persisted well into the 1900s, the influence of the period would dimin-

TYPE HISTORY
The term *leading* is a holdover from the days of hand-set letterpress type. To increase line spacing, thin sheets of lead were placed between the letters. In photo above you can see the strip of lead.

Serif and Sans Serif Typefaces

While all typefaces have unique characteristics, most are classified as either serif or sans serif. Serifs are ornamental flourishes or feet that appear on character strokes.

SERIFS give each character a uniqueness and help increase readability when type is set as body copy.

Serifs

Sans serif

SANS SERIF typefaces do not have serifs and are typified by their evenness of stroke and high readability, especially when read from a distance.

SLAB SERIF
Egiziano Classic

CUPPED SERIF
Garamond

FINE SERIF
Bodoni

SERIF TYPES There are many serif types. For example, Egyptian or slabbed serifs are heavy and hard-edged. Cupped serifs are rounded and curve slightly.

Serif or sans serif typefaces are available in a range of thick and thin designs, referred to as condensed and extended faces.

CONDENSED
Industria Solid

EXTENDED
Bank Gothic

Type Attributes

Many fonts include a range of attributes which include bold, and italic variations.

Palatino

SERIF FACES are also called Roman faces. This is the standard face on which other attributes are based.

Palatino

BOLD TYPE is used for emphasis. Using bold type sporadically in text helps make it easier to skim.

Palatino

ITALICS are also called oblique faces. Their handwritten feel brings an intimacy and casualness to text.

Font Families

Each font is part of a larger typeface family that includes a wide range of attributes and weights.

Futura
Futura Bold
Futura Condensed Bold
Futura Condensed Oblique
Futura Condensed Light Oblique
Futura Condensed Light
Futura Condensed
Futura Bold Oblique
Fut. Cond. Extra Bold
Futura Light
Futura Light Oblique

Garamond Three
Garamond Bold
Garamond Bold Italic
Garamond Italic
Garamond Book
Garamond Book Italic
Garamond Ultra
Garamond Ultra Italic

Most typefaces include a wide range of weights and variations, which can be applied to different tasks and space requirements. Using varying weights within a design can bring a sense of visual hierarchy.

Understanding Tracking & Kerning

While the effects of tracking and kerning appear to be identical, there is a distinct difference. Kerning applies to display type, whereas tracking is applied to body copy.

Uneven Spacing

BEFORE The text above hasn't been kerned. It appears as it would when typed into a text box in QuarkXpress. Quark relies on imbedded kerning tables to determine each font's spacing. Notice the awkward, uneven gaps, especially between *n* and *g*.

Each type pair has its own kern setting ▲ Ligatures

AFTER *Kerning* refers to the space between individual characters. It generally applies to display type. Display type should be kerned so that it is evenly spaced visually. All display type requires some kerning.

Kerning setting

Kerning is essentially applying a specific tracking setting for each pair of characters in a word. To apply kerning in Quark, simply place the cursor between the characters whose relationship you want to affect. Hold down the Option key and increase or decrease spacing. The Option key allows you to adjust the setting in smaller increments.

FRISCO

peace

drifting

How type is kerned depends upon the typeface. Words set in all caps will read as one word despite very loose kerning. Short lowercase words can work nicely kerned tightly. Words set in lowercase are prone to falling apart when loosely kerned.

typeface. For instance, let us say that you have selected Garamond as your serif face and Futura as your sans serif typeface. You will be able to use each font's entire family. This means you may select from the range of available weights, attributes, and variations included with each font. For example if Garamond was chosen as the representative serif face, its bold, oblique, or heavy variations could be incorporated into the design. Using Futura as the sans serif face would include its condensed, extended, or light variations as options.

Type pairing is a great way to approach your type design. While using too many fonts can result in an overly busy design, designing in only one font can lead to uninteresting results. Type pairing represents a happy medium between these two approaches. It is an approach that can add variety to your type. While it simultaneously controls the range of fonts being used, type pairing brings a sense of consistency to the design. By making good use of the selected

The Hicksville Gregory Museum evolved from the collections of local school administrator Gardiner E. Gregory. Fascinated by butterflies and moths, he amassed thousands of specimens. Then he found another passion when a changing science curriculum emphasized the study of rocks & minerals. Granted a temporary charter for the museum in 1963, Gardiner and his wife Anne opened their Cottage Boulevard home to schoolchildren from Hicksville and surrounding communities.

The Hicksville Gregory Museum evolved from the collections of local school administrator Gardiner E. Gregory. Fascinated by butterflies and moths, he amassed thousands of specimens. Then he found another passion when a changing science curriculum emphasized the study of rocks & minerals. Granted a temporary charter for the museum in 1963, Gardiner and his wife Anne opened their Cottage Boulevard home to schoolchildren from Hicksville and surrounding communities.

▲ Tracking setting

Tracking is essentially a kern setting for an entire paragraph. To track a paragraph, highlight its text and apply one setting for the entire paragraph. The text block will tighten up or loosen accordingly. A general rule for tracking paragraph text is not to track more than -4 or +4. Keeping within this range will avoid creating text that is too tight or too loose to be read easily.

The Courthouse was originally the village hall, serving a variety of civic functions; weekly court sessions were presided over by a justice of the peace. In 1915 a new jail was constructed; and when upgraded to Nassau County Fourth District Court in the 1930s,	The Courthouse was originally the village hall, serving a variety of civic functions; weekly court sessions were presided over by a justice of the peace. In 1915 a new jail was constructed; and when upgraded to Nassau County Fourth District Court in the 1930s, a judge's chamber was added. By 1967	The Courthouse was originally the village hall, serving a variety of civic functions; weekly court sessions were presided over by a justice of the peace. In 1915 a new jail was constructed; and when upgraded to Nassau County Fourth District Court in the 1930s, a judge's chamber was added. By 1967 the courthouse was vacant.
Tracking set at +5	Tracking set at -5	Tracking set at -10

TRACKING *Tracking* refers to the word and letter spacing of an entire paragraph. While individual letter pairs of display type are kerned, such manipulation of body copy is unnecessary. Tracking is applied to paragraphs to tighten or loosen the copy so that it reads evenly. In the two samples above, the paragraph on the left is loose and has large gaps between the words. The tracking on the paragraph on the right is reduced, which gives it a more even look and makes it easier to read. Tracking can also be helpful with copy fitting.

GRAY OF THE PAGE One often-overlooked effect of kerning is on what's called the "gray of the page." All body copy has a tonal value, a shade of gray that is created by its text. The tighter the tracking is set, the darker the tone of the paragraph will be.

Condensed typefaces don't need as much word space as wide extended typefaces will need

WORD SPACING Your tracking settings will change according to the qualities of the typeface that you are are using. Condensed typefaces are designed to have their characters sit close to one another, so they require less space between their words. An extended face, because of its width, requires additional word spacing to clearly separate its words. Without the extra space its words would not be clearly defined and separated.

SOURCE: *Designing with Type*, James Craig

font families, a designer can add contrast and emphasis to body copy and in the process avoid boring blocks of gray paragraph text. There are no hard-and-fast rules as to what type combinations will work best. It depends on the project requirements, the qualities of the typefaces, and, most importantly, the designer's personal taste.

Distorting Type
There are very few typographic guidelines that are etched in stone, and most of the guidelines discussed in this text have some exceptions. Designers should be encouraged to question and push the boundaries of design once they are familiar with the basic rules. Having said this, there is one rule that is rarely given

exception, and that is to never distort type. Type is distorted when it is scaled disproportionally so that it appears squeezed or stretched. Typefaces are designed to look and read best in their original proportions. While type is most often distorted so that it can fit within a specific space, there are many other ways to achieve this without distort-

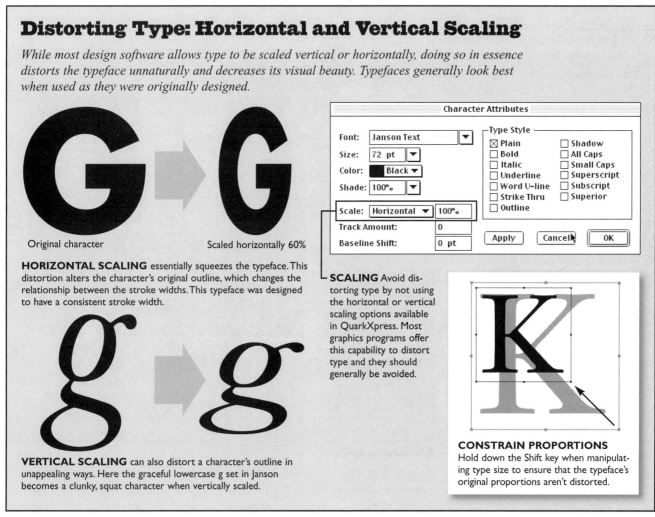

Distorting Type: Horizontal and Vertical Scaling

While most design software allows type to be scaled vertical or horizontally, doing so in essence distorts the typeface unnaturally and decreases its visual beauty. Typefaces generally look best when used as they were originally designed.

Original character

Scaled horizontally 60%

Character Attributes

Font: Janson Text
Size: 72 pt
Color: Black
Shade: 100%

Scale: Horizontal 100%
Track Amount: 0
Baseline Shift: 0 pt

Type Style
- ☒ Plain
- ☐ Bold
- ☐ Italic
- ☐ Underline
- ☐ Word U-line
- ☐ Strike Thru
- ☐ Outline
- ☐ Shadow
- ☐ All Caps
- ☐ Small Caps
- ☐ Superscript
- ☐ Subscript
- ☐ Superior

Apply   Cancel   OK

HORIZONTAL SCALING essentially squeezes the typeface. This distortion alters the character's original outline, which changes the relationship between the stroke widths. This typeface was designed to have a consistent stroke width.

SCALING Avoid distorting type by not using the horizontal or vertical scaling options available in QuarkXpress. Most graphics programs offer this capability to distort type and they should generally be avoided.

VERTICAL SCALING can also distort a character's outline in unappealing ways. Here the graceful lowercase g set in Janson becomes a clunky, squat character when vertically scaled.

CONSTRAIN PROPORTIONS
Hold down the Shift key when manipulating type size to ensure that the typeface's original proportions aren't distorted.

ing the type. These options include sizing, tracking, or using condensed or extended typefaces.

Kerning and Tracking
Kerning and *tracking* refer to the horizontal spacing between words and characters. Kerning deals with the spaces between individual letter pairs and is usually applied to display type. Because of its prominent nature, all display type needs to be kerned to some degree. The amount you kern your display type is a matter of personal preference, but kerning is usually applied uniformly. Applying uniform kerning to display type means not that the

amount of kerning between each character will be numerically the same, but rather that the spacing between each character visually appears consistent. When it comes to kerning, trust your eye, not the software. While type can be kerned either loosely or tightly, the spacing between the letters should appear uniform.

Kerning is often overlooked by young designers, who understandably expect the computer to evenly kern the type. Computer software has limitations, and kerning is largely determined by the designer's subjective preferences regarding type. Understanding how graphics software applications kern type will help explain why type often requires manual kerning. In most software packages, each font has its own "lookup table" that contains kerning information. This table's purpose is to approximate the kerning between different type pairs. QuarkXpress refers to this table to establish the kerning for the type being entered into the text box. Because of the endless amount of possible character combinations, the software is limited in its ability to evenly space the word's characters, and thus type often appears awkward when initially typed.

Like kerning, tracking also

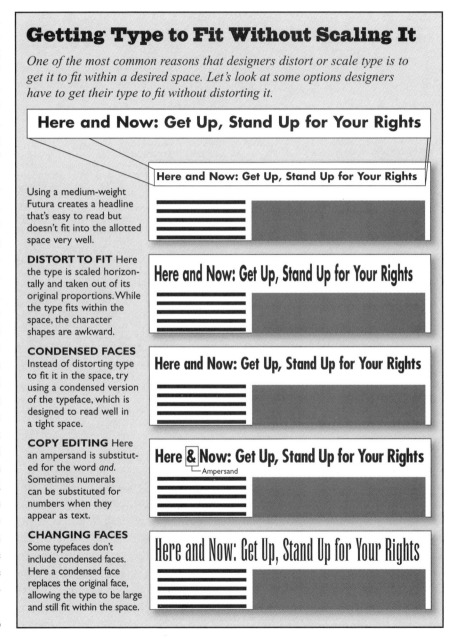

Getting Type to Fit Without Scaling It

One of the most common reasons that designers distort or scale type is to get it to fit within a desired space. Let's look at some options designers have to get their type to fit without distorting it.

Here and Now: Get Up, Stand Up for Your Rights

Here and Now: Get Up, Stand Up for Your Rights

Using a medium-weight Futura creates a headline that's easy to read but doesn't fit into the allotted space very well.

DISTORT TO FIT Here the type is scaled horizontally and taken out of its original proportions. While the type fits within the space, the character shapes are awkward.

Here and Now: Get Up, Stand Up for Your Rights

CONDENSED FACES Instead of distorting type to fit it in the space, try using a condensed version of the typeface, which is designed to read well in a tight space.

Here and Now: Get Up, Stand Up for Your Rights

COPY EDITING Here an ampersand is substituted for the word *and*. Sometimes numerals can be substituted for numbers when they appear as text.

Here & Now: Get Up, Stand Up for Your Rights
└─Ampersand

CHANGING FACES Some typefaces don't include condensed faces. Here a condensed face replaces the original face, allowing the type to be large and still fit within the space.

Here and Now: Get Up, Stand Up for Your Rights

Widows, Orphans, Ladders, and Rivers

One aspect of fine typographic design that gets overlooked is the attention a designer gives to finessing the details of the body copy so that it is readable and doesn't include any awkward gaps.

WIDOWS refer to when the last line of a paragragh falls at the top of a column or on the next page. They also apply to small single words that fall on their own lines at the end of paragraphs. They are also referred to as "one word widows".

ORPHANS, like widows, are a few small words that end a paragraph and fall on their own lines.

POSITIONING of subheads should not be overlooked. Try not to place subheads so that they fall too close to the bottom of a column.

gems.
He amassed thousands of specimens. Another passion arose when a changing science curriculum emphasized the study of rocks.

LOCAL HISTORY
The Heitz Place Courthouse, circa 1895, was originally the village hall, serving a variety of civic functions; weekly court sessions were presided over by a justice of the peace. A new jail was designed and constructed; and when the courthouse status was upgraded to the Nassau County Fourth District Court in 1915.
By 1967 the courthouse was vacant. Museum trustees entered into a long-term lease agreement with the Town of Oyster Bay in 1969, and four years later the building was reopened as the Gregory Museum and was added to the National Registry in 1974.

THE COLLECTIONS
With displays ranging from the

earth sciences to exotic butterflies, the Gregory Museum offers exhibits for the casual visitor (child or adult), interested student, and academic scholar.

THE COURTHOUSE
The courthouse jail remains the historical heart of the museum. One of the original cells has been preserved; the rest of the area is dedicated to exhibits tracing back, using photographs and artifacts, the history of Hicksville. Rotating displays may illustrate: important periods in the area's development; the every-day life of its people; or the many cultural influences of the original inhabitants and the later immigrant groups.

ROCKS AND MINERALS
Minerals on display are a fraction of the 10,000 specimens in the collection. The permanent exhibit serves as an introduction to: the major mineral groups; the economically important ones; and the properties that have made them so

sought after, The Rock and Mineral collection is one of the standout collections in the country both in its size and the diversity and quality of the collections materials.

PREHISTORIC FOSSILS
Fossils in the collection represent most of the major plant and animal groups. Two of the most noteworthy are: a pair of 65 million year old eggs, in one of which are the exposed embryonic bones of a new species of dinosaur; and a Jurassic-age fossil bird.
The museum's growing mineral and fossil collection includes rare and world class specimens, some not seen in major institutions. In keeping with the historical nature of the building, there are exhibits offering insights into the historical background of it. Therefore the Museum isn't a repository for objects, but also excels in using its treasures as teaching tools for young and old. These displays are perhaps the most

RIVERS These are spaces created when subheads align vertically. They cause visual gaps and tend to break up the page. They can be fixed by repositioning art on the page, working with paragraph tracking, or deleting one of the subheads.

LADDERS are series of hyphens that fall on consecutive lines. This can fixed by rebreaking words so that the paragraph rehyphenates. Ladders are most common with justified text.

applies to letter and word spacing, but usually in terms of its effect on an entire paragraph. There is a clear distinction between the kerning and tracking—display type is kerned, while paragraphs are tracked. Kerning applies to the spacing between specific charac-

ters, whereas tracking is applied to an entire paragraph. When designers are copy fitting, they often track paragraph text to accommodate their design. By adjusting the tracking you can add a line of text to a paragraph or to pull the paragraph back a line. Production and

copy edit departments often set limits on how much tracking can be applied to a paragraph before the actual text needs to be rewritten to fit. Most paragraph text requires very little tracking before it starts to become too tight or too loose. A general guideline for paragraph tracking is no more than +5 or less than -5.

Paragraphs should not be tracked so that their characters touch. While it is fine to kern display type quite tightly, even touching, body copy will be difficult to read at such a tight setting. The amount of tracking required also depends on the typeface. Because condensed faces are narrow and their characters are designed to sit close to one another, they some-times require more tracking. The added tracking helps to spread out the characters and make them easier to read. Extended typefaces also have their own tracking require-ments when set as body copy. Because of the width of their char-acters, extended faces generally require more word spacing. When tracked too loosely, the words tend to run into each other and it becomes difficult for the eye to separate and decipher individual words.

Widows and Orphans

Designing attractive and readable body copy also involves manipu-lating specific paragraphs so they take on an attractive form on the page. These adjustments are the final step in designing body copy and should be done when all text is finalized and not subject to later changes. This type of fine-tuning is often the last step before the document gets sent to the printer. In many cases the changes made

Treating Type with Consistency

Most magazine designs are based on two typefaces, one serif and one sans serif, that are used to set almost all text. These typefaces become associated with the magazine's look. Despite the limitations that this might seem to pose, good designers find unlimited ways to design with a limited number of typefaces.

ONE FACE, MANY LOOKS
Entertainment Weekly's design is based around two typefaces, one serif and one sans serif. The head-lines in the layouts are all set in the same serif typeface, Bureau Grotesque, yet each typographic design is unique and varied.

TYPE AS SHAPE The vertical quality of a typeface can be empha-sized. In examples B and D, these designs takes advantage of the vertical, linear quality of the type-face. In these examples the typeface plays a major role in the overall page design.

PLAYING WITH SIZE One way to get exciting type designs is to play with the size of the headline's words. Changing the size of certain words can make for a visually inter-esting type design while giving a sense of hierarchy to the type. In example A, C, and F the type size changes, in some cases dramatically.

USING BASELINE How the type falls along the baseline directly affects the mood it conveys. In example E the type jumps around at different intervals from the baseline, giving it a playful quality.

MIXING CASES In example F the headline is designed with changes in type size and case set-tings. Some characters are in lower-case, while other are seemingly indiscriminately set in uppercase. Some of the letter outlines have been altered, such as the *v* and *h* in the word *everything*.

Many Faces, Many Moods

With the wealth of typefaces available, designers today have access to thousands of fonts that reflect a wide range of emotions and moods. One of the most important decisions designers make is the typefaces they select. Here's a sampling of some novelty fonts with specialized uses.

Elegant
Shelley Allegro

Funny
Curlz

Retro
Wendy

NOUVEAU
Desdemona

Technical
Template Gothic

Formal
Didot

OLD WESTERN
Mesquite

Groovy
Arnold Boecklin

Casual
Brush Script

Distressed
Attic

will involve copy fitting and in larger design companies may be handled by a copy editing department. But since designers are ultimately responsible for how a design's type looks, they need to keep an eye out for these typographic problems.

• **Widows** are short single words that fall on their own line at the end of a paragraph or when the last line of a paragraph falls at the top of a column or the start of the following page. Widows cause unattractive and inconsistent gaps within running paragraph text.

• **Orphans** are small sets of short single words that fall, like widows, onto their own line at the end of paragraphs.

Usually five characters or less constitutes a widow or orphans. These short words at the end of paragraphs need to be "turned up" or pulled back to the previous line, or added to in order to extend the length of the paragraph's last line.

The first step to take when trying to remove widows and orphans is to try applying tracking to the paragraph to either add to the final line's length or to pull the sentence back, shortening the paragraph. If a tracking setting of +5 or -5 will not fix the problem, the text may need to be rewritten, usually by adding or deleting a word or two, so that the widow or orphan is removed.

• **Ladders** are a series of consecutive lines within a paragraph that end with a hyphen, resulting in a "stacking" effect. Ladders can be removed by manipulating the paragraph tracking or rebreaking the text if necessary. More advanced users may also want to try adjusting the Hyphenation and Justification settings in QuarkXpress.

• **Rivers** are vertical gaps that run between columns of text caused when spaces between paragraphs fall in similar vertical positions. They often appear when paragraph text includes subheads with line spaces preceding them. Rivers can be fixed through tracking or copy editing.

Choosing Appropriate Typefaces

One of the most important design decisions involves type selection. The typefaces that are selected contribute directly to the overall feel of a project. Designers today have access to more typefaces than ever before. The rise of digital type design shops has provided designers with an overwhelming array of choices. Designers need to develop a typographic repertoire, a working knowledge of a diverse range of available fonts. A good way to devel-

Still Going Strong: Classic Typefaces

Many typefaces commonly used in contemporary design have long histories. Some typefaces date back to the 1600s. Despite their age, these faces have a timeless quality that always seems to stay in fashion.

Garamond

One of the oldest typefaces in current use, its design dates back to 1617. Its design includes "cupped" serifs. Macintosh uses a condensed version for its logo.

Bodoni

Designed in 1785, Bodoni is characterized by its wide range of thicks and thins. Variations of this face are used by Armani and Calvin Klein.

Avant Garde

This sans serif face was designed by Herb Lubalin in 1968. While it characterized design of the 1970s, it continues to be used and can be seen in the logo designs of Macy's, Adidas, and New Balance.

TRAJAN

Although a relatively new font, the design for Trajan was based on a chiseled Roman typeface. It has been used in movie titles for *Gladiator* and *Titanic*.

Minion

Variations of the Minion face are used in many well-known logos, including those of Sony, Volvo, and Honda.

Selecting Appropriate Typefaces

Selecting typefaces is a subjective choice, but it will in part depend on whether the type is used for body copy or display type. Effective type design involves selecting typefaces that work visually and informatively. With so many available fonts, here are a few ways to narrow your search.

1 MAT COUNTY CREDIT UNION

2 Mat County Credit Union

3 MAT COUNTY CREDIT UNION

4 MAT COUNTY CREDIT UNION

This sample design calls for a typeface to represent a credit union, a financial institution.

1 **SERIF OR SANS SERIF** Here a Helvetica face is used. Helvetica is a sans serif face, relatively modern. One of the first overall design decisions you will make is whether the type should be serif or sans serif. Since one of the qualities a financial institution wants to convey is a sense of stability or dependability, you may want to narrow your search to serif faces, which have an older look and a sense of history.

2 **CHOOSE A CASE STYLING** The next question would be how to style the case of the type. A combination of upper- and lowercase is easiest to read, but it doesn't give off the sense of authority that all uppercase does.

3 **COMPARE TYPEFACES** There is a wide range of serif faces that could apply to such a design. One way to decide is to copy and paste the words numerous times and apply different serif faces and case stylings to compare them.

4 **INTRODUCE ATTRIBUTES** As you narrow down your search to a few typefaces, start to introduce different attributes, such as small caps, which convey a sense of dignity and work well with serif faces. If you're using all caps, you might try kerning them loosely.

op this is to experiment with different typefaces with each new project. This approach will help expand your knowledge and familiarity with a wider range of typefaces.

Begin your search for an appropriate typeface by considering the nature of the project. Does it require a sense of dignity? Does it call for a comical approach? Is its feel a casual one? What typefaces have characteristics that will fit the tone of the piece? Let's say you have a project that represents a financial institution. It will probably need to reflect a sense of strength and stability. There are quite a few typefaces that convey these attributes. Begin your search by making some basic overall decisions about what style of type will be most appropriate. A designer's first inclination in a case like this might be to use a serif face. By their nature, serif faces evoke a classic feel and a sense of history. Because the design of sans serif faces are more modern, their use would probably be less successful here. Small caps, especially when set in a serif face, can provide a dignified feel and might also be considered as an option.

Each font has its own unique characteristics that convey different qualities. This is usually the result of the way the character forms are designed. Hand-rendered faces like Garamond have a formal yet personal quality because of the nature of their outline and cupped serifs. Juxtapose Garamond to a more mechanically formed face like City and you will see two quite different sets of qualities. While City is a beautifully crafted face, its feel is much bolder and more impersonal.

Appreciating Classic Typefaces

In the previous paragraph we discussed increasing your typographic literacy by familiarizing yourself with a range of typefaces. Many of the most commonly used typefaces in design today have been in use for centuries. These are predominantly serif typefaces, since sans serif stylings were not developed until the twentieth century. For instance, Garamond was originally designed and hand-cut in 1617, and Baskerville dates back to 1757. Bodoni, designed in 1785, was considered at its time to represent the height of typographic modernity because of the extreme thicks and thins found in its character forms. Over two hundred years later, Bodoni continues to be used by some of today's most respected fashion designers, including Calvin Klein and Armani. Even recently designed faces such as Trajan, based on Roman chiseled typefaces, reflect a classic quality. Trajan has recently been used for titling of popular movies like *Titanic* and *Gladiator* as well as for the masthead of magazines like *Maxim*. These fonts have remained in use because of their timeless quality. While there will always be fashionable typefaces, and it is a designer's job to be aware of these, these clas-

Type Attributes: Dos & Don'ts

Introducing bold, italic, and other attributes will give a sense of visual hierarchy and variation to your type design.

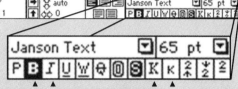

TYPE ATTRIBUTES Some of the type attributes available in the Measurement palette should be avoided. Depending on the final output device, these attributes may not print properly. Always choose the typeface version (e.g., Garamond Bold) rather than applying the Bold or Italic buttons.

Text styled using the Bold and Italic buttons won't print properly on high end printers

All caps and small caps will output properly on high-end printers

AVOID USING QUARK ATTRIBUTES It is preferable to select the bold variation of the typeface rather than apply the bold attribute in the Measurement palette. The Janson Text type below on the left is set the wrong way. It uses bolding attributes, whereas on the right the actual bold variation of the typeface is selected. Notice that the actual font has nice character outlines. Quark's bolding attributes tend to be clunky and awkward.

time
Janson Text — 65 pt
Here the type is set in Janson Text and has been given a bold appearance by applying the Bold button.

time
B Janson Text Bol — 65 pt
Here the type has been bolded by selecting a bold version of the typeface, Janson Text Bold.

time
Janson Text — 65 pt

time
I Janson Text Ital — 65 pt

ITALICIZING TYPEFACES The same rules used for bolding apply to italicizing type. Select the italic font, not the Italic button on measurement palette. The type on the left has been skewed by Quark, whereas the text on the right uses a font designed to be used for italics.

Type Attributes: Small Caps & All Caps

Using uppercase type stylings can be an effective way to handle display text. Uppercase adds a sense of formality and dignity.

▲ Small Caps Button   ▲ All Caps Button

SMALL CAPS Here the type has been set in small caps by using the Small Caps button. Unlike the bold and italic attributes, the small caps attribute will output accurately.

ALL CAPS Here the type appears entirely in uppercase as a result of applying the All Caps button. The all caps attribute will print accurately when output on high end printing device.

THE STATE OF GRACE
THE STATE OF GRACE

SERIF AND SANS SERIF TYPEFACES Small caps can be applied to any typeface, but they will be more successful with some faces, less so with others. Generally small caps work well with serif faces and give them a sense of class and dignity. While small caps can be applied to sans serif faces, they tend to look a little awkward, as the small caps setting tends to accentuate the difference in the stroke widths of the characters.

sic faces always remain in style. They are like the blue jeans of typography in that they never go out of style. Something about their design transcends fashion. The huge number of typefaces available today can make choosing fonts an overwhelming task. Young designers will benefit immensely by familiarizing themselves with these classic faces, as this will help simplify the type selection process.

Searching for a Typeface

The process of design always begins with experimentation and variation. This approach can also be applied when searching for appropriate typefaces. A good way to start this selection process is to type out the words that make up the display type and then create numerous copies of these words. Because the characters of each font have unique features, it is important to see the specific words in the actual typeface. While a particular font might seem ideal for a project, it can be a much different story when that font appears in the form of the actual words. With display type, the shape of the word, especially if it's set in upper- and lowercase, will play a role in your type selection. Because of the different qualities of each typeface and the unique shape that each word forms, finding the right match starts with trying different faces. Creating multiple copies of words and styling them in different faces allows for comparison and can help narrow down a type search. Once you've decided upon a few typefaces, you can start to apply different type attributes and create different typographic variations. Designers have countless typographic options. Consider setting the words in small caps or entirely in uppercase. Try italic and bold variations. Try using these attributes in conjunction with the different weight variations offered within a typeface.

A word of advice: Before you begin to design a finished headline, make sure the title is finalized. You don't want to fine-tune a type design that is subject to change.

Typographic Symbols

Besides selecting and styling type, designers will often incorporate other typographic options when they are made available by the actual text being used. In looking for alternative ways to design type, a designer may try spelling out numbers instead of using numerals or substitute an ampersand (&) instead of using the word *and*. Ampersands are beautiful and elegant typographic characters. There are many dingbat fonts offering a range of typographic symbols that can be incorporated into a design. Because of the cultural influence of the Internet, the at sign (@) is becoming commonly used in place of the actual word. Many contemporary designs will even incorporate an individual number or letter instead of words, for example using the letter *U* in place in place of the word *you*. Some of these options will often be determined by the project and the client, but the designer should consider

Type Attributes: Drop Shadows

Drop shadows are a commonly used design device, and using them with type adds depth to a design and increases a typeface's readability and impact.

The Shadow Knows...

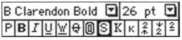

Drop Shadow Button ▲

Quark's drop shadow attribute does not allow you to change the color of the shadow or control the distance or direction in which the shadow falls.

DROP SHADOW ATTRIBUTE It's better to create a drop shadow for your type manually rather than to apply the drop shadow button in the Measurement palette. Quark's drop shadow attribute offers the designer very little control.

Manually Creating Drop Shadows

It's easy to create custom drop shadows that allow the designer to fully control the shadow's color and its positioning.

Shadow ⬇ **Shadow**

Begin by styling and kerning the text. Then copy and paste a second copy of the type. This copy will act as the drop shadow. Give the shadow type a different color. Make sure that both text boxes do not have text runarounds applied. Place the original type over the shadow text.

Shadow **Shadow**

Type with drop shadow behind it.

Shadow Avoid gaps between type and shadow

Make sure that the shadow is placed close to the type so that no gaps appear. Gaps make the type more difficult to read.

them when the actual text used within a design allows for them.

Type Attributes

There is a basic set of type attributes that can be applied to most typefaces. These attributes include bold, italic (or oblique), small caps, and all caps. Each of the attributes has a different quality and introducing them into your design will bring variety to your type.

Working with Text Columns

There are many approaches to building files that require columns of running text. For some projects, separate linked text boxes work best, while for others one text box with multiple columns is appropriate. Let's look at when to use which box.

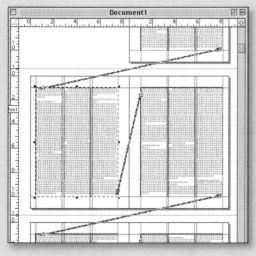

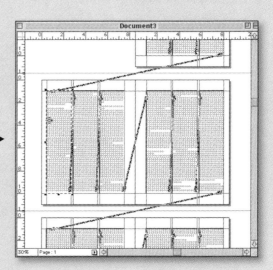

◄**MULTIPLE COLUMN TEXT BOXES** are the most practical method for creating running columns of body copy. They don't require each separate column to be linked, but they can be more difficult to design with, as they require the designer to manipulate text runarounds.

SEPARATE COLUMNS allow ► the designer to quickly lay out a page's composition and not have to rely on text runarounds. Here the separate columns are master items and the running body is linked. In this case each column's depth can be changed manually to accommodate images rather than depending on a text runaround.

• **Bold faces** are used for emphasis. They add contrast to gray paragraphs of body text and can create a sense of visual hierarchy. As the purpose of bold faces is to attract attention, avoid overusing them, as they will lose their impact. Too much bold type can make an overall design busy, as the type fights with itself for the reader's attention.

• **Italic typefaces** are calligraphic in nature and emulate a handwritten form. These qualities give them an intimate, personal quality. The slant of the italic face gives it a unique form, and like bold faces, italics can add variety to running columns of text. There is a wide range of italic faces. While most faces have italic variations, some faces are designed in a specifically ornate calligraphic style. While ornate faces could also be thought of as italic, they are generally considered script faces. When italicizing sections of body copy, the italic ver-

sions of the body copy typeface should be used.

One technical note regarding the standard use of italics: italics are used to denote proper names such as *The New York Times*.

• **Small caps** are a common way to set type, and they can evoke a formal, elegant impression, especially when set in serif faces. For small caps, a word's characters are set entirely in uppercase and the word's initial character is set in a slightly

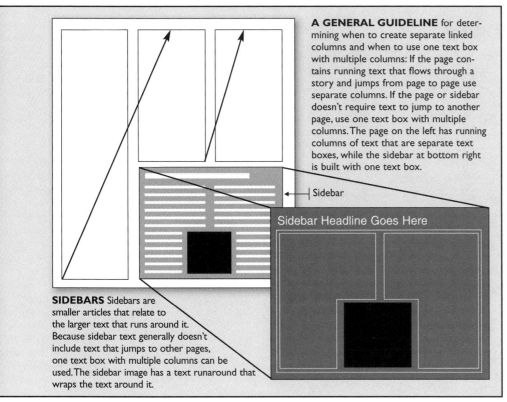

A GENERAL GUIDELINE for determining when to create separate linked columns and when to use one text box with multiple columns: If the page contains running text that flows through a story and jumps from page to page use separate columns. If the page or sidebar doesn't require text to jump to another page, use one text box with multiple columns. The page on the left has running columns of text that are separate text boxes, while the sidebar at bottom right is built with one text box.

Sidebar

Sidebar Headline Goes Here

SIDEBARS Sidebars are smaller articles that relate to the larger text that runs around it. Because sidebar text generally doesn't include text that jumps to other pages, one text box with multiple columns can be used. The sidebar image has a text runaround that wraps the text around it.

larger size.

Unlike the Bold and Italic buttons in QuarkXpress, the Small Caps button on the measurement palette can be used without causing any of the printing problems associated with the bold and italic attributes. The size relationship between the larger and smaller characters for small caps can be adjusted by using the Character Preferences. Some typefaces are designed specifically to be used in uppercase or as small caps. These fonts, which include Copperplate, Bank Gothic, and Trajan, don't offer typical lowercase character forms, but rather small versions of the uppercase letters.

Bold and Italic Attributes

Generally you should avoid using the Bold and Italic buttons on the measurement palette in Quark-Xpress. If you wish to use a bold or italic styling, selecting the version within the type family is a better method. For example, instead of highlighting a word that is set in Garamond and then selecting the Bold button on the measurement palette, choose the Garamond Bold typeface from the font list. There are two reasons for doing it this way. The first reason concerns the visual quality of the typeface. When you select the bold attribute, QuarkXpress creates the bold effect by applying a uniform stroke around the character. This method of bolding creates a clunky, heavy bold. The bold version included in the font family offers a more refined character design. The second reason to avoid applying these attributes is that they create inconsistent printing problems on high-end image setters. While these attributes may print accurately from your local laser printer, they may not output correctly when sent out to a service bureau. High-end image setters often fail to recognize the bold or italic attributes and the type will be printed as if the attribute was never applied.

The Importance of Body Copy

While display type may initially attract the reader, it is the body copy that holds their attention. The display type may hook you, but the

Understanding Baseline Grids

Any project that contains multiple pages with columns of running body copy will require a baseline grid to give the design an integrated, consistent feel from page to page. Baseline grids also help determine the placement of elements within a composition

VIEWING THE BASELINE GRID You can see the baseline grid by selecting View Baseline Grid from the View pull-down menu or by using the Opt + F7 hot key. This is a commonly used key command. It's easy to remember since F7 is view guides, another commonly used hot key. The baseline grid appears as evenly spaced pink guidelines.

ALIGNING TO THE GRID ▶
The bulk of the running body copy here is aligning to the baseline grid. This ensures that the text in the columns cross-aligns and that the layout has a consistent spacing.

BASELINE SHIFT In some cases, especially when type size changes, you may want the text to lock to the baseline grid. In this case the song titles sit slightly above the baseline grid. This is done by applying a baseline shift to the text.

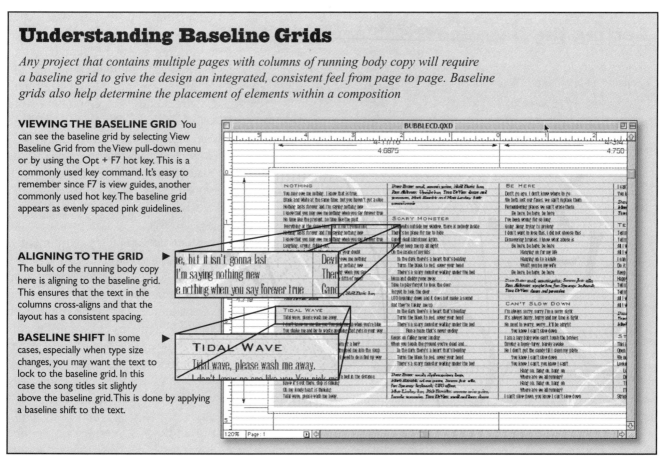

body copy keeps you around. When you consider that the reader will spend more time looking at the body copy than the display type, the importance of setting legible, attractive body copy becomes clear.

Body copy is where the reader goes to be informed. Because of this, you want to create type that is both readable and easy to navigate

through, enabling readers to locate the information they seek. The sense of visual hierarchy that bolding and italicizing brings to text also makes the copy easier to skim through. Setting body copy is a subtle design skill that involves strong typographic and technical skills. Let's look at some things you should consider when designing body copy.

Formatting Page Columns

If you are working on a multipage project, formatting is the first thing you do upon opening a new document. It is here that the page parameters are specified. These parameters include the page's margins, columns, and gutters.

There are many approaches to building the page once it's been

Letting the Baseline Grid Serve as a Guide

Besides being used to cross-align text, baseline grids also help determine the placement of elements on the page. Once you've decided how the images will sit within the text, this relationship can be applied to all images to achieve consistent spacing throughout a design.

WORK THE GRID

When deciding how to align an image with the body text, use the x-height, cap height, or baseline as your guide.

1 The top of the image aligns with the x-height, the bottom with the baseline.

2 The top of the image aligns with the baseline, the bottom with the x-height.

3 The top of the image aligns with the cap height, the bottom with the baseline.

emergence of the city challenged our ideas of what constituted a community. So much that was character- istic of city living, its highly concentrated population, noise and lack of light, absence of natural environment, and the impersonal quality contradict- ed traditional ideals of community. This rearrangement of living patterns left people disoriented as social, political, and religious traditions no longer

seemed relevant in a modern urban soci- ety. Opportunity, autonomy, identity, and status were difficult to establish in the urban world. As American life moved from the local life of the nineteenth century to a vastly more integrated socie- ty, a sense of hope surrounded it as Melvin while responsible to the com- munity became more strained. Urban life and industrial work made it increasingly difficult to

TOP OF COLUMNS

Images placed at the top of columns will often break style with images that fall within the text. Images that align with the cap height appear too high. X-height is a more appropriate position.

COLUMN RULES

When vertical rules are placed between columns, they also are placed in relation to the baseline. Both rules align with the x-height on the top and the baseline on the bottom.

---

formatted. Let us say that your design calls for a three-column format. The most obvious approach to setting up this page would be to use a single text box with three columns. While using one multi-columned text box may seem easier and more efficient, setting up three separate column boxes and then linking them is more conducive to the design process. While this method makes the file a little more complex, it is easier to compose your page when the columns are set in this manner. This approach

allows you to be less dependent upon runarounds, which can some-times be unwieldy and time-con-suming to manipulate. It allows the designer to independently change the depth of each column. This is more difficult to do with a multi-columned text box. Separate linked text boxes are a much more natural and intuitive way to design.

There are situations where using multicolumned boxes is advisable, but these usually involve smaller ele-ments that don't include linked text. Using multicolumned text boxes is

also advisable for multipage docu-ments whose pages include large amounts of running text, such as with a novel or technical report. Because each page within these designs do not change greatly, multicolumned text boxes are prefer-able. The use of separate text boxes will make any design that includes inserted images and smaller support graphics easier to work with. If you are setting up documents in which each page needs to be uniquely designed, separate linked columns are the best design approach.

Cross-Aligning Text

When you are working with linked columns of body copy, the text must cross-align. This means that the baselines of the type in adjacent columns are in alignment with each other. The baseline is the implied line that the bottom of the text sits on. To achieve cross alignment, the baseline grid must first be set to match the leading of the body copy, and then the text is set to snap to this grid. This can be done by first setting the paragraph leading and the baseline grid to the same increment. The baseline grid can be adjusted by editing the document's paragraph preferences. The running text can then be snapped to the grid by using the Style Formats menu.

The baseline grid, along with the column guides, will serve as the underlying structure of the page, in relationship to which all design elements will be placed.

Exceptions to the Rule

As with any of the guidelines offered in this text, there are situations in which they don't apply. In design, unlike mathematics, there are usually numerous solutions to any problem. With that said, there are instances when text may not be required to lock to the baseline grid. In the case of smaller design elements that fall within a larger story, such as sidebars, graphics, or pull quotes, the type within the elements may fall off the grid. In these cases, the baseline grid would not dictate the placement of the type, but it would determine the placement of that element. For instance, the tint box within which the type sits would align to the baseline grid in some manner. While building separate column boxes is preferable for running body copy, these small self-contained elements are an appropriate place to use a multicolumned text box.

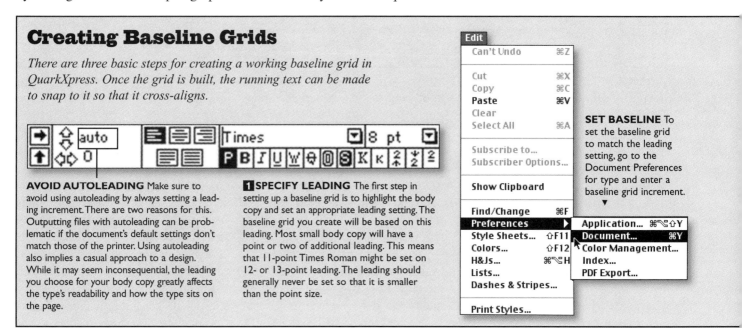

Creating Baseline Grids

There are three basic steps for creating a working baseline grid in QuarkXpress. Once the grid is built, the running text can be made to snap to it so that it cross-aligns.

AVOID AUTOLEADING Make sure to avoid using autoleading by always setting a leading increment. There are two reasons for this. Outputting files with autoleading can be problematic if the document's default settings don't match those of the printer. Using autoleading also implies a casual approach to a design. While it may seem inconsequential, the leading you choose for your body copy greatly affects the type's readability and how the type sits on the page.

1 SPECIFY LEADING The first step in setting up a baseline grid is to highlight the body copy and set an appropriate leading setting. The baseline grid you create will be based on this leading. Most small body copy will have a point or two of additional leading. This means that 11-point Times Roman might be set on 12- or 13-point leading. The leading should generally never be set so that it is smaller than the point size.

SET BASELINE To set the baseline grid to match the leading setting, go to the Document Preferences for type and enter a baseline grid increment.

Choosing Fonts for Body Copy

The typeface that you select for your body copy is an important choice, one that requires a different set of criteria than those used for choosing a font for display type. The most important consideration in choosing a face for body copy is its readability. The typeface and its size will be partly determined by the amount of text the project requires. There is a wide range of serif fonts that serve well as body copy. These fonts include Palatino, Times, Baskerville, Garamond, and Sabon. While all of these fonts are appropriate for use as body copy, each has its own distinctive qualities. It is easy to overlook the subtle nuances in these seemingly similar faces. For instance, Times was created specifically for the *The New York Times*, a newspaper known for its heavy editorial content. The font was designed to maintain readability while also accommodating a high character count per line. This allowed the newspaper to fit more text in a smaller space. This is one example of the subtle qualities that each face brings to a design.

Body copy is almost always set in upper- and lowercase. Generally for multiple-page projects with running text, a serif face is preferable. The typeface's serifs and its variance in line weight help to enhance recognition of the characters' shape, and this directly increases readability. Similarly, setting type in upper- and lowercase helps each individual word take on a unique and recognizable shape, which in turn makes the text easier to read. Conversely, body copy is difficult to read when set entirely in upper case because there is less uniqueness in word shape. This uniqueness of character is found less often in sans serif faces, which typically have evenly stroked line weights. The serifs

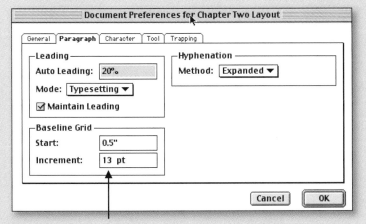

2 SETTING THE BASELINE GRID Since the baseline grid setting is a document-wide setting in that it applies to every page of the document, it is accessed through Document Preferences. Enter an increment setting in Baseline Grid that matches the leading of your body copy. To control where the baseline grid preview starts on the page, enter a measurement into the Start section. Here the baseline grid begins one-half inch below the top of the page.

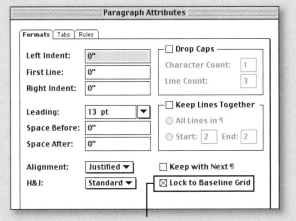

3 LOCKING TO THE BASELINE GRID The last step in getting your text to cross-align between columns is to lock the text to the grid. Highlight the text you wish to affect and go to the Formats menu and select the Lock to Baseline Grid button. The baseline of the text will now align with the baseline grid.

Using the Baseline Grid to Cross-Align

Multiple-page documents that have running columns of text require a working baseline grid upon which the text as well as the graphics will align. Baseline grids help bring consistency to your overall design.

Three separate linked text boxes

VIEW BASELINE If you've set up the baseline grid correctly, you should be able to view the baseline grid (Opt + F7) and see that your body copy is cross-aligning. Any running body copy that is placed into columns should align to the baseline grid.

TOP OF IMAGE The top of the image aligns to the x-height of the type. The x-height is the top of the lowercase characters.

FLOATING CAPTIONS Depending on a photo's composition, sometimes a caption can be placed within a photo. Because the image aligns to the baseline, the caption doesn't have to align to the baseline.

BOTTOM OF IMAGE The bottom of the image aligns to the baseline grid itself.

aps, and All Caps. Each of the attributes have different qualities and introducing them into your design will bring variety to your type.

Bold faces are used for emphasis. They add contrast to gray paragraphs of body text and can create a sense of visual hierarchy. As the purpose of bold faces is to

This rare species of urchin can be found off the African coast in the springtime when tides are low.

attract attention, avoid overusing bold faces as they will lose their impact. Too much bold type can make an overall design busy, as the type fights itself for the reader's attention.

Italic typefaces are calligraphic in nature and their handwritten form has an intimate, per-

sonal quality. The slant of the italic face gives it a unique form and like bold faces, italics can add variety to otherwise monotonous columns of text. There is a wide range of italic faces. While most faces have italic variations, some faces are designed in a specifically ornate calligraphic styles. While ornate faces could also be thought of as italic, they are generally considered script

POSITIONING IMAGES WITHIN THE GRID Photos that fall within the text will be positioned in a direct relationship to the baseline grid. Once you've decided what that relationship is, you will place all photos in the same way. This ensures consistency throughout your pages.

SETTING TEXT WRAPS Here the picture box has text runaround applied to it. The runaround settings are set low for the top and bottom (1–2 points), higher for the left and right (9 points). Make sure to allow enough space between the type and the image and to apply the left and right wraps evenly.

found at the x height also help to guide the eye horizontally across the page. This is not to say that sans serif faces are difficult to read; they are just not as well suited to voluminous paragraph text. In fact, sans serif faces are commonly used on road signage (in upper- and lower-

case) because of their legibility from long distances and readability in small doses.

Readability: Font Attributes
Besides the selection of the typeface, the readability of your body copy also depends upon a combina-

tion of other settings. These include font styling, color, size, leading, tracking, and column width. All of these aspects work in tandem and play a role in how easy or difficult your body copy will be to read. Some of the effects that these attributes have on readability are obvi-

> **I can't say I was an angel...**
> **I've made bad decisions...**
> **but I don't have any regrets**
> *Jamie Moeller at Emmy Awards*

aps, and All Caps. Each of the attributes have different qualities and introducing them into your design will bring variety to your type.

Bold faces are used for emphasis. They add contrast to gray paragraphs of body text and can create a sense of visual hierarchy. As the purpose of bold faces is to attract attention, avoid overusing bold faces as they will lose their impact. Too much bold

type can make an overall design busy, as the type fights itself for the reader's attention.

Italic typefaces are calligraphic in nature and their

handwritten form has an intimate, personal quality. The slant of the italic face gives it a unique form and like bold faces, italics can add variety to otherwise monotonous columns of text. There is a wide range of italic faces. Most faces have italic variations, some very are ornate. ■

The Latest in Burgers

As burgers come and burgers go fast food restaurants constantly in search of the next taste craze. After Sourdough craze past last year many fastfoods have been introducing everything form bacon and sour cream to babagonoush. It seems the both the provincial approach and the international offerings are falling short of enticing America's appetite.

ALIGNING TO COLUMN TOP Elements that are positioned at the top of columns look most natural when they align to the x-height. When they align to the baseline or cap height, they don't appear to align with the top of the column.

COLUMN RULES When vertical rules are placed between columns, they are also placed in relation to the baseline. Both rules align with the x-height on top and the baseline on bottom.

END SQUARES Dingbats, symbols, and logos can be used as end squares, which are commonly used to denote the end of an article.

TOP OF SIDEBAR The top of the sidebar tint aligns with the x-height. Note the consistency of space above this sidebar and above the photo on the adjacent page.

BOTTOM OF SIDEBAR The bottom of the sidebar tint aligns with the baseline. When design elements like this tint fall at the bottom of a column, it is usually best to align them to the baseline. Aligning them with the x-height or cap height would be awkward.

SIDEBAR TEXT While the background tint of the sidebar aligns to the baseline grid, the text within the sidebar can float.

BUILDING SIDEBARS An intuitive way to build sidebars is to use separate boxes for each element. This sidebar uses four boxes: a background tint, a white border, and two text boxes for the headline and body copy. This allows for all the elements to be manually positioned.

ous. For instance, text readability is greatly reduced when type is set at a small size. The effects of other attributes on readability can be much more subtle. Let's look at how these attributes affect readability and some of the pitfalls to avoid when setting body copy.

Readability: Type Stylings

Each typeface has a family of different weights and alternative versions. While some faces, because of the nature of their character forms, will never serve well as body copy, there are other fonts that can, with some manipulation, work well in

paragraph form.

• **Ornate typefaces** usually don't read well at smaller sizes, as the details of the characters tend to get lost, and this obscures readability. Ornate faces are generally designed to be used as display type, at larger sizes in small groups of words, as opposed to in paragraph form. Fonts with extreme variations of thicks and thins are difficult to read at small size because the thin sections will fall out when printed. *Falling out* refers to the loss of detail that can occur when being printed. Depending on your final output device, the printer may not be able to maintain a high enough level of detail to accommodate such typefaces.

• **Condensed faces**, because of their narrowness, tend to fill in when printed at smaller sizes. Condensed typefaces, especially bold versions, can be difficult to read in paragraph form without some manipulation. They require less word spacing, as the letters tend to sit close together. With some condensed faces you may consider adding some letterspacing so that the letters don't run into each other. Extremely condensed faces are also subject to losing detail when output at a small size.

• **Extended typefaces**, when set as body copy, generally require more word spacing. Without additional tracking added, the words are prone to run into each other, causing the reader to have difficulty in deciphering where one word ends and the next one begins. Because of the wideness of extended faces, they

Type Readability

To successfully design with type, you need to basically understand how the human eye perceives and deciphers type. Once you understand this, you can more effectively style your type.

Serif and Sans Serif Typefaces

When it comes to readability, serif and sans serif faces have their strengths and weaknesses. Being familiar with these will help you create easy-to-read text.

S **SANS SERIF FACES** Because of the evenness of stroke that characterizes many sans serif faces, they are very readable when set in upper- and lowercase. Most signage used on roadways is set in medium-weight sans serif faces. They are easily deciphered when seen in small groups of words. While sans serif faces can be used for body copy, serif faces are generally preferable when text is set in multiple pages of running columns.

F **SERIF FACES** Serif faces are characterized by stroke widths that have varying thicknesses. The serifs provide a uniqueness of character that typically you don't get with sans serif faces. When set in upper- and lowercase, serif faces are especially well suited for use as body copy, particularly when there are multiple pages. The serifs help guide the reader's eye across the page and help with character recognition.

iconography
iconography

CHARACTER RECOGNITION Here the same word is set in both serif and sans serif. When you can see only the tops of the characters, the word set in the serif face is easier to read. The serifs bring a uniqueness to the characters and help with the recognition of the letter forms. A limited number of foundation shapes are used to create sans serif faces, and because of the consistency within its type design, it is difficult to decipher one sans serif character from another. Serifs also help the readability by accenting the horizontal flow of the text.

SOURCE: *Designing with Type*, James Craig

Upper- & Lowercase Settings

One of the faculties that we use to read text quickly involves shape recognition. Just like letter forms, words themselves have distinguishable shapes which help us quickly recognize their forms and read faster. Let's look at the effect that setting text in uppercase and lowercase has on readability.

DECIPHER THE TEXT

Uppercase

Decipher the text

Upper- and lowercase

CHARACTER RECOGNITION In these cases the same text has been set in different case stylings, and a shape has been drawn around each word. The shapes drawn around the uppercase words all appear the same, as boxes, whereas the shapes outlining the words set in upper- and lowercase are much more recognizable, thus making the words more distinguishable and easier to read.

Case Settings & Readability

THE HICKSVILLE GREGORY MUSEUM EVOLVED FROM THE COLLECTIONS OF LOCAL SCHOOL ADMINISTRATOR DR. GARDINER GREGORY. FASCINATED BY BUTTERFLIES AND MOTHS, HE AMASSED THOUSANDS OF SPECIMENS. THEN HE FOUND ANOTHER PASSION WHEN A CHANGING SCIENCE PROGRAM DECIDED TO ADOPT

The Hicksville Gregory Museum evolved from the collections of local school administrator Dr. Gardiner Gregory. Fascinated by butterflies and moths, he amassed thousands of specimens. Then he found another passion when a changing science program emphasized the study of rocks & minerals. Granted a charter by the county for the museum to have its home in the former County Courthouse.

PARAGRAPH TEXT In the two paragraphs above, one is set in all caps and one in upper- and lowercase. Both are set at the same size and leading. The text in upper- and lowercase is clearly easier to read.

Knockout Type

Another way to style type is to knock it out, or reverse it. Knockout type refers to any lightly tinted type set on a dark background. As with any type setting, knockout type has its own readability considerations. It can be easy or difficult to read, depending on the typeface used. Because of the varying stroke widths of the serif face, its thin sections tend to break up when knocked out. Because of the high contrast, serif faces have a tendency to visually vibrate more than sans serif faces. Because of the evenness in their stroke weights, sans serif faces are generally more readable when reversed.

The Hicksville Gregory Museum evolved from the collections of local school administrator Gardiner E. Gregory. Fascinated by butterflies and moths, he amassed thousands of specimens. Then he found another passion when a changing science curriculum emphasized the study of rocks & minerals. Granted a temporary charter for the museum in 1963, Gardiner and his wife

The Hicksville Gregory Museum evolved from the collections of local school administrator Gardiner E. Gregory. Fascinated by butterflies and moths, he amassed thousands of specimens. Then he found another passion when a changing science curriculum emphasized the study of rocks & minerals. Granted a temporary charter for the museum in 1963

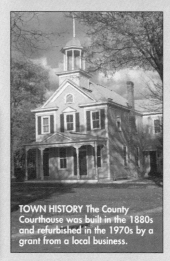

TOWN HISTORY The County Courthouse was built in the 1880s and refurbished in the 1970s by a grant from a local business.

The large, consistent gray area in the foreground of the image accommodates knockout type well.

DISPLAY CASES The museum offers a wide range of displays from sea shells to rocks and minerals. Their

Because this image has areas that change abruptly from dark to light, the caption is difficult to read.

REVERSE TYPE AND IMAGES While sans serif type is generally more readable as reverse type, the quality of the image also affects readability. High-contrast images like the one above, have busy areas of black and white that won't knock out type as well as images with large inactive areas of consistently dark tones, like the image on the left.

Readability and Column Width

Besides typeface, size, and leading, the width of the columns and the way the text is treated within them will greatly affect the text's readability.

NARROW COLUMNS When column widths are set too narrow, the type can be difficult to read. This is especially true with justified text. Narrow justified text can result in text that has large, awkward gaps between its words. These gaps are created because the justified setting forces the text to justify on both the left and right margins.

BIG GAPS Setting justified text at narrow column widths can cause big gaps.

CONSISTENT SPACING The two images set within the text align to the baseline grid in a similar manner: to the baseline on the bottom, and to the x-height on the top.

AWKWARD POSITIONING The image is placed awkwardly in that it leaves only two lines below it, forcing the reader's eye to jump around unnecessarily. Another pitfall of this placement is that the two lines below it could be misread as a caption, rather than as running text. Placing the object at the bottom of the column will fix this. Corners and bottoms of columns are natural places to position elements.

aps, and All Caps. Each of the attributes have different qualities and introducing them ■ into your ■ design will ■ bring variety ■ to your type and design elements.

Bold faces are used for emphasis. They add contrast to gray paragraphs of body text and can create a sense of visual hierarchy. As the purpose of bold faces is to attract attention, avoid overusing bold faces as they will lose their impact. Too much

bold type can make an overall design busy, as the type fights itself for the

reader's attention. Italic typefaces are calligraphic in nature and their handwritten form has an intimate, personal quality. The slant of the italic face gives it a unique form and like bold faces, italics can add variety to otherwise monotonous columns of text. There is a wide range of italic faces. While most faces have italic variations, some faces are designed in a specifically ornate calligraphic styles. While ornate faces could also be thought of as italic, they are generally considered script faces. When design-

> To get equal spacing between the edge of the box and the text, the box aligns to the baseline grid at top and bottom and uses a runaround of 0 points at the top and bottom and 8 points. on the sides.

ing body copy, the italic versions of the body copy face will be used. One technical note regarding the proper use of italics: italics are used to denote a proper names such as *The New York Times*.

• Small Caps are a common way to set type and they evoke a formal, elegant impression when set in serif faces. -

Bold faces are used for emphasis. They add contrast to gray paragraphs of body text and can create a sense of visual hierarchy. As the purpose of bold faces is to attract attention, avoid aps, and All Caps. Each of the attributes have different qualities and introducing them into your design will bring variety to your type. Bold faces are used for emphasis. They add contrast to gray graphs of body text and can create a

ding lics: te a The om- and ele- a set caps 's characters are

callig their an in ity. face and can wise monotono

This Type Is Set Too Wide By only seeing the tops of the characters, the same word is set in both serif and sans serif. The word set in the serif face is easier to read. The serifs bring uniqueness to the characters and help with the recognition of the letter forms. A limited number of foundation shapes are used to create sans serif face here and because of the consistency within its type design, it is difficult

|← ———————————————— 85 characters wide ————————————————— →|

Box handles ⌐ └ Column Guides

BATTLE OF THE BULGE Ever find yourself reading the same line over and over? Most of us have. We tend to blame ourselves, rather than recognize the probable culprit: poor typography. Usually this happens when type is set so wide that the eye isn't able make the transition

smoothly from the end of one line and down to the next line. To solve this problem, try reducing the column width, increasing leading, or creating a two-column format. A general rule of thumb is to avoid setting a line wider than two alphabets, or fifty to sixty characters.

CENTERING OBJECTS One way to center objects accurately is to align their side box handle (which is centered) between the column guides.

Readability: Complex Text Wraps

A nicely placed silhouetted image with a text wrap can make a page's composition more visually interesting. When properly used, silhouetted images can break up the column grid and introduce interesting shapes to a page.

aps, and All Caps. Each of the attributes have different qualities and introducing them into your design will bring variety to your type.

Bold faces are used for emphasis.They add contrast to gray paragraphs of body text and can create a sense of visual hierarchy. As the purpose of bold faces is to attract attention, avoid overusing bold faces as they will lose their impact. Too much bold type can make an overall design busy, as the type fights itself for the reader's attention.

Italic typefaces are calligraphic in nature and their handwritten form has an intimate, personal quality. The slant of the italic face gives it a unique form and like bold faces, italics can add variety to otherwise monotonous columns of text. There is a wide range of italic faces. While most typefaces have italic variations, some typefaces are designed to be detailed and ornate in

their nature. While ornate faces could also be thought of as italic, they are generally considered script faces.

When designing body copy, the italic versions of the body copy typeface will be used. One technical note regarding the proper use of italics: italics are used to denote a proper names such as *The New York Times*.
• Small Caps are a common way to set type and they evoke a formal, elegant impression when set in serif faces. Small caps refers to when a word's characters are set entirely in the upper case and the word's initial

Bold faces are used for emphasis.They add contrast to gray paragraphs of body text and can create a sense of visual hierarchy. As the purpose of bold faces is to attract attention, avoid aps, and All Caps. Each of the attributes have different qualities and introducing them into your design will bring variety to your type.

Bold faces are used for emphasis.They add contrast to gray paragraphs of body

text and can create a sense of visual hierarchy. As the purpose of bold faces is to attract attention, avoid overusing bold faces as they will lose their impact. Too much bold type can make an overall design too busy, as the type fights itself for the reader's attention.

Italic typefaces are calligraphic in nature

their handwritten form has an intimate, personal quality. The slant of the italic face gives it a unique form and like bold faces, italics can add variety to otherwise monotonous columns of text. There is a wide range of italic faces. While most faces have italic variations, some faces are designed in a specifically ornate calligraphic styles. While

STRADDLING COLUMNS
Centering small images between columns in this manner brings variety to a grid.

AWKWARD TEXT WRAPS The image of the butterfly is poorly placed and sized for the column that it sits in. Type size and relative column width cause large word spaces.The image's positioning causes the text to jump around awkwardly.

BIG GAPS Placing the image too deep into the text can result in big gaps.

TEXT JUMPS Avoid setting text in such a way that it causes the reader's eye to jump around unnecessarily.

an overall design busy, as the type fights itself for the reader's attention.

Italic typefaces are calligraphic in nature and their handwritten form has an intimate, personal quality. The slant of the italic face gives it a unique form and like bold faces, italics can add variety to otherwise monotonous columns of text. There is a wide range of italic faces. While most faces have italic variations, some faces are designed in a specifically

KEEP WRAPS EVEN The space between the image and text should be equal on all sides and visually balanced. Using the Non-White Areas runaround will allow the wrap to be manually adjusted. This text wrap type is edited by selecting Item:Edit:Runaround.

PLACING IMAGES A nicely placed silhouetted image can introduce organic shapes to a page and make its composition more visually interesting. Some silhouetted images, like the one above, can work very well when placed between columns.

KEEP IT SIMPLE Complex shapes can create overly elaborate text wraps.Avoid trying to fit words into tricky spaces.

LET DESIGN DICTATE Use text wraps when they're appropriate and the design calls for it.

FINE-TUNING TEXT WRAPS Large gaps and jumps in the text can be fixed by resizing, rotating, and repositioning the image.Text jumps can also be removed by manually adjusting the runaround.

Mastering Text Runarounds

While wrapping text around complex shapes can be beautiful, getting it to wrap evenly requires a sensitive eye and precision control.

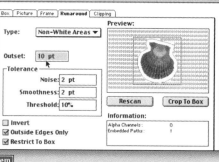

TAKE CONTROL by choosing Non-White Areas as the runaround type. This will allow manual control of the wrap by going to Item:Edit:Runaround.

IMAGE AREA is represented by the picture box border. Because the image has a clipping path, the picture box is larger than the viewable image.

LIMIT POINTS on a text wrap or clipping path. Too many points can complicate a file.

✓ Corner Point
Smooth Point
Symmetrical Point

POINT TYPES are changed by selecting a point and going to the Point/Segment Types on the Item menu.

By the dawn of the twentieth century industrialism had swept its way across the country, leaving nothing untouched in its wake. Seemingly overnight industrialization profoundly changed the face of the nation, influencing every aspect of life. The events that took place between 1885 and 1910 represent the metamorphosis of the country from a society relatively untouched by industrialism to one almost transformed by it. Emphasizing the speed and intensity of industrial advance Samuel Hays states that "seldom, if ever, in American history had so much been altered within the lifetime of a single man." 1

The accelerated rate of technological progress quickly rendered obsolete everything that had provided meaning for members of preindustrial America. These sudden and unprecedented changes left people disoriented and unable to call on previous experience to help understand their changing surroundings. Religious beliefs were fundamentally challenged by scientific advancements, while the

dominance of the Protestant church was threatened by the millions of Catholic and Jewish immigrants who came from Southern and Eastern Europe in the late 1880s.(3A Zinn 261) Urbanization redefined community standards and the rise of the industrial city in the 1880s resulted in the consequential decline of long-standing agrarian ideals which meant much. Mass procant characteristic of the American industrial economy by the 1880s, determined how and where Americans worked, as well as redefined the reasons why they worked. By the 1890s educational institutions had begun restructuring programs according to the specialized needs of industry. International markets, as well as faster modes of communication and transportation changed our perception of time and distance as well as heightening our sense of interdependence. The cumulative effect of these diverse changes created confusion and misperception among even the most forward thinking members.

Changes to traditional work patterns had a profound effect on the autonomy of both the community and the

ADD AND DELETE POINTS Points can be added to or deleted from the text runaround by using the content tool with the Option key. The cursor will change to an X display when you move over a point with the Option key down.

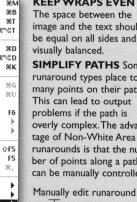

Modify

| Box | Picture | Frame | **Runaround** | Clipping |

Type: Non-White Areas ▾

Outset: 10 pt

Tolerance
Noise: 2 pt
Smoothness: 2 pt
Threshold: 10%

☐ Invert
☑ Outside Edges Only
☑ Restrict To Box

Preview:

Rescan   Crop To Box

Information:
Alpha Channels : 0
Embedded Paths : 1

Item
Modify...	⌘M
Frame...	⌘B
Runaround...	⌘T
Clipping...	⌘⌥T
Duplicate	⌘D
Step and Repeat...	⌘⌥D
Delete	⌘K
Group	⌘G
Ungroup	⌘U
Constrain	
Lock	F6
Merge	▸
Split	▸
Send to Back	⇧F5
Bring to Front	F5
Space/Align...	⌘,
Shape	▸
Content	▸
Edit	▸
Point/Segment Type	▸

✓ Shape   ⇧F4
Runaround ⌥⇧F4
Clipping Path ⌥⇧F4

KEEP WRAPS EVEN The space between the image and the text should be equal on all sides and visually balanced.

SIMPLIFY PATHS Some runaround types place too many points on their paths. This can lead to output problems if the path is overly complex. The advantage of Non-White Area runarounds is that the number of points along a path can be manually controlled.

Manually edit runaround

can be difficult to use as body copy, especially when set justified or at thin column widths.

The bottom line with readability issues is to use common sense. Is the type you've styled easy to read, and does it reflect the project's feel while accommodating the amount of required text? By keeping these considerations in mind, you should

be able to find a highly readable typeface with the appropriate qualities for your project.

Readability: Font Color

The most legible color combination for type is black type printed on white paper. It is especially important to keep this in mind when designing body copy. For this rea-

son just about all body copy is set in black. There are two reasons why black type is the most legible, the obvious one being the high level of contrast created by the black and white. The printing process also makes black type the preferred color for body copy. Let's look at the printing process and how it affects readability.

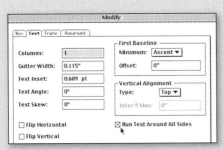

RUN TEXT ON ALL SIDES This allows you to have text "jump over" an image and continue on the other side. This function is best used with small images. This can be done by selecting the text box, not the image box, and then selecting the option from the Modify:Text menu.

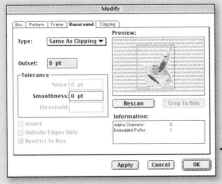

◄**SAME AS CLIPPING PATH** A text wrap can be applied to a silhouetted image, based upon its clipping path. The screen on the left shows the settings for the image in the sidebar above.

duced or how to produce it. This was devastating to semi-independent farmers and craftsmen who were accustomed to playing an integral role in the entire production process. Jack of all trades like the independent, multi-skilled farmer gave way to many interdependent individuals who were skilled in particular functions like the factory worker. There was very little satisfaction to be derived from tedious repetiindustrial labor ods of produca sense of confrom the work notions of work

the performance of tive tasks that the required. New method. have also removed nection to the community process. The local farm epitomized traditional in that it involved both the private and public spheres. The religiously guided calling, one in which God's will determined a person's purpose within society, was replaced by the professional career and industrial labor. The

As standards change in PDA technology, the old business tools pale.

Silhouetted Images and Background Tints

When independent farmers and craftsmen who were accustomed to playing an integral role in the entire production process. Jack of all trades like the independent, multi-skilled farmer gave way to many interdependent individuals who were skilled in particular functions like the factory worker. There was little satisfaction to be derived from the performance of tedious repetitive tasks that industrial labor required.

New methods of production also removed the sense of connection to the community from the work process. The local farm epitomized traditional notions of work

in that it involved both the private and public spheres. The religiously guided calling, one in which God's will determined a person's purpose within society, was The religiously guided calling, one in which God's will determined a person's purpose within society, was replaced by the professional career and industrial labor. The notion of work as a calling implied

ACCURATE PATHS There are numerous ways to use silhouetted image for interesting design solutions. Here the image is placed in the corner so that the telephone breaks off the page, while the pad beneath it is cropped by the page edge. Here the text wrap is expanded to create a space for a caption.

CREATE DEPTH An illusion of depth can be created by using silhouetted images with accurate clipping paths and placing them over a background tint so that parts of the image appear to come out toward the reader.

When your file is output to color separations and later printed, the black plate is printed on top of the other color plates (C,M,Y). Keep in mind that a full-color image can be reproduced using only cyan, magenta, and yellow. Conversely, black can be created by combining cyan, magenta, and yellow. When you consider this, it

would seem as if the black plate was unnecessary. So why is a black plate included in the print process? Were you to specify a black using only cyan, magenta, and yellow, such a black would be liable to falling out of registration during the printing process and thus become blurry and unreadable. A common example of color shifting can often be seen in

the Sunday comics of a newspaper in which the color plates do not align perfectly. This registration shift happens because the lower-quality paper stretches as it rolls through the press and the color plates shift slightly during a press run. If type is printed solely on the black plate, it will remain legible, even if the plate falls out of register.

Setting Captions

Captions are designed to work in tandem with images and to complement the body copy. Here are a few ways to build and group captions with images.

KNOCKOUT CAPTIONS

An image's composition and overall quality may allow the caption to be placed within the image area and knocked out from it.

TYPE PAIRING

Since most body text is set in a serif face, captions are a great way to introduce a sans serif face. They are also less likely to be mistaken for body copy.

SEPARATE BOXES

The caption is placed in a separate text box, not as part of the linked column. This way its position is fixed and will not change as body copy is edited and reflowed.

By the dawn of the twentieth century industrialism had swept its way across the country, leaving nothing untouched in its wake. Seemingly overnight industrialization profoundly changed the face of the nation, influencing every aspect of life. The events that took place between 1885 and 1910 represent the metamorphosis of the country from a society relatively untouched by industrialism to one almost transformed by

Despite personal problems, Ochoa has managed to continue to dominate mountain biking.

it. Emphasizing the speed and intensity of industrial advance Samuel Hays states that "seldom, if ever, in American

ACROSS THE SKY Gustav cuts a path through the clouds on his way on his first gold medal.

history had so much been altered within the lifetime of a single man." 1

The accelerated rate of technological progress quickly rendered obsolete everything that had provided meaning for members of preindustrial America. These sudden and unprecedented changes left people disoriented and unable to call on previous experience to help understand their changing surroundings. Religious beliefs were fundamentally challenged by scientific advancements, while the dominance of the Protestant church was threatened by the millions of Catholic and Jewish immigrants who came from Southern and Eastern Europe in the late 1880s.(3A Zinn 261) Urbanization redefined community standards and the rise of the industrial city in the 1880s resulted in the consequential decline of

JORGE OCHOA
Born: August 12, 1977
Dominican Republic
Olympics: 1998, 2002
Teen contender for Junior Olympics 1994, Silver medalist 1998, Gold medal in 2002

long-standing agrarian ideals which meant much. Mass procant characteristic of the American industrial economy by the 1880s, determined how and where Americans worked, as well as redefined the reasons why they worked. By the 1890s educational institutions

OLYMPIC VILLAGE is comprised of over 700 A-frame cottages located in the South Woods just minutes from the Ski Trails

HOLDING RULES

For images with light areas that match the page tone, use a "holding rule," a half-point black rule to hold the image in place and define its edge. Without the holding rule, the snow on the right edge of the image at far left would match the page white and the edge would not be defined.

INFO CAPTIONS

While captions commonly describe their accompanying photos, they can convey a much broader range of information.

LEAD-INS This is a common way to style captions. Lead-ins are a series of initial words that are styled differently from a caption.

TEXT RUNAROUNDS By using a separate text box for the caption, the column of running body copy jumps around the image and its caption.

USING THE BASELINE GRID While the caption above doesn't lock to the baseline grid, its last line does align with the baseline at the bottom of the adjacent column.

For this reason it is best when setting type at smaller sizes, to specify it as black rather than in color.

Readability: Font Size and Leading

While the typeface you select to use as body copy is important, you also need to consider its size and leading. The type size and its relationship with the leading, has a direct impact on readability. You need to find a relationship between the type size and its leading that will maintain readability while accommodating the amount of text required. For obvious reasons, you should avoid setting the type too small. For general audiences, 10- to 12-point type is generally appropriate for body copy. It is important to make design decisions with your audience in mind. Remember that the young generally have stronger eyesight and have fewer problems reading small type than older people. Many popular magazines publish alternative versions geared toward an older readership that include larger body type.

When deciding on type size, don't judge your type solely by how it looks on the screen. No matter what part of a design you are working on, it is a good practice is to print out samples of the page as you progress. Type that looks fine on the screen may turn out larger or smaller than you expected. Printing samples also provides the opportunity to see the design as it will truly appear on a printed page, rather than backlit on a color monitor.

Leading, the vertical space between the lines of text, is also integral to readability. The term *leading* is a holdover from the days of handset type, when typesetters would actually insert thin sheets of lead between the lines of text to manually spread them apart. The amount of leading you apply to the text will have both aesthetic and practical effects. Leading directly affects how easy it is for the eye to comfortably read through the text, as well as how dense the paragraph appears. In most cases, body copy should have some leading applied to it, but how much depends on the typeface and the size it is set at. For example, type set at 11 point is usually given an extra point or two of

Special Characters: Using Key Caps

There are numerous special characters, including accents and unique symbols, that cannot be created through standard keystrokes. To create these special characters, you'll need to familiarize yourself with Key Caps.

KEY CAPS is a small native application that is included on most Macintosh operating systems. It allows you to view a font's entire character set. By using different key combinations such as Shift + Option, Option, Shift + Option + , you can see which combinations of keystrokes produce which special characters.

CHARACTER SETS include much more than upper- and lowercase characters. The special characters included within these character sets can be diverse, containing accented characters and numerical symbols. Ligatures, type pairs that are actually designed to touch, are also included within these sets.

Shift + Opt + "   Opt + c   Opt + e

additional leading. This proportion will change as the size of the type increases.

A Word About Autoleading

QuarkXpress provides an autoleading option, which many designers strongly recommend not using. The reasoning behind this is based partly on principle and partly for practical reasons. Autoleading is by default set at 120 percent of the type size. This means that if

the size of your type is set at 10 point, the leading will be set at 12 point. While this relationship may be an appropriate one, its use implies an indifference on the part of the designer. There is nothing automatic about graphic design, and designers should be making conscious decisions about every aspect of their design. The practical reasoning for avoiding autoleading is that it is susceptible to output problems. Autoleading is a Quark document preference, and should your service bureau have a different set of default preferences, the running text within your document might flow differently into the columns, causing awkward line breaks or lost type.

Readability: Column Widths

Along with type size and leading, column width is a third factor in determining the readability of your paragraph text. Overall readability is the result of the relationship of type size and leading to its column width. Successful body copy design is largely a result of balancing these three factors.

Column width directly affects the readability of the text. When a column is set too wide, the eye has a hard time jumping from the end of one line down to the next, and hence readers find themselves reading the same line over again. Everyone has experienced this at some time, and typically we think that we as readers are at fault, when in actuality it is the result of ineffective type design.

There are a few adjustments you can make to fix this problem without reducing the column width. The type size could be increased, in essence making the column width appear less wide. Increasing the leading will also create more separation between the paragraph's lines and help guide the eye downward. A general rule

---

Styling Captions

While captions generally are used to describe the images they are grouped with, they can also be used as an informative vehicle and as a design element.

By the dawn of the twentieth century industrialism had swept its way across the country, leaving nothing untouched in its wake. Seemingly overnight industrialization profoundly changed the face of the nation, influencing every aspect of life. The events that took place between 1885 and 1910 represent the metamorphosis of the country from a society relatively untouched by industrialism to one almost transformed by it. Emphasizing the speed and intensity of industrial advance Samuel Hays states that "seldom, if ever, in American history had so much been altered

The pocket-sized box includes a die-cut and specialized front tab. The use of a rotated ellipse also works well.

STRONG VERTICAL Image and caption work nicely when they are set into a column. The text and image should be sized so that they don't make the text column too narrow.

NATURE'S POWER has been harnessed to produce hydroelectricity for eastern seaboard cities as far away as Boston and Portland.

By the dawn of the twentieth century industrialism had swept its way across the country, leaving nothing untouched in its wake. Seemingly overnight industrialization profoundly changed the face of the nation, influencing every aspect of life. The events that took place between 1885 and 1910 represent the metamorphosis of the country from a society

SELF-CONTAINED Tint boxes can be grouped with the photo and caption to form a small group of elements that brings contrast and color to the page design.

By the dawn of the twentieth century industrialism had swept its way across the country, leaving nothing untouched in its wake. Seemingly overnight industrialization profoundly changed the face of the nation, influencing every aspect of life. The events that took place between 1885 and 1910 represent the metamorphosis of the country from a society relatively untouched by industrialism to one almost transformed by it. Emphasizing the speed and intensity of industrial advance Samuel Hays states that "seldom, if ever, in American history had so much been altered within the lifetime of a single man." The accelerated rate of technological progress quickly rendered obsolete everything that had provided meaning for members of preindustrial

TRANSLUCENCE Macintosh's introduction of translucent plastics into their product line, competitors are following suit.

COMPLEXITY Basing a text runaround on an elaborate clipping path can bring interesting organic shapes into the page. The caption is placed so that it offsets the body copy.

regarding column width is to limit the number of characters on a single line to about fifty to sixty characters.

Just as wide columns are subject to readability problems, so is text set in very narrow columns, which do not accommodate large type well and can cause awkward line breaks when justified.

Once you understand the criteria you should consider when setting body copy, the task becomes much easier.

Knockout Type

Another typographic option is knockout or reverse type—light-colored type placed on a dark background. There are a couple of things to consider when using knockout type. While it can give a dramatic feel to a design, it is generally more difficult to read than black type on a white background. Because of the evenness in their stroke weights, sans serif typefaces tend to work better as reverse type than serif

faces. Serif faces have varying stroke weights with thin sections that tend to break up when knocking out. The high level of contrast created by the thin stroke widths and the dark background tend to make serif text visually vibrate when it is knocked out.

Using knockout type is a great way to add emphasis to type while also breaking up and offsetting repetitive columns of gray text. Another option designers have is setting knockout type in color. While white is the most legible for knockout type, using a light tint that relates to the design can help to integrate the type with the design.

Knockout Type and Images

Type can also be knocked out from a background image instead of a solid color. This common treatment can be very dramatic and attractive. How effective the knocked-out type is depends on the image being used and the placement of the type within that image. When it comes to type positioning, always let the image dictate the type placement. This means placing type within the inactive areas of a photo so that it doesn't obscure any of the photo's pertinent areas. The images that best accommodate knockout type

NOT FORGOTTEN New plans are being discussed on how to rebuild the area and commemorate the fallen heroes.

By the dawn of the twentieth century industrialism had swept its way across the country, leaving nothing untouched in its wake. Seemingly overnight industrialization profoundly changed the face of the nation, influencing every aspect of life. The events that took place between 1885 and 1910 represent the metamorphosis of the country from a society relatively untouched by industrialism to one almost transformed by it. Emphasizing the speed and intensity of industrial advance Samuel Hays states that "seldom, if ever, in American history had so much

TINT BOXES Captions in a tint box can be positioned so that they float over an image. This approach works best with images that have inactive areas that can accommodate the box.

By the dawn of the twentieth century industrialism had swept its way across the country, leaving nothing untouched in its wake. Seemingly overnight industrialization profoundly changed the face of the nation, influencing every aspect of life. The events that took place between 1885 and 1910 represent the metamorphosis of the country from a society relatively untouched by industrialism to one almost transformed by it. Emphasizing the speed and intensity of industrial advance Samuel Hays states that "seldom, if ever, in American history had so much been altered within the lifetime of a single man." 1

The accelerated rate of technological progress quickly rendered obsolete every-

GRILLED CHICKEN Deluxe

Despite an aggressive commercial campaign sales performance has been lower than projected.

thing that had provided meaning for members of preindustrial America. These sudden and unprece-

CREATING DEPTH By their nature, images with clipping paths bring a sense of depth to a page. When used in conjunction with a tint box, that effect can be increased.

Creating Drop Caps in QuarkXpress

Drop caps help make introductory text more visually interesting and bring variety to a page design. Let's look at how to set up standard drop caps in QuarkXpress.

This drop cap is set by highlighting the first paragraph and setting a 5-line drop cap in the Formats menu. Then refine the drop cap size by highlighting the drop cap and changing its percentage in the measurement palette.

Initial paragraph text is set larger and with looser leading. Following paragraphs are styled in smaller text size.

Habits of the Heart: Individualism and Commitment in American Life explores the current relationship between individual character and society. Its focuses on how Americans make sense of their lives, envision themselves, and how their ideas and actions are related to these values. This survey interviews people from diverse demographic groups and questions their views on personal and social obligation, freedom, religion, and personal relationships. Finding separation to be a prominent characteristic of twentieth century society, the study is divided into two sections: private and public life.

Pre-industrial forms of republican and biblical individualism have become overshadowed in modern society and replaced by a new dominant utilitarian form of individualism. These older social and moral standards have become less relevant to modern life. It explores how traditional notions of self-reliance, freedom, commitment, community, and status take shape in the present day. The results of the study finds Americans to be success-oriented, materialistic, self-centered, and inarticulate, without any foundation based on tradition.

Contradictions in current notions of status, individualism a nd empowerment are evident today. Older notions have changed as American life has shifted from agrarian to industrial and then from industrial to tech-

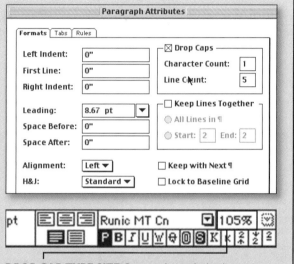

DROP CAP TYPE SIZE Once you've applied a drop cap to the paragraph, the initial letter is sized according to the number of lines deep it was set at and the leading setting. The drop cap no longer has a point size but appears as a percentage in the measurement palette. These drop caps can often appear visually small, and it is not uncommon to size them up slightly.

are those that have consistently dark areas that are sizable enough to comfortably fit the text. If your image is a high-contrast one or has large busy areas of light and dark tones, there is a strong possibility that these qualities will interfere with the typeface's readability. Knockout type requires a relatively consistent background so that the character's edges are well defined and recognizable. When the type's edges are not well defined, the type does not appear to sit above the image, and thus lacks the separation it needs to read well. When type is knocked out from an image, character edges should be well defined so that the text "pops" from the image.

Designing with Type: Text Wraps

Runarounds, or text wraps, involve the interplay of image and text in which body copy is manipulated to follow or wrap around an image's outline. Runarounds range from basic to complex manipulations depending on the image being used. They can be based upon the boundaries of an image's picture box or upon an imbedded clipping path created in Photoshop. Runarounds are often effectively used to push type around silhouetted images. Running type around silhouetted images can help break up the rigid column grid and introduce interesting shapes to a design. Text wraps are especially effective when they are applied to elements that straddle, or sit between, text columns. Silhouetted vertical objects work particularly well when straddling columns of justified body copy. They break up the page nicely and deemphasize the strict column grid.

A couple of commonsense guidelines for using text wraps: Generally some buffer space should be placed between the type and image so that the text doesn't butt into an image's edge. Overly complex runarounds can make type read awkwardly and force the reader's eye to unnaturally jump around the page in order to read the text. Text wraps that force type to run into very narrow columns should also be avoided, as they cause awkward word spacing.

QuarkXpress offers a wide, and sometimes confusing, array of runaround types. You really only need to master a few of these runaround types to be able to achieve your design goals. There are two runaround types that should address most design needs. The item runaround is the most common and simple to use. This option simply wraps text according to the picture box edges. While it is easy to use, its editing capabilities are limited. For more elaborate runarounds, most

Styling Custom Drop Caps

Besides using standard drop cap setting in QuarkXpress, there are an unlimited number of ways to build, refine, and stylize custom drop cap treatments. Here's a sampling of some of the ways.

This is a standard drop cap set using one character that is three lines deep.

While fragments of preindustrial culture persisted well into the 1900s, their influence would decline dramatically by century's end. Contemporary America looks to its past more for a sense of nostalgia than for cultural reference. As America welcomes the technological future it might

"I thought the influence of social, political, and religious traditions which previously guided citizens had become attenuated in modern society. As the world gets increasingly complex, our sense of control over events outside of our own personal

Words can also be used to start paragraphs. Use Quark drop cap settings with multiple characters.

Large, lightly tinted initial characters can be placed behind actual text.

Urbanization and consumerism have contributed greatly to America's growing individualistic nature. The isolation and unfamiliarity which characterize modern life have caused us to look inward. Consumerism also encouraged us to focus on personal well-being. As our priorities shift, Americans show less regard for earlier models of family, reli-

Ernest Hemingway observes that the most resonant of all contemporary American values, personal freedom, is one which differs greatly from earlier notions of individuality. Personal freedom today implies exclusion from obligation and commitment to others. Despite this revised version of self-sufficiency,

Drop caps can be placed outside the text margins. This drop cap is placed in a separate text box.

Because of their narrowness, condensed faces can be styled so that they sit deep in the paragraph.

The most resonant of contemporary American values, personal freedom, is one which differs greatly from earlier notions of individuality. Personal freedom today implies exclusion from obligation and commitment to others. Despite this revised version of self-sufficiency, Americans are more dependent on large complex insti-

Robert Bellah observes that the most resonant of contemporary American values, personal freedom, is one which differs greatly from earlier notions of individuality. Personal freedom today implies exclusion from obligation and commitment to others. Despite this revised version of self-sufficiency,

This drop cap was created by changing type size and face. It is not a true drop cap, as it doesn't "drop" into the text.

A separate box is used to wrap the text around the letter form.

The influence of social, political, as well as religious traditions which previously guided citizens has become attenuated in modern society. As the world gets increasingly complex, our sense of control over events outside of our own personal experiences is vanishing. Democratic ideals of participating politically to effect change

In his latest overview on American social values Robert Bellah observes that the most resonant of contemporary American values, personal freedom, is one which differs greatly from earlier notions of individuality. Personal

A separate box with no tint or border is used to push the text around the letter form.

COMPLEX WRAPS Here an empty shape is created to follow letter form. Text wrap is applied to this shape. In this case the drop cap is separate from the text.

The influe cal, as we which pre has become att

— Edit shape to push type around letter form

While fragments of preindustrial culture persisted well into the 1900s, their influence would decline dramatically by century's end. Contemporary America looks to its past more for a sense of nostalgia than for cultural reference. As America welcomes the technological future it might be well served to consider its relatively recent industrial past. While industrial advancement increased standards of living, and improved health care, it has also resulted in increasing materialism, isolation, and individualism. As America welcomes the techno-

KERNING DROP CAPS Adjust the space between the drop cap and paragraph text by placing the cursor between them and adjusting the kerning.

often associated with complex silhouetted images, the Non-White Areas option is probably best because it is editable. This runaround type can be manually adjusted, allowing the designer to specifically control the runaround's effect. Most runaround types cannot be manually edited.

There are instances when you may need to create the effect of a text runaround for complex images without actually applying a runaround to the image's picture box. This can be done by placing an empty shape above an image and applying the Item runaround to this shape. No runaround is applied to the image in this case, and the empty box is used to wrap the text. In essence this technique creates a free-floating runaround that is independent of the image itself.

When QuarkXpress applies an image runaround, it can sometimes add more points than are necessary. By limiting the number of points in a text runaround (or a clipping path) you will simplify the file and speed up your output time.

Soft Returns

In some cases you may want to avoid applying a runaround to an image and simply set the text manually so it appears to wrap around a shape. This involves inserting paragraph returns into the text so that the line breaks form the appearance of a runaround. This approach is most often applied to small amounts of text that is not subject to change. The best way to manually shape text is to enter "soft returns" into the text. Soft returns are inserted by using Shift + Return. Instead of a standard paragraph return, or "hard return," line breaks created by soft returns are not treated as new paragraphs. This means that any attributes that are applied to the paragraph such as indents or drop caps will not be applied to the new line.

Setting Captions

Just as type takes on one of two forms depending on its function—

Ornate Drop Caps

Collections of ornate and period-style initial caps can be an invaluable resource for designers. Many are available in both print and electronic formats.

DOVER BOOKS has a wide collection of visual design materials such as ornate drop caps, Victorian, and Art Deco borders as well as collections of period art such as advertisements. Besides being a great resource for design research, much of the work can be used royalty-free.

Styling Paragraphs

How you style the initial paragraph of text sets the tone for the design piece. By experimenting with column formats, rules, and type size, you can come up with your own customized paragraph style.

While urbanization and consumerism have contributed greatly to America's growing individualistic nature, the isolation and unfamiliarity which characterize modern life have caused us to look inward. Consumerism also encouraged the focus on personal well-being. As our priorities shift, Americans show less regard for earlier models of family, religion, and community. Since our preindustrial past seemingly bears little personal free

SIZE REDUCTION
Here the font size decreases until it reaches the standard body copy size. This involves great attention to word breaks, tracking, and hard and soft returns.

SUBDIVISION
A common way to break up the vertical column grid is to subdivide colums. In this sample the paragraph is initially set at a wider column width and a larger font size.

Urbanization and consumerism have contributed greatly to America's growing individualistic nature. The isolation and unfamiliarity which characterize modern

life have caused us to look inward. Consumerism also encouraged us to focus on personal well-being. As our priorities shift, Americans show less regard for earlier | models of family, religion, and community. Personal freedom today implies exclusion from obligation and commitment to others and despite this

RIGHT AT THE DAWN OF THE TWENTIETH CENTURY INDUSTRIALISM HAD SWEPT ITS WAY ACROSS THE COUNTRY, LEAVING NO STONE UNTURNED IN ITS WAKE AND SEEMINGLY OVERNIGHT INDUSTRIALIZATION PROFOUNDLY CHANGED the face of the nation, influencing every aspect of life. The events that took place between 1885 and 1910 represent the metamorphosis of the country from a society relatively untouched by industrialism to one almost transformed by it. Emphasizing the speed and intensity of industrial advance Hays states that "seldom, if ever, in American history had so much been altered within the lifetime of a single man." The accelerated rate of technological progress quickly rendered obsolete everything that had provided meaning for members of preindustrial America. These sudden and unprecedented changes left people disoriented and unable to call on previous experience to help understand their

TYPE AS SHAPE
Here the initial cap was converted to a graphic using Text to Box and then a text wrap was applied. Run Text on All Sides allows the text to jump over the bottom of the *R*.

STEP AND REPEAT
Lightweight rules complement standard paragraph stylings nicely. Here they are used in conjunction with a large drop cap.

Urbanization and consumerism have contributed greatly to America's growing individualistic nature. The isolation and

life have caused us to look inward. Consumerism also encouraged us to focus on personal well-being. As our priorities shift, Americans | show less regard for earlier models of family, religion, and community. Since our preindustrial past seemingly bears little Personal free-

Mr. Bellah observes that the most resonant of contemporary American values, personal freedom, is one which differs significantly from earlier notions of individuality. ¶ Personal freedom today implies exclusion from obligation and commitment to others. Despite revised versions of self-sufficiency, Americans are more dependent on large complex institutions than ever before. ¶ While technology has provided us The influence of social, political, and religious traditions

USING IMAGES
An image that relates to the text can be used as a drop cap.

CONTINUOUS TEXT A paragraph symbol is inserted (Opt + 7) instead of a standard line break. The symbol becomes a design element.

display type and body copy—so do photographs. Large, dominant photographs often appear on the opening pages of magazine articles and on covers of CDs, books, and brochures. Often these projects contain smaller supporting photographs that provide more specific information than the large opening photo, which is usually more decorative in nature.

Because of the informative nature of these small photos, they are often accompanied by captions. Captions typically consist of one or two sentences, but they can sometimes include as much as a paragraph. As with working with any form of body copy, styling captions is a subtle skill. Depending on the complexity of the material covered in the caption, there are many approaches to styling captions. Designing captions involves creating a type styling that complements the photo while clearly conveying its information. Just as

Show Invisibles

In order to control the finer details of paragraph text, you need to understand how invisible formatting characters work.

FIRST-LINE INDENTS should be set by using the first-line indent setting in the Paragraph Attributes menu.

INSERTED TABS are used for aligning text in columns, not for paragraph indents as shown here.

WORD SPACES are shown as dots between words. These are commonly used by copy editors to check for extra spaces in the copy.

Bold·faces·are·used·for·stress.··They·add contrast·to·gray·paragraphs·of·body·text·and·can create·a·sense·of·visual·hierarchy.··As·the·purpose of·bold·faces·is·to·attract·attention,·avoid··over-using·bold·faces·as·they·will·lose·their·impact.·· Too·much·bold·type·can·make·an·overall·design· busy,·as·the·type·fights·for·a·reader's·attention.¶
→Italic·typefaces·are·calligraphic·in·nature and·their·handwritten·form·has·an·intimate,·per-sonal·quality.·The·slant·of·the·italic·face·gives·it variety·to·monotonous·columns·of·text.↵
There·is·a·wide·range·of·italic·faces.··While·most faces have·italic·variations,·some·faces·are·in·a

HARD RETURNS indicate that a paragraph return has been inserted here. A hard return is inserted by hitting the return key.

SOFT RETURNS are inserted to turn a line, so that Quark won't handle it as a new paragraph. In this case the line after the return does not automatically indent because a soft return is inserted. Soft returns are inserted by using Shift + Return.

SHOW INVISIBLES is a way to access hidden formatting characters. Select Show Invisibles from the View pull-down menu. Invisible characters represent paragraph formats like spaces, tabs, and hard and soft returns.

there are many types of photographic treatments, such as ghosting, silhouetting, and vignetting images, there are an equal number of ways to style captions.

Selecting Type for Captions

While captions can be set in serif or sans serif faces, because of their small point size, simpler faces tend to work best. As discussed earlier, ornate faces are meant to be used as display type, and their detail falls out when printed small. Select your caption typeface according to the project. If you are designing an informative poster, a serif or sans serif typeface is fine. If the project includes running body copy set in a serif typeface, try styling the captions in a sans serif face. Setting captions in a sans serif face avoids the risk of having the reader confuse the caption as part of the running text. It also introduces a second font into the design and breaks up the columns of running serif text. Because of the evenness of the sans serif stroke, the caption text will appear in a different, often darker shade and add contrast to the overall tonality of the type.

Lead-ins and Subheads

Because readers tend to like to be able to browse through an article's content and quickly locate information, it's important to design type so that it is easy to navigate through. One way to do this is to style type so that it includes lead-ins and subheads. Lead-ins and subheads are small groups or phrases of words that precede a caption or paragraph text. They are usually set in bold face or all caps. Their purpose is to quickly summarize content and help increase the skimmability of a design.

While lead-ins and subheads are visibly similar, there is a subtle difference between them. In a lead-in, the initial words of a sentence are bolded. A subhead is a short title, usually two or three words, that is a separate thought, followed by a separate sentence. The running text in this book includes subheads throughout its design.

Complex Caption Styling

A wide variety of information can be included within a caption. How much descriptive information that is included with the photo depends on the project. While many captions are simple, more informative captions will require more advanced styling techniques. One way to add variety and create a sense of visual hierarchy is to introduce different type weights and styles to your captions. For example, let's say a project includes a series of company profiles accompanied by a photo. Each profile will provide similar information about its representative company. This information might include product, financial or contact information, and company history. In this case you will need to create an attractive caption treatment that will accommodate all this information in a consistent manner. There are many design elements that can be integrated, such as bullets, indents, tint bands, drop shadows, and rules, to dress up the caption information.

Type Styling: Drop Caps

Drop caps refer to when the initial letter of a paragraph is set at a larger size than the rest of the paragraph text. They are called drop caps because they drop or fall into the paragraph text. Using drop caps is an effective way to add visual variety to a design as well as breakup the text and provide visual relief for the eye. The use of drop caps can be traced back to the Middle Ages,

Controlling Indents and Insets

Setting indents and insets allows the designer to maintain and finely control the paragraph settings.

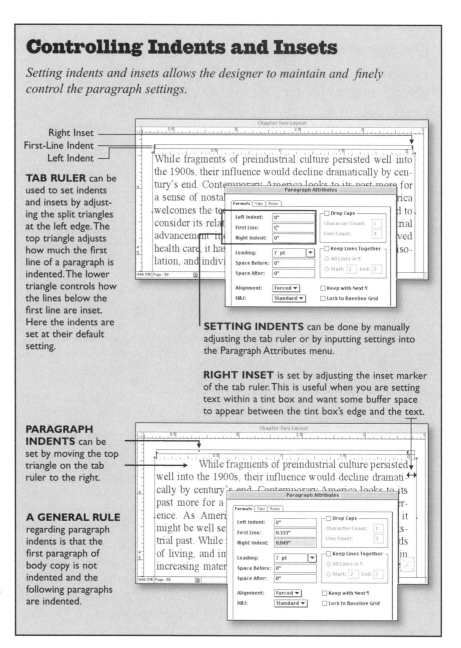

Right Inset
First-Line Indent
Left Indent

TAB RULER can be used to set indents and insets by adjusting the split triangles at the left edge. The top triangle adjusts how much the first line of a paragraph is indented. The lower triangle controls how the lines below the first line are inset. Here the indents are set at their default setting.

SETTING INDENTS can be done by manually adjusting the tab ruler or by inputting settings into the Paragraph Attributes menu.

RIGHT INSET is set by adjusting the inset marker of the tab ruler. This is useful when you are setting text within a tint box and want some buffer space to appear between the tint box's edge and the text.

PARAGRAPH INDENTS can be set by moving the top triangle on the tab ruler to the right.

A GENERAL RULE regarding paragraph indents is that the first paragraph of body copy is not indented and the following paragraphs are indented.

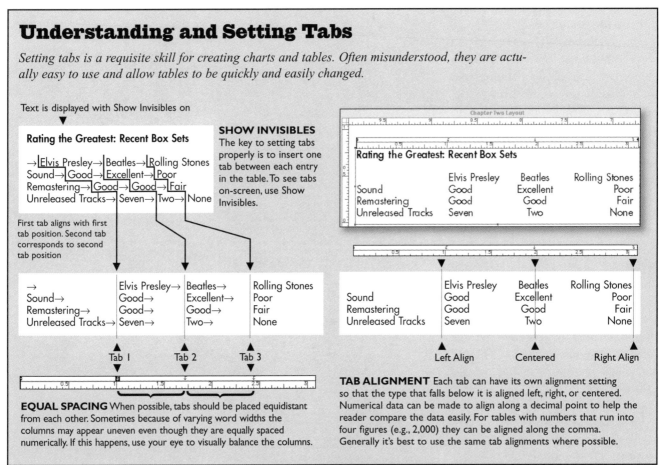

Understanding and Setting Tabs

Setting tabs is a requisite skill for creating charts and tables. Often misunderstood, they are actually easy to use and allow tables to be quickly and easily changed.

Text is displayed with Show Invisibles on

Rating the Greatest: Recent Box Sets

→ Elvis Presley → Beatles → Rolling Stones
Sound → Good → Excellent → Poor
Remastering → Good → Good → Fair
Unreleased Tracks → Seven → Two → None

SHOW INVISIBLES The key to setting tabs properly is to insert one tab between each entry in the table. To see tabs on-screen, use Show Invisibles.

First tab aligns with first tab position. Second tab corresponds to second tab position

→	Elvis Presley →	Beatles →	Rolling Stones
Sound →	Good →	Excellent →	Poor
Remastering →	Good →	Good →	Fair
Unreleased Tracks →	Seven →	Two →	None

Tab 1   Tab 2   Tab 3

EQUAL SPACING When possible, tabs should be placed equidistant from each other. Sometimes because of varying word widths the columns may appear uneven even though they are equally spaced numerically. If this happens, use your eye to visually balance the columns.

Chapter Two Layout

Rating the Greatest: Recent Box Sets

	Elvis Presley	Beatles	Rolling Stones
Sound	Good	Excellent	Poor
Remastering	Good	Good	Fair
Unreleased Tracks	Seven	Two	None

Sound	Elvis Presley	Beatles	Rolling Stones
Remastering	Good	Excellent	Poor
Unreleased Tracks	Good	Good	Fair
	Seven	Two	None

Left Align   Centered   Right Align

TAB ALIGNMENT Each tab can have its own alignment setting so that the type that falls below it is aligned left, right, or centered. Numerical data can be made to align along a decimal point to help the reader compare the data easily. For tables with numbers that run into four figures (e.g., 2,000) they can be aligned along the comma. Generally it's best to use the same tab alignments where possible.

when elaborate and ornate sets of characters were developed for use in illuminated manuscripts.

Designers have many options in setting drop caps. Drop caps can be set in a different typeface from the body copy. They can be positioned in different relationships to the paragraph and its margins. Drop caps can be set in QuarkXpress by specifying the number of initial characters you wish to affect, as well as the number of lines deep you want the drop cap to be. This function can be found in the Formats section.

The size of the drop cap will be determined in part by the column width. When wide, extended typefaces are used for drop caps and are dropped too deeply into a paragraph, they can become too wide for the column width. Condensed typefaces make great drop caps because they can sit deep into paragraph text without becoming too wide. Drop caps are generally used at the beginning of sections and should not be applied to every paragraph. Too many drop caps on a page can give the page a busy or "buckshot" look, in which too many small elements on the page fight for the viewer's attention.

While the drop cap options available in QuarkXpress are often adequate for most design needs, there are instances when drop caps need to be set manually. Separate type boxes containing drop caps can be manually positioned over the paragraph. This approach provides more control, but because it is separated from the running text it will need to be repositioned should the text change.

Another method is to use resource materials for drop caps. There are great sets of illustrative initial characters available that are in the public domain and can be used royalty-free. These characters are particularly useful in period pieces and can be scanned in and manually placed before a paragraph. Another method of adapting this illustrative approach to drop caps is to place a small image that relates to the text's subject where a drop cap would appear. For example, if your text deals with an upcoming election you might use a campaign button or presidential seal in place of a drop cap.

Using Columned Tables

Another approach to preparing tabular material is to use columns instead of tabs. Although it offers less control, for simple charts it can be useful.

USING COLUMNS instead of tabs to set up a table can be easily done by using the enter key on the numeric pad of the keyboard to move the cursor into the next column. Start by setting up a four-column text box. Type into the first column and then use the enter key to move the cursor into the next column.

STYLING TEXT Multi-column text boxes are well suited for tables that include large sections of paragraph text. Some options for styling text include:

• **LEADING** can be changed to group relative information together.

• **TYPE WEIGHTS** can be varied to create visual hierarchy within the text.

• **RULES** can be used as a design element and to separate information. Here they give the heading text cohesiveness.

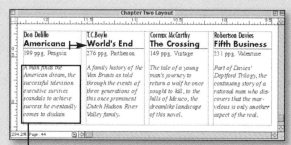

MULTIPLE-LINE CELLS are created by typing directly into the table entry or cell. No paragraph returns or tabs are necessary using this method. Actual final layout using this method is shown below.

Tabs and Indents

Setting and controlling tabs in text will save you a lot of time when designing tables and charts. Tabs are easy to set in QuarkXpress, and it is a skill that is well worth the small amount of time it takes to learn. The first time most designers attempt to build a table, they often resort to using spaces and multiple tabs to push the type into column positions. While this method may

Designing and Styling Text Tables

Designers are often required to design charts and tables. Don't let the cold numbers intimidate you—tables don't have to be strictly the purveyor of sterile data and, in fact, with a little effort can be styled quite attractively.

APPLYING RULES Thin rules can run between the lines of a chart to give it a cohesive look. The rules also help guide the reader's eye across the chart. This is important with wide charts, which are more difficult to locate information on.

RULES AND TEXT The best way to create rules in the table is to apply rules to the text, rather than draw each rule manually. Applying rules to the text allows the rules to move with the text and isn't a problem should the text be edited and reflowed.

OFFSETTING RULES Rules should be offset so that they are centered horizontally between the lines of text. Here a black half-point rule is set to fall 3 points below the baseline of the text.

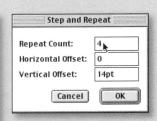

Paragraph Attributes

Formats | Tabs | **Rules**

☐ **Rule Above**
Length: [Indents ▼] Style: [_____▼]
From Left: [0"] Width: [1 pt ▼]
From Right: [0"] Color: [Black ▼]
Offset: [0"₀] Shade: [100%₀ ▼]

☒ **Rule Below**
Length: [Indents ▼] Style: [━━━━━▼]
From Left: [0"] Width: [1 pt ▼]
From Right: [0"] Color: [Black ▼]
Offset: [3 pt] Shade: [100%₀ ▼]

CDs by the Numbers: A Look Back on 2

	Redd Kross Show World	Tom Waits Blood Money	Bjork Vespertine	Radiohead Kid A
Sound Quality	Good	Good	Excellent	Poor
Highest Chart Rating	2	11	23	7
Weeks in Top 100	19	9	42	79

└─ Row Heads   └─ Column Heads

COLUMNS AND ROWS Usually row and column headings are set in bold text. This creates a sense of visual hierarchy, as well as increases the table's readability and skimability.

▲ **APPLY RULES** before or after a line. The rule's width, color, or style can be set. Its horizontal position is controlled by the offset setting. Set offset in points rather than percentage, which can be difficult to estimate. **Note:** Rules are applied only after hard returns. If you want rules below each line in a paragraph, insert a hard return at the end of every line.

Styling Tables with Tint Bands

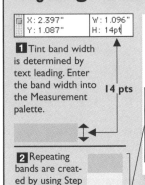

X: 2.397" W: 1.096"
Y: 1.087" H: 14pt

1 Tint band width is determined by text leading. Enter the band width into the Measurement palette.

14 pts

2 Repeating bands are created by using Step and Repeat, and then placed behind the text.

CDs by the Numbers: A Look Back on 2004

	Redd Kross Show World	Tom Waits Blood Money	Bjork Vespertine	Radiohead Kid A
Sound Quality	Fair	Good	Excellent	Good
Highest Chart Rating	52	23	11	7
Weeks in Top 100	19	9	42	79
Advance Sales*	55	13	9	14

Step and Repeat

Repeat Count: [4]
Horizontal Offset: [0]
Vertical Offset: [14pt]

[Cancel] [OK]

STEP AND REPEAT Create a set of tint bands by using Step and Repeat. Vertical offset is set at 14 points, the same as the leading. Bands will be spaced to align with the rules in the table.

ALTERNATING TINTS Another way to add variety while assisting the chart's readability is to apply alternating tints behind the lines of the chart. You can also use a series of graduated tints that go from darker to lighter to give a rhythm to the chart.

KNOCKOUT TINTS
Another way to apply rules to the chart is to set the rules so thick that they in essence act as tint bands. Here the rules are set at 13.5 points. The leading is set at 14 points, so there is a half-point space between the rules. The half point of negative space between the rules creates the appearance of half-point white rule between the tint bands.

CDs by the Numbers: A Look Back on 2004

	Redd Kross Show World	Tom Waits Blood Money	Bjork Vespertine	Radiohead Kid A
Sound Quality	Good	Good	Excellent	Poor
Highest Chart Rating	2	11	23	7
Weeks in Top 100	19	9	42	79
Advance Sales*	55	13	9	14

ROW INDENTS Indenting the text so that it sits slightly inside the rules works nicely with knockout tint bands. Highlight text and apply a first-line indent. In this case a 3-point indent is applied

STEP AND REPEAT The half-point white rules are an illusion, created by a half-point gap between thick dark rules. These rules are 13.5 points wide, offset by 3 points from the baseline.

USE IMAGES
Whenever possible try to find a way to make the material more interesting. Introducing images and illustrations is one way. If the space allows for it, look for ways to illustrate the material and make it more visually interesting. In this case photos of the CDs being reviewed are shown above the columns.

COMPLEX CELLS
Some tables offer in-depth information for comparative purposes. As with any chart, one tab should be placed between the entries. To style a chart like this requires a clear understanding of how tabs work.

CDs by the Numbers: A Look Back on 2004

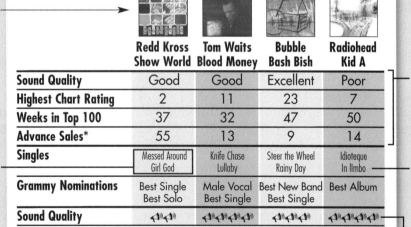

	Redd Kross Show World	Tom Waits Blood Money	Bubble Bash Bish	Radiohead Kid A
Sound Quality	Good	Good	Excellent	Poor
Highest Chart Rating	2	11	23	7
Weeks in Top 100	37	32	47	50
Advance Sales*	55	13	9	14
Singles	Messed Around Girl God	Knife Chase Lullaby	Steer the Wheel Rainy Day	Idioteque In Ilmbo
Grammy Nominations	Best Single Best Solo	Male Vocal Best Single	Best New Band Best Single	Best Album
Sound Quality	◁))◁))	◁))◁))◁))	◁))◁))◁))	◁))◁))◁))◁))

VERTICAL COLUMN TINT BOXES Another way to increase readability is to create background tints for each column. This method will help guide the reader's eye down the page and is especially effective when charts are deep.

DESIGN ELEMENTS
Don't overlook elements such as title and background tint. Every element in the table can be handled to work in an integrated manner.

READABILITY Adding a heavier rule at intervals throughout a table will help separate and group information. This is especially important when charts are large, wide, and unwieldy.

CONDENSED TYPE
This works well for larger table entries, because they can accommodate a high character count per line.

IN-LINE SYMBOLS These are often used in charts to provide rating information. Symbol and dingbat fonts work well.

appear to work, it is inaccurate and inflexible. As a general rule, type should never be positioned by using paragraph returns, spaces, or multiple tabs. The proper way to build a table is to insert a single tab between each entry in the table. Using single tabs is the key to building clean tables. Sometimes it can be difficult to tell how many tabs have been inserted between the table's entries. In this case QuarkXpress' Show Invisibles feature can be used to display the positioning of all spaces, returns, and tabs.

Once single tabs have been inserted into the table's text, its columns can be created by positioning the tabs on the tab ruler. The tab ruler appears above the text box in the document after the text has been highlighted and Tabs has been selected. While the tab window is active, select apply to see the results and then continue to manipulate the tabs until they align correctly.

Setting tabs in this manner will allow you to create a flexible table that can be fine-tuned quickly and easily. When setting tables with multiple columns, try to evenly space the tabs so that the table's columns are positioned equidistant from each other. Each tab can have its own alignment attributed to it, which means that the table's columns can be set aligned left, right, centered, or on a decimal point if the table includes numerical data.

Designing Tables and Charts

Once the table's tabs are set, you can begin to design the table. Many of the elements and techniques previously discussed can also be applied to designing tables and charts. Type variations, lines, tint boxes, and drop shadows can all be applied to designing charts. While there are some accepted methods for handling tabular information, there is also a lot of room for creative experimentation. Because of the nature of tabular information, you want to create tables in which the design doesn't interfere with the clarity of the information. By their very nature tables can be difficult to read, and this makes the need for a clean, simple design paramount. Tables should be made as easy to read as possible and the designer must help facilitate the reader as much as possible. One standard way to style tabular type is to bold the row and column heads. Color can also be applied to the category heads to differentiate them from the tabular entries. Using condensed sans serif faces can also help keep the cells in your table narrow. *Cell* refers to each separate entry within the table.

Charts and tables that contain large amounts of information with many columns and rows can be especially difficult to navigate. As the table gets wider, it is more difficult for the eye to move across the table and locate the desired information. When designing such large and unwieldy tables, consider inserting horizontal rules at fixed intervals throughout the table. These rules will help guide the reader's eye across the table's columns. Vertical tint boxes can also be placed behind the table's rows. Additional line space can be added to help separate the chart's categories.

Summary

While large, dramatic display type tends to get all the attention, the small type contributes greatly to how well a design ultimately works. Body copy and captions represent a major part of a typographic design, and knowing how to style them properly will help bring a sense of visual hierarchy to your text, increase the skimmability of the content, and make the type design attractive and easy to read.

Chapter Three
Designing with Photographs

Designing with dramatic and beautifully shot photography can be one of the most satisfying parts of graphic design. Photographs play a major role in contributing to the overall feel of the project. The right image can make a project shine. Working with photos can also be challenging, especially when the designer is provided with less than perfect images to work with and is faced with finding a way to integrate them into a design successfully. No matter what the quality of the imagery, almost all images require some manipulation. Photos rarely fit perfectly into a design without requiring some cropping or resizing. While there are many ways to affect images by applying filters in Photoshop, a strong, well-composed shot rarely needs this type of manipulation.

This section primarily addresses how to work with photos in QuarkXpress. It will also clearly delineate what the roles of Photoshop and QuarkXpress are in regard to image manipulation. It begins by covering some basic guidelines for successfully designing with imagery. These guidelines will help to maximize the visual and informative impact of the imagery. Many of the guidelines used for type apply to photos as well. Because photos convey their information in a less literal way than type does, there are fewer rules for using photos than for type, and most of these require a sensitive eye and some common sense.

This chapter looks at designing with photography as a two-part process: the act of design and the preparation of images for production. The design process is the act of creative decision making, one that is separate and uninfluenced by production considerations. These decisions are made purely in the interest of reaching a successful design. They involve the sizing, cropping, positioning, or rotating of an image. Once a solution has been reached, the production concerns need to be considered. This second, more technical side of the design process usually involves manipulating and preparing the image for final production in Photoshop.

Respecting Image Integrity

Designers need to handle photography with the same respect they show to typography. Designers have many options available to them, but it is essential to maintain the image's integrity. While designers may consider the positioning, cropping, or sizing of an image as well as its color mode, they generally will not distort the image. *Distortion* refers to altering an image's original proportions or its orientation.

Distorting Images

While QuarkXpress allows designers to distort images by taking them out of their original proportions, this is not an advisable practice. Images that contain common objects whose shapes and proportions we are familiar with will seem incorrect. For instance, when any image of a person, be it a portrait or body shot, is distorted by squeezing or stretching, it will appear unnatural. Another example is a computer monitor has a screen that is typically in a fixed 3:4 ratio. Distort the photo and the monitor will appear too wide or narrow. Even subtly distorting image proportions will draw the attention of the reader for the wrong reasons. The most common reason for taking an image out of proportion—and for distorting type, for that matter—is to get the image to fit within a specific space. A better approach would be to recompose the photo by resizing or cropping it so that it will fit within the allotted space while still maintaining its original proportions.

Flipping Images

QuarkXpress enables designers to horizontally and vertically transpose or "flip" images. Flipping is another form of distortion, and for similar reasons it is an inadvisable way of treating images. Images that contain familiar objects are likely to look unnatural when they are flipped. Some examples of flipping images are more obvious than others. In subtle cases, readers may not recognize what is specifically wrong with the image, but they may sense it subconsciously. If your image is of a well-known place or celebrity, the transposition will be even more noticeable. For instance, if you horizontally flipped a portrait of model Cindy Crawford, the birthmark on her

Maintaining Image Integrity

Photography has unique characteristics that need to be considered when designing. Here are a few guidelines for creating photographic treatments that handle the imagery with integrity.

Image Distortion: Scaling

Like type, photos can be scaled, but they should not be distorted and taken out of their original proportions.

SCALE PROPORTIONATELY As a designer, you want to treat photography properly and maintain its integrity. This means using images in their original proportions and avoiding distortion through scaling or flipping. Designers may crop, rotate, or scale an image's size up or down proportionately when working with photos. The size of an image can be changed as long as its X and Y ratios remain the same. This means if an image's width is scaled down 70%, its height should also be set at 70%.

IN DESIGN MODE When designing, images can be sized (but not distorted) in any proportion you wish. The photos will be adjusted later so that their size in the final Quark page design is as close to 100% as possible.

Scaled proportionately
Original size

Scaled proportionately
Reduced size

X% : 60%   X+ : 0"   0°
Y% : 100%   Y+ : 0"   0°

CONDENSING Taking images out of their original proportion gives them an obviously unnatural look. Here the X and Y settings don't match. The width (X) setting is set lower than the Y setting, producing an overly thin image.

X% : 100%   X+ : -2.008"
Y% : 60%   Y+ : -0.212"

SQUEEZING Here the height (Y) setting is not proportional to the width (X) setting. This takes the image out of its original aspect ratio and creates unnatural and awkward results.

Image Distortion: Flipping Photos

Flipping an image vertically or horizontally is another form of distortion that can awkwardly change an image's content.

FLIP HORIZONTAL AND VERTICAL

Just as changing an image's aspect ratio can create an awkward visual image, flipping images horizontally or vertically will produce a similar unnaturalness in an image's content. Flipping produces visual anomalies, telltale signs to the reader that an image is flipped. These anomalies include reversed type, unnatural orientations, and distinguishing features like birthmarks appearing on the wrong side of a face.

FLIP IMAGE ICONS on the Measurement palette are often mistaken for adjustment buttons for an image's X and Y scaling.

FLIP VERTICAL

Occasionally a design project may require an image to be flipped upside down. In this case, make sure to rotate the image 180 degrees in Photoshop before the project goes final. This speeds up output time.

 X%:100%   X+:0"
Y%:100%   Y+:4.914"

▲
Flip Vertical setting

FLIP HORIZONTAL

Depending on the image, flipping horizontally can produce unnatural results. In this case, any distinguishing facial characteristics such as birthmarks or nose rings will appear on the wrong side of the face.

X%:100%   X+:3.244"
Y%:100%   Y+:0"

Flip Horizontal setting

What's Wrong with This Picture?

Society today is increasingly visually literate and sensitive to image anomalies. The effects of flipping an image are sometimes subtle, sometimes obvious. Here's a sampling of the results of flipping or distorting imagery.

FAMILIAR FORMS like the human body appear noticeably wrong when distorted. Here the image has been clearly squeezed. Because we're sensitive to subtlety in facial features, distorting faces is also obvious.

CELEBRITY IMAGES Our familiarity with certain images makes any distortion more obvious. Facial characteristics such Cindy Crawford's birthmark or Elvis' sneer appear reversed when they are flipped.

COMMON OBJECTS that are used in specific orientations will look wrong when flipped. Even people who don't play the guitar are familiar enough with it to sense when it is being played backward.

REVERSE TYPE Any text within an image will appear reversed when the image is flipped. Reversed type is a sure sign that an image has been flipped. Watch out for logos, clocks, sports uniforms, and signage.

LANDMARKS Famous places like the Statue of Liberty have well-known forms that will immediately appear incorrect when they are flipped. Cityscapes are also subject to this.

Understanding Linked Images

Understanding how QuarkXpress imports, displays, and handles images is important, especially when preparing finished designs for accurate, high-end output.

IMAGE LINKS Unlike Photoshop, which allows you to place an image directly into a file, images placed in Quark remain separate files that are linked to the document. When the document is sent to print, the image link is used to access the image information. Rather than embedding images directly into the Quark document, links are used to help speed up software performance.

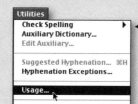

USAGE This dialogue box can be accessed through the Utilities pull-down menu. Usage provides status information regarding which fonts and images are being used within the document.

MAINTAINING IMAGE LINKS Image links must be maintained for accurate output. Image link status can be checked by using the Usage utility. To see if all the images are linked to the document, go to Usage: Pictures and note the status of the images. Status of all should be OK. If any image is missing or modified, it should be updated or placed into the document again.

BASIC IMAGE INFO Directory location, page placement within the document and other information appears in the image listing.

DON'T TRUST THE SCREEN Just because the image appears within the document on-screen doesn't mean that its link is intact. Quark uses a low-resolution preview to display the image and does not depend upon the link being active to display the image.

MORE IMAGE INFO This provides specific information about the selected image's color model, resolution, file size, and format. Before going to final output, check all images to make sure they are high-resolution, CMYK images in either .EPS or .TIF format.

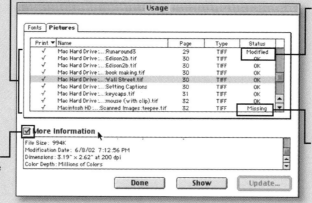

MODIFIED LINKS When the status of an image is Modified, it means that the image has been altered from the state it was in when it was originally placed within the page document. This often happens after an image is placed and then later reopened in Photoshop for resizing or color correction. The link is still active, but the image has changed.

MISSING LINKS If the status of any of the images is Missing, it means that the original image has been deleted or moved from its original directory. To fix this, either relocate the image (it may have been moved or may be on removable disk) or re-create the image and then update it or replace it in the page document.

UPDATING LINKS Images that require updating are subject to having their sizing or positioning change after being updated. Always check the image after updating its status.

cheek would appear on the opposite side of her face. While Elvis Presley sneered, he did so only from the left side. Even without such distinguishing marks or mannerisms, human faces by their nature are not perfectly symmetri-cal, and when you flip them, they look wrong. Flipping photographs has a similar effect on common objects contained within a photo. Flip a photo of a car and suddenly you are in England, driving on the left side of the road, as the steering wheel appears to be on the right side of the car. Transposing photos will also cause any type within the image to read backward, perhaps the most telltale sign to a reader that an image is flipped.

Having to flip images is usually

the result of not thoroughly planning and thumbnailing a project before beginning the design. If you must flip an image, make sure that it does not fall prey to any of these pitfalls. In a brochure for an earth science museum, the designer flipped an image of a gemstone. In this case it did not cause any visual problems, and only the curator of the museum, who was familiar with this specific stone, was aware of the transposition.

If you flip an image, as in the gemstone case, remember that before you go to final output you should flip the image in Photoshop and then update the image link in QuarkXpress. Any manipulation regarding flipping, cropping, or sizing that you do during the design stage in QuarkXpress should be made to the image in Photoshop prior to final output. If you leave the image flipped in Quark, it will increase the output time. While it's fine to rotate, crop, or resize your images in Quark while you design a project, when you reach the production stage these adjustments must be made to the image in Photoshop.

Formatting Imagery

There are three formatting concerns that designers need to under-

Formatting Images for Print

To ensure that your images print accurately they have to be formatted properly in Photoshop. This involves choosing the correct color model, resolution setting, and appropriate format for print.

PROPER RESOLUTION
All print images must be high-resolution. Go to Image Size and check that the image resolution is high, somewhere between 266 and 300 dots per inch. 300 dpi is an optimum setting for outputting to high-end color devices.

CMYK COLOR MODE
All print images should be converted to the CMYK mode. Color mode can be adjusted by selecting CMYK from the Image: Mode pull-down menu. Print images can be set in either grayscale or CMYK models. The RGB color model is not used in print and is subject to output problems.

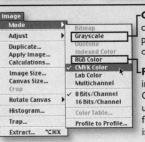

GRAYSCALE images are commonly used for print projects. They are composed of 256 shades of gray.

RGB MODE means the image is composed of Red, Green, and Blue. Web design uses this mode because its final output is a screen that is composed of the colors.

PRINT FORMATS Images that are used for print design must be saved in the proper file format. The two most commonly used file formats are .EPS (encapsulated PostScript) and .TIF (tagged image file) formats. Other formats can also be used, but these two are the most stable.

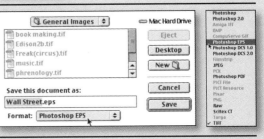

DON'T USE WEB IMAGES for print. .JPEG and .GIF formats are low-resolution RGB files, designed and optimized for screen output and Web use. Their low resolution and improper color model will result in poor image quality. RGB images print in grayscale when output on high-end printers.

DON'T COMPRESS image files for print. Compression applies to images being used for Web design. Lossy compression can reduce image quality and its palette each time the image is used.

Manipulating Images Properly

QuarkXpress, Illustrator, and Photoshop have defined roles in the print process. While they share similar tools and functionality, it's important to know which program to use for certain tasks.

THE RIGHT TOOL You need to clearly understand the function of each software program. QuarkXpress is for page layout, Photoshop is for manipulating images, and Illustrator is for creating vector drawings.

IMAGE MANIPULATION All images must be sized, rotated, and color-corrected in Photoshop before the files are sent out to a service bureau.

IMAGES IN QUARK Since images are linked to the Quark document and don't actually reside in the document file, the images are not actually rewritten when they are sized and rotated in the Quark document.

LOW RESOLUTION PREVIEW Quark displays images in a low-res preview. Because of this preview quality it's difficult to color-correct them using Quark's imaging features.

Just Say No: Quark's Imaging Tools

While QuarkXpress provides tools that allow users to adjust image quality, they should be avoided.

THE RIGHT TOOL Ever try taking a bottle cap off using a screwdriver? It'll do the job, just not with any control. The same applies to Quark's imaging tools. You can use them, but Photoshop's tools offer more control and accuracy for adjusting images.

Imaging controls included in Quark, like Negative, don't change the actual image file, only its display. Changes like this can only be done in Photoshop.

SHADING that is applied to grayscale or color images in Quark will print properly. It's still a good idea to use Photoshop for changing image opacity.

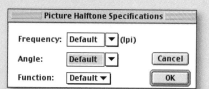

HALFTONES are the dot pattern that an image is composed of when printed. Unless you're knowledgeable in pre-press production, let your printer determine these settings.

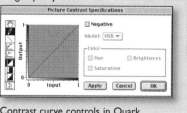

Contrast curve controls in Quark

---

stand when designing print projects with photos. The first concern is that the photo must be in the proper format. Full-color image files that are intended for print must be set at a high resolution, usually 266 to 300 dpi, depending on the final line screen being used. These images must also be in the CMYK color model. The image should also be saved in the proper format. Typical formats for print are .EPS and .TIF.

Understanding Linked Images

The second concern involves understanding the mechanics of placing an image into QuarkXpress. When you place a photo into a picture box, the photo is not actually part of the document in the way that an image becomes part of a Photoshop file when it is pasted into it. The image that appears in QuarkXpress is placed, and this means that the image is linked to the document file and exists outside and separate from the Quark document. This link must remain intact in order for the images within the design to print correctly. When a QuarkXpress file is output it calls to this linked file to get its information. If you break the link by moving, deleting, or manipulating the image file, the image will

Image Types: One Color, Two Color...

Images can be formatted in many different color modes, depending on the type of project you're working on. The project's budget and final output will determine what color options are available.

CMYK: The Four-Color Process

The four-color process uses four colors, cyan, magenta, yellow, and black, to emulate a natural color space. For each color a film/plate separation is output. When all four of these plates are aligned and printed they combine to create full-color images.

CMYK PLATES are combined and registered to create full-color images. Each plate prints over the other plates to create the illusion of a continuous-tone image, when in actuality the image is created of a dot pattern. Each plate's dot pattern is set at a different angle so that dots don't print directly over each other

BLACK PLATES are printed on top of the other three colors. A black can be made by mixing values of C, M, and Y. So why is a black plate necessary? For type. If black type was created using C, M, and Y it would be subject to becoming blurry if the plates shifted out of registration.

FOUR-COLOR PROCESS combines the four plates and prints them in registration to create the illusion of a continuous tone image.

FIFTH AND SIXTH COLORS are sometimes used on high-budget jobs. After the four-color process is finished the project has another color printed over it, such as a metallic Pantone color like gold or silver that cannot be reproduced accurately in CMYK.

Color Models

Like image formats, there are many types of color models, and you need to understand how and when to use each model.

• **GRAYSCALE** images are composed of 256 shades of gray. This is the most commonly used format in print design because it is the least expensive process.

• **CMYK** is the four-color model used for all full-color print jobs. This color space is composed of four colors: cyan, magenta, yellow, and black.

• **RGB** is the three-color model used for all screen output in Web design. These colors, red, green, and blue, correlate to the three color guns in a computer monitor. RGB images cannot be used for print unless they are first converted to CMYK. RGB images print on high-end output devices as grayscale.

• **PANTONE** colors are used as "spot colors" in projects with budgets that limit the printing to two or three colors. The Pantone system consists of pre-mixed inks and are not mixed the way CMYK values are. Pantone colors are sometimes used in tandem with CMYK jobs as fifth and sixth colors.

• **BITMAP** images consist of only two colors, black and white, and don't include any shades of gray. Every pixel is either black or white. This format is handy for certain imaging procedures. Because of their reduced palette, bitmap images are easy to make selections from.

not output properly. The status of this link can be checked in Quark's Usage utility. Keep in mind that despite the fact that you can view the image when the document is open, this does not ensure that the link is intact.

Beginning designers often comment on the low quality of the image when it is viewed in QuarkXpress. This is done intentionally to improve the software's performance. In order to speed up its performance QuarkXpress displays a low-resolu-

tion preview of the image on-screen. If Quark were to display its imagery at high resolution, it would drastically reduce the software's performance, taking longer to redraw the screen and pan around the document. Photoshop displays its image

Manipulating Images & Picture Boxes

Using the Measurement palette for placement, sizing, and rotation is a great way to accurately control the elements in a design.

X: -2.566" Y: 2.429"	W: 2.125" H: 1.267"	⊿ 4° 𝕂 0"	→ X%: 45% ↑ Y%: 45%	✧✧ X+: -0.033" ✧ Y+: -0.092"	⊿ 0° ⬭ 0°
Page Position	**Box Size**	**Corner Radius Box Rotation**	**Image Size Flip Image**	**Image Shift**	**Image Skew Rotate Image**
Used to compare object placement within a design. Copy and paste info from one object to another to align accurately.	Used to compare the size of elements. Copy and paste info from one box to another to perfectly match sizes.		Flips an image vertically or horizontally. Avoid applying to images.	Enter amount by which you want to move an object. For example, enter +3pt to move an object 3 points to the right.	Rotate the image within the box. This setting affects only the image, not the picture box (see below).

Rotation Settings

Quark's rotation tool is hard to use and unwieldy. The best way, although less intuitive, is to simply enter a rotation setting into the Measurement palette. The image and its picture box can be rotated, or the image can be rotated separately without affecting the box. If you choose to rotate an image in Quark, remember that you will want to make adjustments to the actual image in Photoshop before the project goes final.

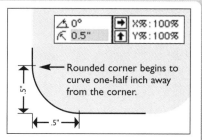

ROTATE IMAGE BOX Both image and image box are rotated as one.

ROTATE IMAGE Only the image is rotated, while the picture box remains unchanged.

Corner Radius

The corner radius setting on the Measurement palette controls the roundness of rectangle corners. These shapes are frequently used today and reflect the tabbed windows found in Web design. The white background shape that this type sits on is built by applying the Merge tool to overlapping rounded rectangles, or roundtangles, as they are also called. This technique is discussed further along in this chapter.

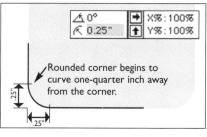

⊿ 0° 𝕂 0.25" → X%: 100% ↑ Y%: 100%

Rounded corner begins to curve one-quarter inch away from the corner.

.25"   .25"

⊿ 0° 𝕂 0.5" → X%: 100% ↑ Y%: 100%

Rounded corner begins to curve one-half inch away from the corner.

.5"   .5"

Corner radius can also be set by selecting Modify Box and entering a value into the corner radius setting.

⊿ 0° 𝕂 0.07"	→ X%: 100% ↑ Y%: 100%	✧✧ X+: 0" ✧ Y+: 0"	⊿ 0° ⬭ 0°

files at a higher resolution because it has a different purpose than QuarkXpress does. Photoshop requires a high-resolution preview because it is based upon this preview that decisions are made concerning the image's overall color quality, as well as its sharpness and contrast.

Photoshop's role in the design process is sometimes misunderstood by beginning designers. Photoshop is predominantly a photo manipulation package whose purpose is to enhance image quality. While there are many illustrators who use Photoshop as an illustration tool, its primary function in the design process is image preparation.

Most designers who have been using QuarkXpress for a while have gotten comfortable designing with a low-resolution preview. They have viewed the image in Photoshop and manipulated it to maximize quality output. Knowing this, they are able to design with the low-resolution image preview and do not get caught up in the lack of photographic detail. Some third-party vendors have designed plug-ins that enable images to be viewed with a high-resolution preview in QuarkXpress, but they can be impractical without a lot of available memory.

The third thing that you need

Image Types: Monotones, Duotones...

Duotones are a great way to add a color tone to black and white images. This versatile format is great for projects that have limited budgets.

Grayscale Image

Duotone Image

Monotone Image

1 CONVERT TO GRAYSCALE
To access the duotone setting from the Image: Mode pull-down menu, the image must first be converted to grayscale.

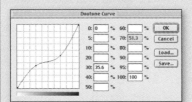

3 BALANCING DUOTONES
The amount of either color is adjusted by clicking on the curve icon next to the color. Adjust the curve to change the colors, effect on shadow, midtone, or highlight.

2 DUOTONE COLOR
When duotone is selected a second active color swatch will appear on the list. Click on the color swatch to select the second "tinting" color. Usually Pantone colors are used for specifying a second color in duotones. Only two pieces of film are output for duotones: black (K) and a second Pantone color.

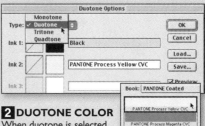

4 SAVE FILE
Duotone files should be saved in an .EPS format to retain the separate color information. You can also use duotones in four-color projects. In this case reconvert the duotone to the CMYK model.

Type, Image, & Readability

Getting display type and imagery to complement each other involves selecting appropriate typefaces and properly positioning the type.

WATCH GUTTER When placing large images over two-page spreads you need to make sure that no pertinent information conveyed by the photo is being obscured or lost in the gutter of the magazine.

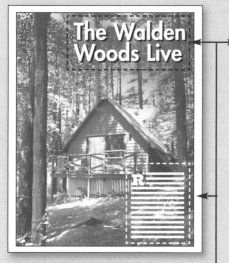

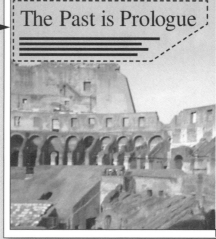

IMAGE DICTATES TYPE PLACEMENT Image composition and color quality will greatly determine how the display type is styled and where it's placed. Large inactive areas in a photo accommodate headlines well.

INACTIVE IMAGE AREAS In both examples the type is placed in inactive areas. On the left, the inactive area is busy, so a drop shadow is placed behind the display type to help with readability. Because of the image's consistent tone no drop shadow is required on the text above.

EXTRA KERNING When type runs across the gutter between two facing pages, extra kerning needs to be added to maintain the readability of the headline running across it.

to keep in mind before going to final output is that your images should be proportionally sized in QuarkXpress as close to 100 percent as possible. A general rule is to increase or reduce the final size of the image in QuarkXpress by no more than 15 percent. This means that your image size could fall between 85 and 115 percent and still print properly. With this said, it is always preferable to have your final images sized at exactly 100 percent.

When initially designing with imagery in QuarkXpress, do not concern yourself with the technical details—size the image up as much as your design requires. When in design mode, you should be concerned only with the page design. Once a design is finalized, you can then resize or rescan any image that requires it, and crop out any areas within the image that are not shown in the final design. Remember that any image area

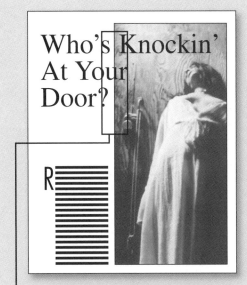

Who's Knockin'
At Your
Door?

R

RUNNING TYPE ACROSS AN IMAGE This helps integrate the page design and allows the type and image to work together, but the type needs to be styled and positioned to maintain readability.

**Who's Knockin'
At Your
Door?**

SANS SERIF TYPE Because of its evenness of stroke, medium-weight sans serif faces are more readable than serif faces, whose varying thick and thin stroke weights can get lost in a busy image.

**Who's Knockin'
At Your
Door?**

DROP SHADOWS Using these can help increase readability by clearly defining the type's edges.

DETROIT
FOLK
CITY

B

DETROIT
FOLK
CITY

SUPERIMPOSE COLOR TYPE Placing type over busy, colorful images can be difficult. Quick contrast changes can obscure type. If an image is consistently dark, bold white type can be knocked out. Colored type may work, but finding the right color can sometimes be difficult. If type color is prevalent in the image, the type may get lost. Here the white type at top works best.

Here Comes

Here Comes

THICK AND THIN The readability of display type placed over an image will depend on the typeface, its size and color, and the quality of the image. Busy images can interfere with type readability. Here a medium-weight sans serif face is easier to read than the thinner serif face.

---

cropped out by the picture box also should be cropped out of the actual image during this final stage of preparing for production. If you don't crop out the image's unused areas, the document will take more time to output. Just because you can't see this information doesn't mean it's not there.

Avoid Color Adjusting in Quark
While QuarkXpress does allow the designer to do some basic image manipulation within the program, such as contrast, halftone, and shading adjustments, these imaging functions should generally be avoided. QuarkXpress is a page layout program and its strengths lie in page

composition and designing multiple-page documents. Unlike Photoshop, it is not an image manipulation program, and its tools for such tasks are limited. Any good craftsman, regardless of discipline, uses the right tool for the job. Always choose a program according to its strengths. Most programs that do a lot of things don't

Type & Image: Composing Page Layouts

Whether working on a vertical or horizontal format, the display type and images you're working with will influence the design and page composition.

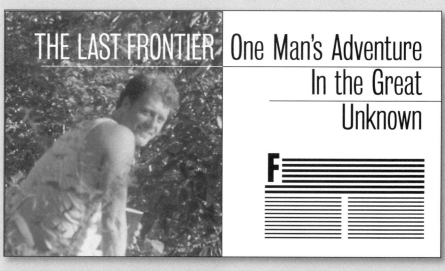

ENGAGE THE READER Magazine covers and movie posters generally have the image of the celebrity looking directly at the viewer. This helps to engage the reader.

GUIDING THE EYE Page composition can directly affect how a reader's eye moves through the layout. Here the person in the photo leans into the page while looking directly at the reader. The headline placement also moves across the page horizontally. Both help guide the reader's eye across the page and into the story. Images that point off the page and away from the story are less engaging.

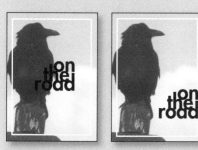

FOCAL POINT shouldn't be obscured by type. Type and image should be used to balance the composition. Here the type on the left is obscured by the image.

CENTERING PHOTOS is one layout option as long as none of the image's important information gets lost in the gutter. Here the type is positioned so the gutter falls between the words.

DIVIDED IMAGES can be used to give a sense of continuity. A sense of confrontation can also be achieved by placing images, such as those of politicians, so that they face into each other.

Vertical & Horizontal Compositions

Vertical and horizontal compositions each have there their own innate characteristics and can be employed to convey different feels.

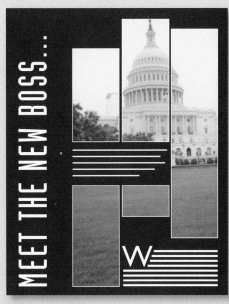

STRONG HORIZONTALS convey a more placid, calmer feel than vertical layouts. Horizontal compositions reflect a sense of landscape and imply space. Vertical compositions tend to have a more imposing and tenser feel.

LOST IN THE GUTTER Placing images across a two-page spread can be an effective way to treat a photo layout as long as the image's focal point does not get obscured by the gutter.

ROTATED TYPE is one way to create an interesting juxtaposition with imagery. It also allows the type to be sized larger than it could be if it were set horizontally. The type is rotated here so that it reads into the page.

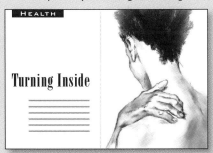

WHITE SPACE within a design creates a lightness and sense of space. Content-heavy projects often don't allow for it. Using plenty of white space is the antithesis of filling up pages with type and image. Take advantage of the uncluttered feel that white space creates.

TILTING IMAGES changes the direction of a composition and creates interesting spaces. Overtitling can create awkward spaces. A little rotation goes a long way.

INSET PHOTOS provide in-depth information while not competing with the larger image.

DARK BACKGROUNDS can be dramatic but are not well suited for pages with much body copy, as small knockout type is hard to read.

ONE DOMINANT IMAGE has more visual impact and is generally more effective than a group of smaller images.

Type & Image: Page Composition

Some basic compositional considerations can help you create interesting layouts that invite the reader to read the story.

LARGE IMAGES have more visual impact than a series of small images. Small, similarly sized images fight for attention. Use the strongest image at a large size. If a layout requires using many images, there are ways to make it work.

VARY SPACE AND SIZE ▶
of the images to bring a sense of variety and visual hierarchy to the design. When all the images are sized and spaced equally, the composition can become predictable and uninteresting.

BACKGROUND IMAGE adds texture to the layout while acting as support material, as the image relates to the story's content. This image was ghosted using Photoshop.

◀ **SENSE OF MOTION** can be achieved by using parallelograms or shapes that have a tilt to them.

◀ **PICTURE BOX SHAPES** that are unusual or custom can introduce organic, technical, or curvilinear shapes to a composition.

TYPE FOLLOWS IMAGE ▶
and can be made to wrap around a silhouette. Both display type and body copy work around image edge.

◀ **ASYMMETRICAL** compositions can be more interesting than perfectly symmetrical ones. Here the shapes divide the page, but not perfectly in half.

◀ **ITALICS HELP** enhance the sense of motion. The font tilts forward and reinforces the direction of the page.

do all of them very well. With this in mind, all image manipulation should be done in Photoshop, which is designed expressly for such tasks. Besides its limited tools and functionality, QuarkXpress's low-resolution image preview makes it impossible to accurately manipulate imagery. How can an aesthetic decision concerning image quality be reached when the image can't be viewed accurately?

Color and Black and White Photos

There are different color options available to designers, and often it is the client's specifications and the project's budget that will determine what those options will be. These options range from standard four-color or black and white models to duotones, tritones, and monotones. Some jobs offer more latitude in how images may be treated. For instance, if you are working on a four-color project, you have all of these options available to you. Let's look at the range of available color options and the effect that they can have on a design.

Four-color images are also referred to as full-color images. Full-color images that are intended for print should be specified in

The Perfect Unbalance: Asymmetrical Design

While symmetrical layouts have a natural balance and logic to them, they are often not as visually interesting as asymmetrical designs.

◀ **EACH ELEMENT** contributes to the overall design. How those elements are placed on the page is integral to how cohesive the design will be. Experiment with placement early in the design process.

DON'T FILL UP THE PAGE with elements. The elements in the layout on the left completely fill the page. This layout has no empty space for the eye to rest. Spacing and sizing elements equally can result in static, uninteresting layouts.

REARRANGE ELEMENTS but make ▶ sure to place emphasis on appropriate elements.

WHITE SPACE adds a sense of space to a design and allows the eye to rest.

VISUAL HIERARCHY creates successful communication clearly by placing emphasis appropriately. Not all elements need emphasis. When emphasis is spread evenly among design components, they fight for reader's attention.

CURVILINEAR shapes break up the design grid interestingly.

EVENLY SPACED OBJECTS make sense, and in some cases consistency in spacing is desirable. Because this page is entirely filled up, there are no interesting relationships between its objects.

OVERLAPPING design elements can create a sense of visual depth. Overlapping type and image can also dramatically reduce readability.

MULTIPLE IMAGES when grouped can act as a larger image, perceived in the composition as one element.

REPETITION OF SPACE The vertical spaces between the type, images, and page edge are consistent. Look for relationships that exist between the design elements.

PLAY ON WORDS Consider how a word's literal meaning can be reflected in a type design. To give an impression of looking into the past, the word *back* is reversed.

RANDOMNESS occurs when positioning seems arbitrary. Top and bottom photos crop differently, suggesting randomness and implying space beyond the page edge.

STEP AND REPEAT is used here to create accurately spaced picture boxes.

SHAPE REPETITION is used in that the width of the image and the column of text are the same. They are not horizontally centered on the page, but actually shifted to the right.

---

the CMYK color model. *Four-color* refers to the separate color plates—cyan, magenta, yellow, and black—that make up the image. In the simplest terms, the four-color process uses a method of overlaying the four plates so that their colors mesh and produce a full-color image. Four-color printing is expensive and requires high-end output devices.

Black and white images are composed of 256 shades of gray. Because only a black (K) plate is produced, these files are a quarter of the size of a CMYK image. (The black plate in the four-color process is represented by *K*, rather than *B*, which could be confused with blue.) While many beginning designers often perceive black and white as less attractive and powerful than four-color, when used effectively it can be as dramatic

Focusing In: Cropping Techniques

Cropping can be used to change an image's shape or shift its focus. Most images can be cropped to fit into just about any fixed space.

Original Image

Distorted scale stretches image

Resized proportionately to fit.

VERTICAL INTO HORIZONTAL It's a challenge to fit a vertical image into a horizontal space. Adjusting how the image is sized and cropped will allow the image to fit without having to distort it.

HEADSHOTS Cropping at the top of the head can allow an image to appear closer. This is a common way of cropping used on magazine covers.

OFF WITH THEIR HEADS Be sensitive. Tight cropping like this can objectify women and be offensive.

Crop out unused image in Photoshop before final output.

EDGE ACTIVATION If you crop the image off the page edge, you can resize and tilt the image to accommodate the type.

CHANGE FOCUS Cropping can dramatically change an image's focal point, direction, and composition. Cropping is a powerful way to manipulate the story an image tells.

and have as much impact as a four-color image.

There are many ways to heighten the effect that a black and white image can have. Experiment with dot or halftone screens, or try a different paper stock—a wide selection of laser-safe papers is available in art and office supply stores.

Duotones are widely used in design and are a great way to add subtle color to photos. They are essentially a black and white image that has a second color applied to it that tints the image. Duotones are composed of two color plates, usually black and a second Pantone color. They can be very effective when a project's budget calls for a limited use of color, particularly two-color jobs. Other tinting variations work in a similar manner, including tritones and monotones. Tritones incorporate three colors, while monotones substitute the grayscale with a monochromatic palette. These variations are relatively easy to create in Photoshop. For true duotones the file should be saved in the .EPS format.

The Lure of Photoshop Filters

Beginning designers are understandably drawn to Photoshop's wide array of image filters. While their effects are showy and dramat-

Creating Soft Drop Shadows

Applying soft drop shadows to images or type is a great way to add depth to a page. Here's one method for building shadows in Photoshop that are designed specifically for your Quark layout.

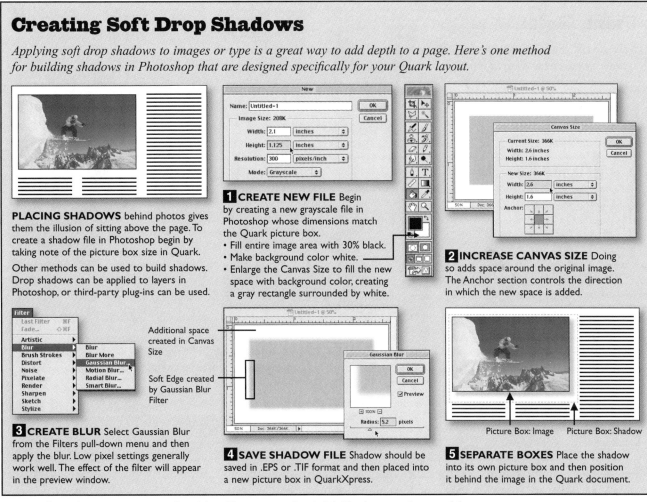

PLACING SHADOWS behind photos gives them the illusion of sitting above the page. To create a shadow file in Photoshop begin by taking note of the picture box size in Quark.

Other methods can be used to build shadows. Drop shadows can be applied to layers in Photoshop, or third-party plug-ins can be used.

1 CREATE NEW FILE Begin by creating a new grayscale file in Photoshop whose dimensions match the Quark picture box.
- Fill entire image area with 30% black.
- Make background color white.
- Enlarge the Canvas Size to fill the new space with background color, creating a gray rectangle surrounded by white.

2 INCREASE CANVAS SIZE Doing so adds space around the original image. The Anchor section controls the direction in which the new space is added.

Additional space created in Canvas Size

Soft Edge created by Gaussian Blur Filter

3 CREATE BLUR Select Gaussian Blur from the Filters pull-down menu and then apply the blur. Low pixel settings generally work well. The effect of the filter will appear in the preview window.

4 SAVE SHADOW FILE Shadow should be saved in .EPS or .TIF format and then placed into a new picture box in QuarkXpress.

Picture Box: Image   Picture Box: Shadow

5 SEPARATE BOXES Place the shadow into its own picture box and then position it behind the image in the Quark document.

ic to a first-time user, most should generally be avoided. A high-quality photograph, with a strong composition, is almost always preferable to a filtered image. Filters are often used to hide an inadequacy or enhance a mediocre image. While filters may be initially impressive, applying them in their default settings does not represent a creative act on the designer's part. As a designer, you want to use the computer to achieve what you personally envision, but using a filter in this manner represents an act of deferring to the computer to determine a design treatment. While using filters like this may offer a solution, rarely do they reflect a designer's vision or sense of personal style. Using straight preset

Using Holding Rules

When an image's edge falls out to white its boundaries become undefined and the image tends to float on the page. A holding rule will help define its edge and hold it in place.

IMAGE FLOATS Without a holding rule, the image's positioning to the baseline grid is lost, as the image border is undefined. It doesn't sit in a relationship with the other page elements. ▼

EDGE DEFINITION Holding rules help define image boundaries and ensure that its edges don't fade into the page background and cause it to float upon the page awkwardly.

CONSISTENT EDGES Images that have clearly defined dark edges usually don't require a holding rule. This consistent tonal quality defines the picture boundary. ▼

distance as well as heightening our sense of interdependence. The cumulative effect of these diverse changes created confusion and misperception among even the most forward thinking members.

Changes to traditional work patterns had a profound effect on the autonomy of both the community and the individual. Advances in transportation, communications, and manufacturing pulled semi-autonomous local societies into a vast integrated national market. As society became increasingly complex, citizens began to feel the growing influence of large impersonal forces, like Wall Street, railroads, and big business, upon their lives. Consequently, many felt their ability to control their lives slipping away.

No longer did the business of life revolve around natural cycles of season and sun as the work day became determined by regulated procedures and

the clock. Wage earning reduced laborer's time to monetary measurement, assembly line techniques removed the worker from a sense of participation in production, and college educations replaced systems of apprenticeship. Specialization and scientific management stripped the worker of any input into what was being produced or how to produce it. This was devastating to semi-independent farmers and craftsmen who were accustomed to playing an integral role

in the entire production process. Jack of all trades like the independent, multi-skilled farmer gave way to many interdependent individuals who were skilled in particular functions like the factory worker. There was little satisfaction to be derived from the performance of tedious repetitive tasks that industrial labor required.

New methods of production also removed the sense of connection to the community from the

HAIRLINE RULES refer to rules that are thinner than a half point wide. Because of their fineness they may print inconsistently and should be used with caution. Talk to your printer to see if their press can handle that level of detail. The rule between the paragraph columns in the graphic above is a hairline rule.

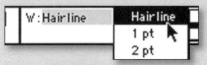

STANDARD SETTINGS A typical holding rule is a half-point black rule.

HOLDING RULES To help define an image's edge when it is placed over an image or background tint that has colors similar to those found within the image, use holding rules.

FRAME SETTINGS Always use a frame setting to create box borders. Do not draw separate lines around the picture box.

filters should not be thought of as a creative act; they are merely a display of the computer software's capability.

Filters have their uses, and as with any tool, designers need to find their own personal way to master them. Developing a personal style is the goal of all designers, and it takes time, experimentation, and an understanding of the filters.

When experimenting with a filter for the first time, try applying it in an extreme fashion so that you clearly see the effect. The effects that some filters have can be unnoticeable when applied in a subtle manner, so this approach lets you see exactly what the filter does. This is a good way to approach any new tool you encounter for the first time. Once you understand how the filter works, a good guideline is to avoid applying too much of an effect to an image. Apply your effect in increments, as you can always apply more later if necessary.

This does not mean that designers don't use filters; in fact, there are several that designers use relatively often. Most of these deal with production concerns such as sharpening, blurring, and feathering. Both technical and creative applications of filters will be covered in the following chapter on image manipulation. Once you understand a filter's effects, you can then experiment with using filters in conjunction with each other. This process may lead to finding your own way of manipulating images, one that is in line with your personal aesthetic. Default filter effects rarely do this.

Large Photos and Display Type
As type and imagery are the dominant elements used in design, designers strive to get the most impact from photos and display type. Getting the type and image to work together as a unit and to complement each other is one of the most obvious design tasks. While a design may include other elements, it is the interplay between the dominant image and display type that is the crux of a design, one that sets the tone for the entire project.

When you superimpose type over an image, it should be positioned so that it doesn't interfere

Basic Frame Types in Quark

The shape of a picture box can be simple or complex. Here's a look at the pros and cons of Quark's seven default picture box types.

A RECTANGLE BOXES are the most commonly used type of picture box. They can be used for images with clipping paths even though their shape doesn't relate to image shape.

C ROUNDED CORNERS are frequently used in contemporary design. These shapes reflect the look of tabbed menus. The roundness of the corners can be controlled through the Measurement palette.

F PARALLELOGRAMS can be created by using a Bézier picture box. These boxes are manually drawn using a pen tool and can be composed of curved and straight lines

B D CONCAVE CORNER and beveled corner boxes are most obviously representative of Quark. They are rarely used in design without some customization.

E ROUND SHAPES are effective when centered between columns of text. Running body copy wraps nicely around them, while they introduce organic shapes to the design.

G FREEHAND SHAPES allow designers to draw box shapes intuitively. This tool is hard to control. It's best to start with a general shape and then edit the shape.

Editing Picture Box Shapes

Creating custom picture boxes by using the pen tool and manipulating its points opens up new possibilities for the shapes that images can be placed within.

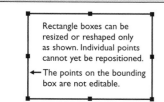

Rectangle boxes can be resized or reshaped only as shown. Individual points cannot yet be repositioned.

← The points on the bounding box are not editable.

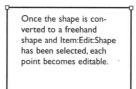

Once the shape is converted to a freehand shape and Item:Edit:Shape has been selected, each point becomes editable.

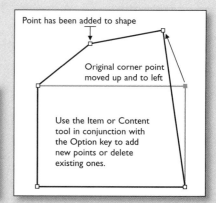

Point has been added to shape

Original corner point moved up and to left

Use the Item or Content tool in conjunction with the Option key to add new points or delete existing ones.

CONVERT FIRST

Picture box shapes must first be converted to freehand shapes before their points can be edited individually. Once a picture box is converted, its shape can be changed by moving, adding, or deleting its points.

FREEHAND SHAPE

must be selected from the shape type list to convert the selected picture box into an editable shape.

EDIT SHAPE

allows the designer to edit a shape's outline by manipulating its individual points. The Content tool is used to alter the shape. Hot keys are used in conjunction with the Content tool to add or delete points. Note: Edit Shape will not work without first converting a picture box to a freehand shape.

Either the Content or Item tool can be used to manipulate a shape. These tools are used in conjunction with the key combinations listed below to add, delete, or select multiple points.

ADD POINTS by holding down the option key and clicking on the shape's outline with the Item or Content tool.

DELETE POINTS by moving over the point that you want to delete and then hold down the Option key and click to delete the point.

MOVE A LINE SEGMENT by placing the cursor between two points. The cursor changes accordingly. Click and drag to move.

MULTIPLE POINTS can be manipulated simultaneously by holding down the Shift key and selecting specific points.

with an image's focal point or obscure any of its pertinent information. Conversely, you want to place the type without having the image interfere with the type's readability. A golden rule for attaining this balance is to let the image dictate the type placement. Most photos include areas that

will naturally accommodate type. Large unfilled areas that have a consistent tonal quality are especially well suited for type placement. The color of your type and its relationship to the color quality of the image will greatly affect the readability of the type and its ability to "pop" or appear to sit above

the image. If the type color is too close to those found within the image, there will not be enough contrast between the two. To achieve this sense of separation, a balance must be reached where the type does not get lost within the image or take away from it. The type and image need to be separate

Complex Shapes & Bézier Curves

Understanding how Bézier curves and points are used to alter shapes is an essential skill for every designer.

PLACING POINTS ▶ can be done in two ways. Click once to place a corner point, or click and drag to get a smooth point with handles.

BEZIER TOOLS These tools can be used to create a picture box, text box, or shape. The pen tool works the same way for any box type.

CURVE HANDLES These will appear after you click and drag with the Bézier pen tool. Don't confuse them with shape outline.

TWO-PART PROCESS Creating the exact shape you want often involves moving the point position and the handles.

LESS IS MORE The fewer points used to create a shape, the faster it will output.

RESET EDIT SHAPE MODE If you don't reset this mode when you're finished reshaping the box, it may result in altering the shape accidentally.

CORNER POINTS are placed by clicking once with the Bézier pen tool. Corner points do not have handles.

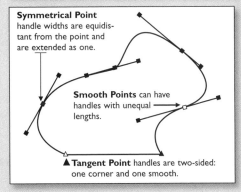

Symmetrical Point handle widths are equidistant from the point and are extended as one.

Smooth Points can have handles with unequal lengths.

▲ **Tangent Point** handles are two-sided: one corner and one smooth.

Pinching points allows each handle to be moved independently of the other. Select the handle point with the Control key to pinch the curve.

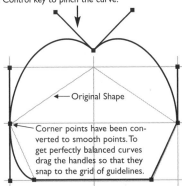

← Original Shape

← Corner points have been converted to smooth points. To get perfectly balanced curves drag the handles so that they snap to the grid of guidelines.

SMOOTH POINTS are placed by clicking and dragging with the Bézier pen tool. Once you begin dragging, the handles will appear.

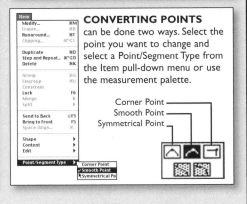

CONVERTING POINTS can be done two ways. Select the point you want to change and select a Point/Segment Type from the Item pull-down menu or use the measurement palette.

Corner Point
Smooth Point
Symmetrical Point

---

and at the same time complement each other.

Knocking out type from an image is another option designers have, but its success depends on the image from which it is knocked out.

If an image has large, consistently dark areas, knocking out type may be a viable option. But if the image is a high-contrast one with a busy quality, the edges of the type may appear undefined.

Drop Shadows for Type

Because of the wide range of qualities an image can have, it can sometimes be difficult to find a color for the type that will achieve a sense of separation. One simple

Custom Shapes: Using the Merge Tools

The Merge tools are a great way to build complex shapes without having to manually adjust outlines using the pen tool.

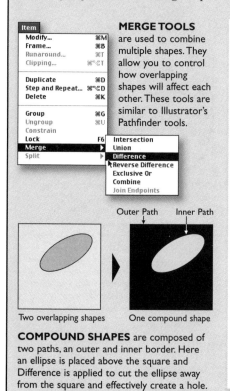

MERGE TOOLS are used to combine multiple shapes. They allow you to control how overlapping shapes will affect each other. These tools are similar to Illustrator's Pathfinder tools.

COMPOUND SHAPES are composed of two paths, an outer and inner border. Here an ellipse is placed above the square and Difference is applied to cut the ellipse away from the square and effectively create a hole.

Two overlapping shapes — One compound shape
Outer Path — Inner Path

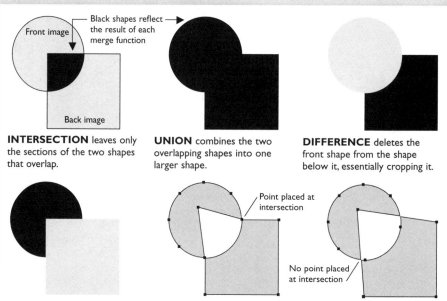

Front image
Black shapes reflect the result of each merge function
Back image

INTERSECTION leaves only the sections of the two shapes that overlap.

UNION combines the two overlapping shapes into one larger shape.

DIFFERENCE deletes the front shape from the shape below it, essentially cropping it.

REVERSE DIFFERENCE deletes the shape in the back from one in the front. Use the Difference tools according to the shape's positioning.

Point placed at intersection
No point placed at intersection

EXCLUSIVE OR AND COMBINE EFFECTS appear to affect overlapping shapes the same way. They both create shapes in which the overlapping area is cropped away. The difference between the tools is how they position points where the lines intersect. This is least commonly used of the Merge functions.

---

way to remedy this might be to place a drop shadow behind the type. This helps separate the type from the image by creating a sense of depth. The best way to create a drop shadow in QuarkXpress is to select the text box and then copy and paste it so you have two identi-cal text boxes. The copy that you use as a drop shadow can be specified in a dark or light color and then placed directly behind the original text box. Offset the shadow slightly to give the illusion of depth. The offset distance of the shadow from the type doesn't have to be large to work well. The further away you place the shadow, the greater the appearance of distance between type and image. When drop shadows are offset too far from the type, especially when used with typefaces that contain narrow stroke widths, readability can actually be

The Big Picture

The Merge tools can be useful for creating large complex shapes for picture boxes, especially when the picture box bleeds off the page.

LARGE SHAPES can sometimes be difficult to work with because Quark will not allow shapes to be positioned over its page clipboard. One method that works around this problem is to use the Merge tools to crop the picture box to the page size.

The final box shape at the right is created by applying the Intersection tool.

Original Picture box

Quark limits the positioning of large elements off the page. Try building the shape at a smaller size and then scale it up to fit.

Shape represents page proportions

THE IRON HORSE

Cropping Box

WHAT NEXT?
Ten Contemporary Composers to Listen For

COMPOUND SHAPES can be used to create image borders. Here a cropping box is centered over the image. The Difference tool is applied to create a hole in the picture box.

SHADOWS can be used with compound shapes to create depth and a sense of light. Images that are used as borders should contain enough detail to be recognizable when cropped.

reduced, defeating the original purpose of the drop shadow. When the shadow is placed too far from the type, gaps will occur in which the image can be seen between them, and the effect can become overly busy and distracting. Drop shadow distance is generally less of an issue with sans serif faces because of the evenness of their stroke widths.

A couple of other things regarding the use of drop shadows with type: Avoid using the drop shadow attribute in QuarkXpress, as it offers no control and creates output problems. The drop shadow attribute is set at a fixed distance and color, leaving the designer no control over them. Also, when setting drop shadows on numerous text boxes that fall on the same page, make sure that all of the drop shadows are offset equally and placed at the same angle. A drop shadow gives the impression of a light source, and the shadows should fall consistently from one block of text to another. You may also want to apply a soft drop shadow, one in which the shadow blurs and fades, giving a transparent quality. These can be done in Photoshop or by using a third-party plug-in for QuarkXpress, such as Shadowcaster. (see bibliography)

Cropping Photographs

One way to increase the impact of an image is by manipulating its composition to get the proper emphasis. This recomposing is primarily achieved through cropping. Cropping helps position the image's focal point so that it works within the design. The focal point of any design or image is the area to which the reader's eye is attracted first. Because cropping can be used to alter the image's composition, it will also help you successfully integrate the display type.

Complex Shapes: Advanced Techniques

The Merge tools can be used in advanced ways to create a range of complex shapes for images or tint boxes.

Tabbed Windows

Tabbed windows are commonplace in design today and reflect the influence of Web design on print.

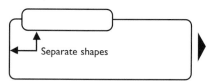

Separate shapes

TABBED WINDOWS can be built by combining shapes and elaborated upon by using a range of Merge tools.

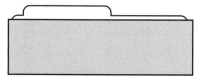

HEADER BARS are created by placing a rectangle over the tabbed shape and applying the Difference tool. This crops away the rectangle from the tabbed shape and creates the bar. Make sure to copy the original tabbed shape before creating the band.

COMBINE SHAPES by placing them over each other and using the Union tool to combine them.

VARIATIONS The header band can then be placed over any number of different shapes.

Slicing Images

Picture boxes can be sliced up to give the effect of transparency.

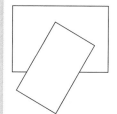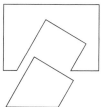

INTERLOCKING SHAPES To get separate shapes that fit accurately into each other, create two shapes and copy them. Apply Difference to one set and Reverse Difference to the other. This will result in two shapes that interlock.

◄ Transparency is the effect of interlocking shapes. Same image is placed in each box with different shades applied.

Cropping is easy to do in QuarkXpress. Import a photo into a picture box and size it so that part of the photo is cropped away by the boundaries of the picture box. Using the Content tool, place your cursor over the picture box, and when the hand cursor appears you can pan the photo around within the box until you get an appealing composition. Finding the right composition often involves a combination of simultaneously repositioning the image and resizing it. Sometimes it also includes rotating the image within the picture box.

There are two ways to rotate an image in QuarkXpress: rotate the entire picture box or simply rotate the image without affecting the picture box. Remember that once you get the desired composition, any changes to the image's size, rotation, or cropping in QuarkXpress

Label Design

Elaborate label design shapes are easy to create by merging multiple shapes.

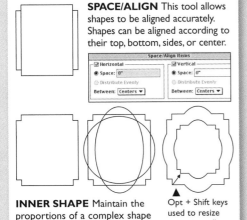

SPACE/ALIGN This tool allows shapes to be aligned accurately. Shapes can be aligned according to their top, bottom, sides, or center.

INNER SHAPE Maintain the proportions of a complex shape by using the Opt + Shift keys when sizing.

▲ Opt + Shift keys used to resize proportionally

You can build up increasingly complex shapes that fit into each other by resizing the shapes and merging them to get interlocking shapes.

Compound Shapes

Using compound shapes as a cropping device can lead to complex picture boxes and interesting photographic effects.

STEP AND REPEAT Begin by creating one line of circles by using the Step and Repeat function.

Step and Repeat	
Repeat Count:	7
Horizontal Offset:	0.25"
Vertical Offset:	0"

GROUP CIRCLES Then apply Step and Repeat to create a perfect grid of circles.

MERGING CIRCLES For the circles to act as a unified shape, ungroup and reselect each separately. Then apply the Union tool. Convert the shape to a picture box and place one image inside the circles.

REVERSE EFFECT Place a rectangle behind the unified circles and then apply the Difference tool.

IMAGE RECOGNITION Make sure that the image placed within the compound shapes remains recognizable.

IMAGE GRIDS These use the same techniques as the circle grid. Here a grid of squares is united and rotated. A larger rectangle is placed above it and Reverse Difference is applied. The shape is then converted to a picture box.

◀ Reverse Difference applied

Difference ▶ applied

SHATTERED Here a series of rectangles are reshaped to create a shattered look.

will have to be adjusted accordingly in Photoshop before going to final production.

Design Intuitively with Hot Keys When you are working with photos, hot keys will help make designing a quicker and more intuitive process.

By their nature, designers use their eyes to determine what they want. Taking advantage of QuarkXpress' hot keys will help you work more effectively and avoid having to repeatedly enter numerical data, which is a slow and indirect way to get the results you want. One of the

most useful hot keys allows designers to resize an image proportionally on the fly, seeing the results immediately. Simply select the image with the Content tool and use ⌘ + Opt + Shift in conjunction with the < or > symbol to increase or reduce the image size. This is a much more intuitive way to design. There is another hot key combination that can be used to resize both the image and its box proportionally at the same time. Holding down ⌘ + Opt + Shift with the Item tool will allow you to select the box corners and change its size.

As has been previously stressed throughout this book, you want to avoid using functions in which the software makes aesthetic decisions for you. With this in mind, there are a couple of hot keys for automatic image sizing that should be avoided because they remove the designer from the design decision. One of these allows for the image to be centered directly in the middle of the box. While this hot key can be useful when an image is not displaying properly within a box, it should not be used to center images. Another hot key will automatically force the image to fit within the picture box dimensions. This Fit to Box function often takes the image out of its original proportions, stretching or squeezing it to accommodate the request. The software has no design sensibilities of its own; it simply positions and resizes the image mathematically. Designers should always use their eye to base such decisions and not defer to the software to determine

Placing Images into Text: Text to Box

Placing imagery into type can be an effective design approach depending on how the type is styled and what type of image is used.

Style type and select Text to Box   Text to Box creates an editable picture box   Place image in box and position

TEXT TO BOX converts type outlines to a picture box, allowing an image to be placed within the type. To apply Text to Box highlight the type you wish to affect. Text to Box will convert only one line of text at a time. After Text to Box is selected, a copy of the type in picture box form will appear. An image can then be placed within the text.

IMAGE QUALITY plays a role in how recognizable an image is when it's placed in type. Detailed images are less successful than large, dominant images that are able to remain recognizable when broken up. These images allow the eye to fill in the missing areas.

CONDENSED BOLD type will accommodate the image's readability better than thinner typefaces.

UPPERCASE letters are larger and less varied in shape than lowercase and help hold the image together.

KERNING type tightly helps hold the image together, allowing more of it to be seen continuously.

ODD GAPS are created by the shape of some letters (A,W,V) and can reduce image legibility.

SERIF TYPEFACES have varying stroke widths that show less of the image and make it harder to distinguish.

Thin strokes make an image hard to see.

when the image is centered or fitting within the box.

Engaging the Reader

There are many compositional techniques that designers use to engage the reader. Through the use of visual hierarchy, a design can be composed to help guide and direct the reader's eye. This can be done through the positioning and sizing of objects within a photograph.

Combining Text to Box with the Merge Tools

Text that's converted to an editable shape can be used with any of the Merge functions.

1 ONE LINE AT A TIME Text to Box converts only one line of text at a time to a picture box. If you have more than one line of text to convert, each line must be converted separately. The separate picture boxes can be positioned to simulate their original leading.

2 TWO LINES, ONE SHAPE To get the separate picture boxes to act as one, place the boxes so that they overlap and then combine into one shape using the Union tool.

3 CUTTING TYPE OUT To cut type out from a background, place a type shape over an image. Then select both and apply the Difference tool.

DROP SHADOW creates a sense of depth. Without it the type would appear to be flat, as if it were placed on the image's surface.

Separating Compound Shapes: Split Paths

Individual images can be placed into the separate paths of a compound shape.

SHAPE AND IMAGE depend on each other for this technique to work. Getting each face to be recognizable in such odd shapes involves a combination of sizing, positioning, and rotating the image.

SEPARATE IMAGES can be placed into the individual letters. By default Text to Box creates one picture box. To divide each letter into its own picture box apply Split Paths: Outside Paths.

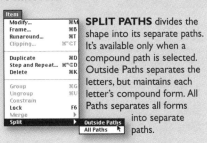

SPLIT PATHS divides the shape into its separate paths. It's available only when a compound path is selected. Outside Paths separates the letters, but maintains each letter's compound form. All Paths separates all forms into separate paths.

Typically, asymmetrical compositions are more interesting than perfectly centered ones. The nature of symmetrical compositions is to be at rest and inactive. This is true for page layout as well as photo com-positions. Whenever applicable, you should also have the direction or thrust of the photo lead into the page. This will guide and invite the reader into a design. If the direc-tion of the layout or photo is one that moves off the page, this is inevitably where the reader's eye will go.

Another guideline is that one large image will generally have more impact than a series of smaller ones. A series of small photos can often be busy, creating a composition that lacks a dominant element. Each photo will compete with the others for attention. Good compositions usually have dominant and subordinate elements that give a sense of visual hierarchy.

Portraits and Head Shots

Photos of people engage the viewer in different ways than landscapes or still lifes do. We relate to these photos in a more personal and intimate way. Keeping in mind the direction of the photo, portraits or head shots should be designed so that the subject looks into the page. This will direct the reader's attention into the story.

Large portraits that appear prominently within a design can also be shot so that the subject looks into the reader's eyes. This technique has long been used by painters to engage their audiences. One of the captivating aspects of Leonardo da Vinci's Mona Lisa is that she appears to look directly at the viewer regardless of what

Organizing Annotated Photo Layouts

Annotated photo layouts are common in design and involve type and image working together to get information across clearly.

EVERY PICTURE TELLS A STORY While some photos are designed to serve as cover or opening art, intended to draw a reader's interest, other photos are designed to provide specific, in-depth information. These photos are often accompanied by caption material that illuminates the features of the object included in the photograph. There are a wide range of ways to annotate or point out these features.

ORDER FROM CHAOS When approaching an annotated layout, begin by locating the highlighted elements and roughly figuring out the caption positions. Try to avoid pointer lines being placed at arbitrary angles, as they can create a chaotic, unorganized look. One way to give the graphic an orderly feel is to use a common angle for the pointer lines,

COPY AND PASTE A PROTOTYPE Rather than building each pointer individually, create a series of prototype pointer designs. Once a final design is reached, copy and paste it and input text so that all pointers are consistent.

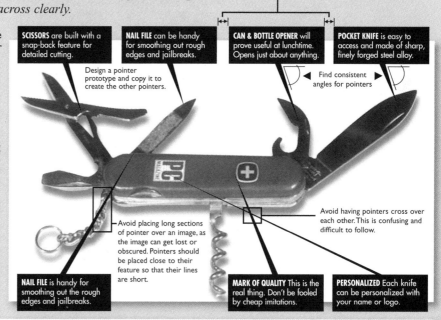

Find a grid to bring order to the pointer placement.

SCISSORS are built with a snap-back feature for detailed cutting.

NAIL FILE can be handy for smoothing out rough edges and jailbreaks.

CAN & BOTTLE OPENER will prove useful at lunchtime. Opens just about anything.

POCKET KNIFE is easy to access and made of sharp, finely forged steel alloy.

Design a pointer prototype and copy it to create the other pointers.

Find consistent angles for pointers

Avoid having pointers cross over each other. This is confusing and difficult to follow.

Avoid placing long sections of pointer over an image, as the image can get lost or obscured. Pointers should be placed close to their feature so that their lines are short.

NAIL FILE is handy for smoothing out the rough edges and jailbreaks.

MARK OF QUALITY This is the real thing. Don't be fooled by cheap imitations.

PERSONALIZED Each knife can be personalized with your name or logo.

DON'T LOSE LINES Make sure the lines don't get lost when placed over an image. Adjust the pointer's line width and color so it doesn't get lost in the image.

CROSS PURPOSES Try to find a way to lay out your pointers so that none of the pointers cross over each other. Crossing lines can cause ambiguity and confusion.

FINDING AN ANGLE One way to clearly organize an annotated photograph so that its information is easy to read and locate is to find a common angle for your pointers.

KEEP LINES SHORT Long lines can force the reader to do unnecessary work in connecting the image with its associated text. Doglegs can be added to pointer lines but should be kept simple.

POSITION CAPTIONS Position the descriptive captions as closely as possible to their associated feature. This will help enhance the effectiveness of the graphic.

STRAIGHT LINES You can use these exclusively or in conjunction with a common angle. Either approach can be used to add a sense of organization.

angle she is viewed at. Magazine covers almost always use this technique.

When using head shots, remember that they can be cropped at the top of the head if necessary. The entire top of the head doesn't need to be seen. Television newscasts often do this to get close-ups.

Picking up Colors from Photos

One way to give your design an integrated feel is to use the colors found in the photo as a reference for other elements within the design. By applying these colors to a range of design elements such as box tints, drop caps, or rules, your design will have a consistent color palette and an overall integrated feel. For instance, let's say you've got a drop cap whose color you would like to match to the photograph. You could use your eye to create a custom color that matches the image in QuarkXpress, but this is difficult to do because of its low-resolution preview. A more accurate method is to open up the image in Photoshop, use the color picker to select a color from the image, and take note of its CMYK values. Using these values, you can then set up an identical color in QuarkXpress and apply it to the drop cap. This method allows you

to be sure that these colors will accurately match when output on a high-end image setter. This method of color sampling can be used for creating overall palettes for a project and will help give it a consistent color sense.

Using Holding Rules

Just as image qualities determine how and where type will be superimposed over an image, it also determines how an image will be framed. Just as a busy or high-contrast image will affect the sharpness of the edges of the type characters, it also affects how a photo sits on a page. Images that have a consistent tone, one that doesn't get overly light, can be used in a picture box without a border. But images that have very light tones, particularly on their edges, require holding rules. Light tones around an image's edge create a lack of definition between the photo and the page white. Holding rules help to define the image border. A holding rule is typically a half-point black rule that holds the picture in place. If you use a holding rule on one picture, it is probably best to apply a holding rule to all the images found within that design. This will help to maintain a consistent feel throughout the design. Holding rules can also have

a color applied to them to help reinforce the consistency of the design's overall color palette.

Frame Types

There are numerous borders that can be applied to picture boxes, some simple, some very elaborate. While image quality will in part determine if a border is required, a frame can be used for design's sake. In most cases a simple frame is usually all that is necessary, but in some instances an elaborate border can work well. The elaborate border types offered in QuarkXpress should be used judiciously when a project calls for it. Young designers have a tendency to overuse these preset borders. Since QuarkXpress doesn't make it easy for designers to create custom borders, you might try creating them in Photoshop or Illustrator.

Picture Box Types

QuarkXpress offers a wide range of shapes for picture boxes. The most commonly used preset shapes are rectangles and ovals. To maintain a consistency throughout a design, it's best to limit the number of frame types used. Rectangle boxes with rounded corners have become popular recently with the influence of Web design on print. The rounded rectangle, or roundtangle, mimics the tabbed windows that are commonly found within Internet and software design.

Some of the other types of boxes QuarkXpress offers include beveled and concave borders. These box shapes can be awkward, and like other preset features offered by software, their use makes one aware of the software used to create the project, not the designer's personal touch. Many of the preset options have a limited range of applicability. For instance, using concave boxes might be handy for a project that reflects a retro feel, but other appropriate applications for them are limited.

While using these frame types in their default preset modes is not advisable, they can be used as a starting point for building more original frame types. These frame types can be manipulated by adding and subtracting other shapes from them using the Merge functions. These frames can also be reshaped manually. This is a preferable way to build customized frames that are specifically designed for your project.

Complex Frames: The Pen Tool

For most projects the standard picture box shapes should be suffi-

---

Styling Pointers & Annotations

Once you've sketched out a layout of the pointer positioning, start styling the pointer and its descriptive caption so that they work as a unit.

DESIGN PROTOTYPE Whether designing annotation pointers, graphic sidebars, or factoids, an efficient way to approach the design is to build a master prototype first.

SIMPLE CAPTIONS Build on these by adding other elements such as rules, title bars, and lead-ins and by using a variety of type weights and attributes.

Pointer boxes are an effective way to annotate photographs.

1 Create two boxes. Here a rectangle and thin triangle are used.

2 Place the shapes over one another, select both, and combine them by applying Unite tool.

3 Adjust the pointer position by manually editing the shape.

SNAP PEDDLES are easy to work, especially on steep uphill grades. The open construction and reflective gearings make them comfortable and the choice of most long distance bikers.

POINTER STYLES

HEAD GEAR
Molded & lightweight, these helmets offer protection, as well as comfort.

Title bar added

EYEWEAR
• **UV Sports Visor**
Combines Ultra Violet protection and style. Form fitting, non-pinching. Ultra Wear Styles, San Francisco 1-800 456-2419 ultrawear.com

Tabbed shape, expanded info

GLOVES
X-RUN RIPPLE GRIP ZS
Textured gortex gives added grip while reducing hand numbness. **DunkNGroove, Sante Fe NM** WWW.DUNKNGOOVE.COM

Tabbed shape and band, section rules used

SHOES
NIKE XTRAIN
Lightweight, tread textured grip soles don't slip. WWW.NIKE.COM

Inset photo used

BUILD A MASTER PROTOTYPE Once you've designed an attractive pointer and caption, use it as a master element by copying and pasting it to build each separate pointer. This ensures that the type positioning in all the pointers is consistent.

Great Falls — Horseshoe Falls — Rainbow Bridge — Changing to white rule helps readability — Canada

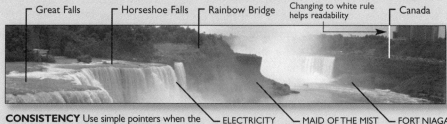

CONSISTENCY Use simple pointers when the design dictates. Pointers are equally spaced, and lines have consistent angles on top and bottom.

ELECTRICITY generated from falls helps supply NYC

MAID OF THE MIST runs tours hourly from noon to 9 p.m.

FORT NIAGARA was built in 1765 for protection

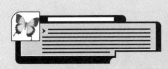  

BUILD VARIATIONS When initially designing elements with complex shapes, experiment with applying the Merge tools to different shapes. Above is a series of design treatments for an infographic. The larger version at right represents the final.

MASTER SHAPES Make sure to copy a set of original shapes before you apply the Merge tools. These extra shapes often prove useful when adjustments need to be made later on.

HAND-DRAWN SHAPES The indented arrow at the beginning of the paragraph was created using the pen tool in conjunction with a grid of guidelines. Points are placed using Snap to Guides.

BUTTERFLY COLLECTION
Butterflies & moths from around the world are reminders of the museum's origin as a natural history collection. The many exotic butterflies show the immense diversity of nature, and the beauty of the moths, often hidden by night's darkness, is exposed here.

MIXING CORNER TYPES The background shape contains a combination of squared and rounded corners.

Higher Ground
Climbers rely on their equipment to stay alive. Faulty or low quality tools can prove deadly.

HEADGEAR should include helmet & UV goggles

BELTS should be tested before every climb

CLAMPS are placed upon the belt in size order

TOE HOLDS must be tight and laced appropriately

ANY SHAPE can be used for a pointer design. Ellipses introduce curvilinear shapes into the design.

ADD DEPTH to the layout by placing pointers so that they overlap the image edge.

AVOID CUTTING across images in awkward ways. Here the pointers cuts across the climber's neck.

WINTER SPORTS include skiing, hockey, and snowboarding. Snow is common year round.

MOUNTAIN BIKING Hundreds of trails for all levels of bikers. Bring your bike or rent.

ENJOY THE POOL Heated pool is available with water polo and fun slide for the kids.

The Great North
There's plenty to do at this undiscovered sporting paradise

By the dawn of the twentieth century industrialism had swept its way across the country, leaving nothing untouched in its wake. Seemingly overnight industrialization profoundly changed the face of the nation, influencing every aspect of life. The events that took place between 1885 and 1910 represent the metamorphosis of the country from a society relatively untouched by industrialism to

THE GREAT OUTDOORS Come hike the many mountain trails. Guided nature hikes included.

INSIDE THE BOX When an image contains large inactive areas, like the sky in this image, captions can be knocked out of the background and still be readable. The pointer is created with straight 1-point rules with manually drawn square heads.

TEXT WRAPS Especially when the type is set justified, it wraps nicely around elliptical shapes. Placing the annotation so that it butts into the body copy helps to integrate the infographic with the rest of the page.

IMAGE MIDTONES The medium tonality of the image allows the headline and subtitle type to be styled in a variety of ways: knocked out or printed as black.

Creating Legends for Photographs

Legends function similarly to annotations in that both are used to point out specific information contained within an image.

LEGENDS are used, like annotations, to describe specific areas or objects found within an image. When numerous items are being illuminated, the layout can become busy.

READABILITY should be considered when deciding to use a legend. Legends require the reader to locate the correlating information. Because annotations include pointers that directly lead to the associated information, they are easier to read.

IMAGE QUALITY will determine whether to use pointers or a legend. Busy images that don't include inactive areas where pointers can be placed are usually best annotated by using a legend. Legends are also recommended when large descriptions need to be placed in close proximity to one another.

BULLET PLACEMENT should be handled so that bullets are easy to see. Letter C bullet is placed over a dark area and is getting lost. Color bullets can help readability.

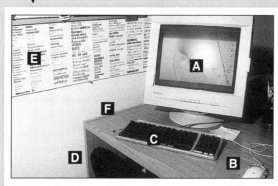

A MONITOR should be large enough so that images can be previewed at actual size.
B INPUT DEVICE Optical mice are preferable for graphic design work.
C KEYBOARD Keyboards should be full sized and positioned to avoid discomfort.
D SURGE PROTECTORS are highly recommended to reduce effects of power surges.
E WALL SPACE should be accessible for posting important and frequently used data.
F DESK SPACE should be ample so that you can work neatly and unincumbered.

STANDARD LEGENDS These place the information in close proximity to the photograph they are describing. Here lead-ins are used in conjunction with bullets to increase skimmability.

1. **HELMET** is a must and should be tightly fit to head and chin
2. **PROPER ATTIRE** will give you a sense of style when you're biking
3. **GLOVES** help maintain a ure grip and reduce hand numbness
4. **HAND BRAKES** Should be checked and maintained on regular basis
5. **FOOT GEAR** helps maintain solid contact between feet and pedal.

LEGEND PLACEMENT Legends can be placed within the image area if the image composition allows for it. Here a tinted box is placed overlapping the image and the legend information is knocked out from the tint.

cient. But some projects require a more advanced approach to creating image boxes. One method might be to draw out the desired shape using the pen tool. While this is the most obvious approach, there are other ways to achieve custom shapes. In QuarkXpress, pen tools are limited and don't offer the functionality that an illustration program does. This doesn't mean that you can't create boxes using the pen tool, but there are some methods that can be used to help you get better results. One way is to begin by dragging out a series of guidelines whose lines intersect at points that reflect the desired shape. By using Snap to Guides, the pen will automatically snap to the intersecting guidelines and into the shape you need. While you can use the shift key to constrain the line to perfect horizontal and vertical positions, the guidelines also ensure accurate measurements and equal line lengths.

BUILDING BULLETS While there are some bullet typefaces available, they can also be built by combining shapes with letters. Bullets often use knockout type, and bolder sans serif faces usually work better.

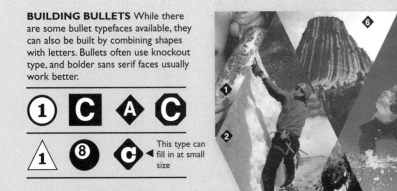

This type can fill in at small size

MAPS Because of the complex nature of maps and the amount of information needed in a small space, legends are good way to handle annotating.

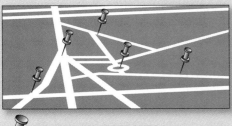

ILLUSTRATIVE BULLETS In some cases illustrative icons can be used as bullets. Because of their small size, illustrative icons should be kept simple and not include too much detail.

PHOTO LAYOUTS These are good places to incorporate a legend because their descriptions don't interfere with the imagery.

COLOR CODING Colors can be used with bullets so that the bullet color corresponds with the color of the caption lead-in type. This allows the reader to quickly locate information.

ICON BULLETS Icons can be used to provide expanded information that standard bullets aren't able to do. For example, a set of icons could be placed on a map to show the location of troops, planes, or warships.

Either method will ensure straight, even lines.

Using the pen tool is the most obvious and direct way to create a custom box shape. QuarkXpress offers tools that provide easier ways to get the shape you want. Unless you are using the Snap to Guides approach, avoid using the Freehand box tool. While it is the most direct method, the shapes created with it are often awkward and have an uncontrolled look.

A word about the pen tool and Bézier curves: Being able to use them properly is a prerequisite for anyone entering the field of graphic design. You cannot avoid using them, and you need to invest the time necessary to understand how they work and are manipulated. Understanding how handles and points work is difficult and confusing for all beginning designers. While they are not the most intuitive tools, they are standardized and generally work they same way in Photoshop, Illustrator, and QuarkXpress. This means that once you've learned how to use them in one program, you can use them in all programs.

Custom Frames: Merge Tools

Another way to create custom boxes that doesn't require the manipulation of points is to combine preexisting shapes to create more complex ones. QuarkXpress offers a series of Merge functions that combine, crop, or divide overlapping shapes. For instance, overlapping shapes that have the Union feature applied to them will be combined. This new shape can then be added to or have its outline refined by using the pen tool. The Merge functions work in very much the same way as Illustrator's Pathfinder filters. Shapes can be aligned accurately by using the Space/Align function before you apply the Merge functions. For instance, if you need to have shapes perfectly centered over one another, the Align function is more accurate than using your eye.

Annotating Photographs

One common type of photographic layout that designers encounter are annotated photographs. These layouts include images that are informative in nature and contain numerous elements that require accompanying text descriptions. For instance, the photo might be of a mountain biker and the purpose of the layout is to describe the gear that he is wearing, such as helmet, gloves, and shoes. One common method of pointing out these features is to use annotations. *Annotation* refers to a pointer and an associated caption that highlights each of these features. Treatments previously discussed in relation to standard captions, such as lead-ins and subheads, can also be applied to annotation design.

One of the biggest challenges with annotating a photo is caption placement. Once again, let the image dictate the type positioning. The annotations should be placed in close proximity to the features they are highlighting. Finding an attractive layout can be accomplished by following a few guide-

lines. A good approach is to roughly position the separate captions around the image to get a sense of the overall layout. Once you've got the general positioning worked out, you can focus on finding an appropriate type styling and pointer design.

One way to create an organized, easy-to-navigate annotated photograph is to limit or control the number of angles that are used by the pointer lines. One method is to limit the range of line angles to strict horizontal and vertical lines. While this is an effective way to avoid an overly busy look, it can be a little rigid. Try to position the captions so that the pointer lines don't intersect, which could be confusing to the reader. One attractive approach is to have your pointer lines share a common angle. This common angle can also be used in conjunction with horizontal and vertical lines, giving you a mix of straight and angled pointer lines.

Legends

Another way to annotate a photograph is to use a legend. Instead of pointers, legends make use of numbered or lettered labels placed over or near their associated features. These labels have associated text

descriptions. Legends are used when the features of a photo or map require more information than can comfortably be placed over or around an image or when the concentration of highlighted elements makes annotating with a caption-and-pointer approach difficult. Legends are also appropriate and effective when pointer placement is not a viable solution, such as when extraordinarily long pointers would be unavoidable. While legends provide a cleaner look, they are not as direct and user-friendly as pointers because they require the reader to locate the associated captions.

Summary

Whether you're working with large opening headlines, captions, or annotations, understanding the way in which type contributes to the design is essential to the design process. No matter how small or seemingly unimportant a piece of type may appear, all type needs to be finessed to some degree. While you may not spend as much time laboring over a page number as you would over splashy display type, good designers give some attention to and make conscious decisions about all of the type found within their designs.

Chapter Four
Advanced Typography

In this section we explore more advanced typographical techniques using Adobe Illustrator. All of the techniques covered in this chapter will adhere to the guidelines discussed in the previous chapters regarding type. Those guidelines include not distorting the type, being sensitive to kerning and word spacing, and maintaining readability. Because

QuarkXpress has limited illustrative capabilities for such typographic techniques, we will primarily deal with creating type treatments in Illustrator and then importing these designs into QuarkXpress. The following examples are best applied to display type. In general, any body copy or caption material that is included in a design should be created in QuarkXpress, which provides more control for this kind of type than Illustrator.

Styling Type in Illustrator
For many design projects, Quark offers enough functionality to effectively style display type. While Quark allows type to be converted to editable shapes or positioned along a curve, sometimes these features are not sufficient to style type in more elaborate ways. In these

cases it is probably best to design your type in Illustrator. Because Illustrator is a drawing program, it offers a wide range of illustrative tools, features, and filters.

Just as with any project, begin

your type design by creating sketches and exploring possible type treatments. This will help figure out how to get the type to work as a unit and how it will be placed within the page composition. Along with this sketch you should also consider which typefaces will be appropriate for the feel of the project. Understanding the message and feel the type should convey as well as the general layout that the type will be placed in will help you develop an approach before you begin to design the type on the computer.

Converting Type to Outlines
In most cases, the type treatment that you create in Illustrator will

WORKING IT OUT ON PAPER Included in this thumbnail layout is a rough type design. Before starting to design type on the computer, rough sketches should be done to get an idea of how the type will work as a unit, as well how it will fit into the page design.

Using the Character and Paragraph Palettes

One of the keys to fine-tuning type is understanding all of the settings included in the Character and Paragraph palettes. Here's an overview of each feature.

CHARACTER PALETTE Understanding how the settings in the Character and Paragraph palettes affect type will help you refine your type design. These palettes are accessed through the Type pull-down menu.

A TYPE SIZE controls the size of the type.

B LEADING controls the vertical space between the lines of text.

C KERNING sets specific horizontal space between individual characters.

D TRACKING sets overall word spacing for entire paragraphs of text.

E VERTICAL SCALE changes the height of type and distorts it. Avoid using this setting.

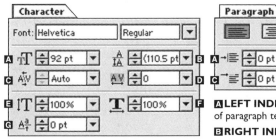

F HORIZONTAL SCALE changes type width and distorts it. Avoid using this setting.

G BASELINE SHIFT moves type so it sits above or below its baseline.

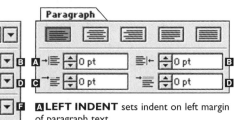

A LEFT INDENT sets indent on left margin of paragraph text.

B RIGHT INDENT sets right margin indent.

C FIRST LINE INDENT sets how deeply the first line of the paragraph is indented.

D SPACE BEFORE PARAGRAPH sets horizontal space between paragraphs.

KERNING HOT KEYS Kerning type using key commands is the easiest way to kern because its results are seen immediately. Place the cursor between the characters and use the left and right arrow keys with the Option key to change the letter spacing.

SIZING TYPE ON THE FLY Type can be resized by using hot keys. Highlight the text and hold down ⌘ + Opt + Shift while using the greater or lesser sign (< or >) to increase or decrease the type size. This method allows the changes to be seen immediately.

FREE TRANSFORM Type can be resized by using the Scale or Free Transform tools. Use the shift key when applying either tool so the type is not taken out of its original proportions. The Shift key is used to constrain proportion.

involve converting your type to outlines so that it can be manipulated in complex ways. While some of these techniques can be emulated in QuarkXpress, it is a much more difficult task because of Quark's less sophisticated illustration tools. While converting type to outlines has its benefits, it is not without its pitfalls. Being able to manipulate a character's outlines is a powerful tool in the right hands. However, outlines can just as easily be used ineffectively and produce unattractive and illegible type. Probably the biggest downside of working with type outlines is the ease with which type characters can be distorted.

In most of the examples contained in this chapter the type is converted to outlines, but in no instance will the type be distorted in a manner inconsistent with its original text outline and design. In each case the integrity of the typeface's original design is maintained.

Preparing the Type

The first step to take after entering the type and selecting a typeface is to kern the type. Since the techniques covered in this chapter apply predominantly to display type, you need to kern the individual spaces between the characters manually. It is easier to kern the text before converting it to outlines. Kerning can be done a few ways in Illustrator. You can place your cursor between the characters and then enter a kerning setting in the Paragraph menu. An easier and more intuitive method is to place your cursor between the characters to be kerned and use the Option key in conjunction with the arrow keys. This allows you to see the kerning change immediately on the screen.

From Font to Shape

Once you've selected, sized, and kerned your type roughly, you can then convert the type to outlines by selecting, not highlighting, the type and choosing Create Outlines from the type pull-down menu. Once the type is converted to outlines, it becomes a shape and can

---

Curves Ahead: Creating Outlines

The first step in creating complex typographical treatments is often converting the type to curves by using the Create Outline function.

KERN BEFORE CONVERTING It is easier to control kern settings before the type is converted to curves. Once converted to curves, each character becomes an individual shape and must be then selected individually and moved to change the space between the characters.

CONVERT TYPE to outlines by selecting the type with the Selection tool, not by highlighting the text. Then select Create Outlines from the Type pull-down menu. Once the type is converted, it becomes a vector object and can no longer be highlighted and edited.

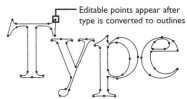

Editable points appear after type is converted to outlines

EDITABLE SHAPES Once type is converted to outlines, it becomes a shape with points that can be edited using the Direct Selection tool.

Curves: The Pros & Cons

There are inherent benefits and pitfalls to converting type to curves.

OUTLINE QUALITY Once converted, type is no longer a font, which means a slight loss in the quality of its outlines. Typefaces have more refined shapes than outlines.

PRINTING One of the benefits of converting to outlines is that because it is no longer an actual typeface, the font does not need to be presently loaded for it to print well. This can make it easier to transport files and open them when the font is not available.

MORE CONTROL While curves enable type to be treated in ways not possible when it remains as a font, it can also open the door for type to be distorted easily.

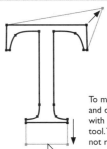

Corner point is selected and moved using the Direct Selection tool. Point is active when it appears blue.

To move a segment, click and drag between points with the direct selection tool. This method does not require points to be selected first

DIRECT SELECTION This tool is used to select and move points. To select specific points, first click on the path and then select the point.

Controlling Type Outlines

Once type has been converted to outlines, its shape may be altered in countless ways. Understanding both the Bézier pen tools and the Selection tools is a prerequisite to getting the results you want.

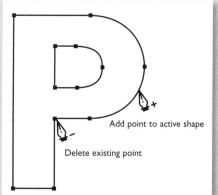

Add point to active shape

Delete existing point

THE PEN TOOLS can be used to draw original shapes or to manipulate shapes that have been created using other tools. The pen tools in Illustrator and Photoshop work in identical ways.

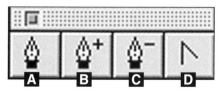

A PEN TOOL is used to directly place original points to create lines or shapes.

B ADD ANCHOR POINT will add points to a selected shape.

C DELETE ANCHOR POINT will delete points from a selected shape.

D CONVERT POINT converts smooth points to corner points and vice versa.

SELECTION TOOLS Illustrator offers three selection tool options; the Selection, Direct Selection, and Group Selection tools. Each tool selects points and shapes differently.

SELECTION TOOL is used to select and move entire objects or groups of objects. It does not select individual points.

DIRECT SELECTION TOOL selects specific points. To select a point click directly on it. To select multiple points click on the points using the Shift key or click and drag to surround points.

GROUP SELECTION TOOL selects specific objects within groups. It enables the placement of a grouped element to be changed without ungrouping.

ADD AND DELETE POINTS Choose the appropriate pen tool and click on point to delete it or click on the path to add a point.

CONTEXT-SENSITIVE Points can also be deleted using the standard pen tool. The pen tool is context-sensitive, which means it will change its functionality as you move over existing points. Its cursor changes as you move over existing points.

TEAR-OFF MENUS For projects involving intense point editing, "tear off" a separate pen palette for quick access. Click and hold on the pen tool icon in the toolbox and select the arrow at the right of the tool set. A floating menu of pen tools will appear.

no longer be highlighted and edited as text. By converting it to outlines, each character shape can now be altered. Once it is converted to a shape, any number of illustration tools and techniques can be applied to it. One downside of this is that the character outlines lose some quality in the translation from font to shape. The upside of converting type to outlines is that

since it is no longer a font, the font will no longer need to be present for it to print properly. This can be handy to remember when displaying or outputting a file on a computer where the font may not be available.

Working with Type Outlines

Once type is converted to outlines, its character outlines can be manip-

ulated. Perhaps the most important thing to remember is that the character shapes should be altered in ways that are consistent with the typeface's original design. The most common methods of adjusting outlines to create original type designs involve creating ligatures, extending ascenders, descenders, and serifs, and sizing type proportionately.

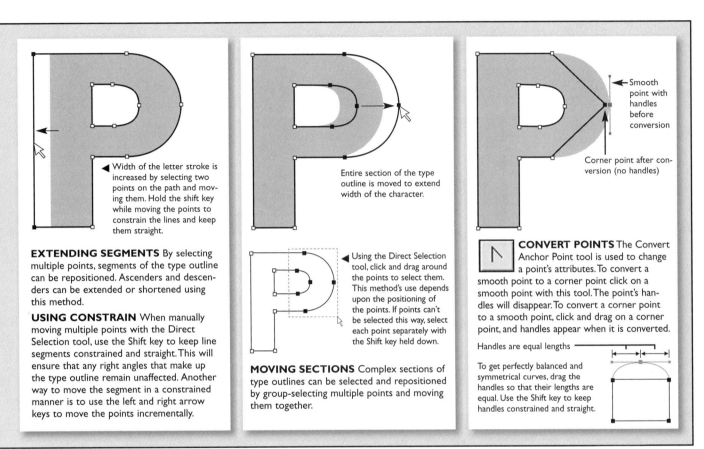

Width of the letter stroke is increased by selecting two points on the path and moving them. Hold the shift key while moving the points to constrain the lines and keep them straight.

EXTENDING SEGMENTS By selecting multiple points, segments of the type outline can be repositioned. Ascenders and descenders can be extended or shortened using this method.

USING CONSTRAIN When manually moving multiple points with the Direct Selection tool, use the Shift key to keep line segments constrained and straight. This will ensure that any right angles that make up the type outline remain unaffected. Another way to move the segment in a constrained manner is to use the left and right arrow keys to move the points incrementally.

Entire section of the type outline is moved to extend width of the character.

Using the Direct Selection tool, click and drag around the points to select them. This method's use depends upon the positioning of the points. If points can't be selected this way, select each point separately with the Shift key held down.

MOVING SECTIONS Complex sections of type outlines can be selected and repositioned by group-selecting multiple points and moving them together.

Smooth point with handles before conversion

Corner point after conversion (no handles)

CONVERT POINTS The Convert Anchor Point tool is used to change a point's attributes. To convert a smooth point to a corner point click on a smooth point with this tool. The point's handles will disappear. To convert a corner point to a smooth point, click and drag on a corner point, and handles appear when it is converted.

Handles are equal lengths

To get perfectly balanced and symmetrical curves, drag the handles so that their lengths are equal. Use the Shift key to keep handles constrained and straight.

Creating Ligatures

One of the most common reasons for creating outlines is to create type ligatures. A ligature is typically a pair of adjacent characters that overlap and touch each other to form one overall shape. Many typefaces have special ligature characters designed for specific type pairings, which because of the nature of their forms tend to have too much space fall between them. Two of the most common true ligatures include *ffl* and *fl*. Note that these characters have not been kerned to appear close to one another but actually represent a single character. Ligatures such as these will be present only when the ligature setting is selected in the Quark preferences.

It is not uncommon for designers to create custom ligatures by converting text to outlines and then uniting overlapping characters by applying the Unite filter in the Pathfinder menu. The decision to create ligatures generally implies that the type is set tightly overall. Remember that however you decide to kern your type, it should be spaced consistently. This means that visually the characters appear

KPT Filters: An Interface Primer

KPT's interface design doesn't use standard sliders and buttons and takes a little while to get used to. Here's a basic primer on how its interface works.

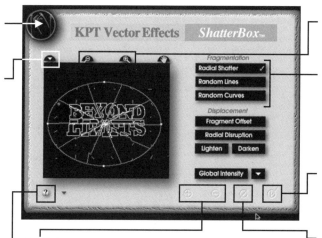

PREVIEW WINDOW In some of KPT's filters you can click on the KPT icon to view the filter effects in a full-screen preview.

FILE MENU From this pull-down menu you can select viewing options, reset filter settings, or show unselected art. The viewing choices include wire-frame mode and rough or full previews (full preview takes longer to render). Showing unselected art enables you to see unselected objects in the Illustrator file. Other settings like Render Hidden Faces will render all the shapes created by the filter, not just those that are visible.

PRESETS Most of the KPT filters include a set of customized filter settings that can be accessed here.

CUSTOM FILTER SETTINGS can be saved for later use. This feature can save time and ensure accuracy when multiple objects require similar filter manipulations. To save a setting click on the plus sign. To delete a setting click on the minus sign.

VIEWING SETTINGS To view the selected art at a larger or smaller settings click on the magnifying glass icons to zoom in or out.

FILTERS SETTINGS The KPT interface uses its own slider design. To change the amount of a filter setting click inside the black bar and hold down. A blue slider line will appear and you can move the cursor back or forth to change the filter's effects on the art. You cannot enter a numerical setting.

SAVE EFFECT Once you are finished applying a filter and are happy with the results, click on the check mark icon to exit KPT Vector Effects and reenter the original Illustrator document.

CANCEL EFFECT If you do not like the results of the filter and do not want them to be applied to the selected object, exit KPT Vector Effects by clicking on the cancel icon.

---

equidistant from each other. Don't rely on the word spacing numbers to set kerning intervals; just because the setting may be the same numerically, this does not guarantee that they are evenly spaced visually. The typeface you select will also determine how you handle the letterspacing. While some typefaces look great when they are kerned tightly, others are designed to have greater spaces between their characters.

Case settings also play a role in determining the letterspacing. Type that is set in uppercase can be kerned extremely loosely and still hold together as a unit and maintain its readability. The opposite is true of type set entirely in lowercase. Frederic Goudy, a legendary type designer, once stated that anyone who would loosely letterspace lowercase type would "shag a sheep." While this may be a questionable characterization, the effects of letterspacing on lowercase characters is well known. Because of the wide range of shapes that make up lowercase characters, words tend to fall apart when kerned very loosely.

Another factor that will influence how type is styled is the fashion of design at the time. Just as typefaces move in and out of

Original Shapes

CONVERT FIRST Most of the KPT filters require type to be converted to outlines before the filters can be applied.

TOO MANY SHAPES When applying KPT filters, try to limit the number of steps and shapes the filter creates so that it doesn't become too complex and subject to possible printing problems.

NEON creates a neon sign effect by creating a stepped blend in which the colors emanate from dark to light.

SHADOWLAND can be used to create standard drop shadows or a series of stepped shapes.

SHATTERBOX will divide a shape to appear as if it has been broken into shards.

3D TRANSFORM will rotate shapes on their x, y, and z axes as well as extrude and bevel them to create three-dimensional shapes.

VECTOR DISTORT allows shapes to appear rounded as if printed on a concave or convex plane.

EMBOSS will create a series of stepped shapes to create the illusion of an embossed or recessed shape.

WARP FRAME affects grouped objects using a bounding box, enabling them to be shaped as one unit.

FLARE places a starburst shape inside the selected shape and lets you control how the flare graduates outward from the shape.

style among designers, so do the methods of styling it. In the mid-eighties, when specing type by hand was still a common practice, type was often specified as "TNT," which signified "tight, not touching." It was the common practice of the time. Today it is not uncommon to see type styled with tight leading settings that would have been unheard of twenty years earlier.

Extending Serifs

Another common way to manipulate character outlines is to adjust serifs. This method works especially well with faces that have slab serifs. Slab serifs, also referred to as Egyptian serifs, are usually the same weight as the font's downstroke and are often squared off at their ends. Common typefaces that have slab serifs include City, Clarendon, and Century Schoolbook. Because of the thickness of these serifs, extending or shortening them can be effective.

Ascenders and Descenders

Besides manipulating a character's serifs, ascenders and descenders can also be reshaped. Ascenders and descenders are the sections found on lowercase characters that fall above the x-height and below the baseline. Once the type is converted to curves, they can be lengthened or shortened accordingly. While this approach can be applied to many type styles, it can be particularly effective with italic faces that have graceful ascenders and descenders. To extend these character elements you need to select multiple points from the outline and then move them simultaneously.

Antiquing Type

Sometimes a project's design will call for an older style, one that reflects an earlier design sensibility. Let's say you are working on a design that needs to evoke colonial America of the late 1700s. One way to approach such a project is to find documents, posters, advertisements, and public announcements from the period. You might also try searching through type books for fonts that are representa-

Creating Custom Ligatures

True ligatures are special characters available in some fonts' character sets. Overlapping characters in tightly kerned type will often form ligatures that can be united to form one complex character.

SPACE RELATIONS The unique shape of each character affects the amount of kerning required. Letters like A, V, or W often need tighter kerning because of their shapes. This variety of shapes is why one kern setting does not always produce evenly spaced characters.

Letters like *A* and *V* have shapes that often require tighter kerning.

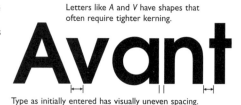

Type as initially entered has visually uneven spacing.

KERN TYPE FIRST Type should be kerned before it is converted to curves. It's easier to kern type while it is still a font. Kern settings can be adjusted in the Character menu or by placing the cursor between the letters and using the Option key with the left and right arrow keys.

Type can be kerned tightly so that characters overlap.

When type is kerned properly its spacing appears visually even.

Convert type to an editable shape by selecting the type and applying Create Outlines. The text outlines will be grouped after Create Outlines is applied.

Type becomes separate editable shapes after conversion.

Once Create Outlines is applied, select the letters and apply the Unite filter.

Select both shapes and apply the Unite filter.

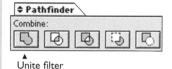

Unite filter

Unite filters creates a ligature, one editable shape.

---

tive of the time. One common way to get a period feel is to antique the type. Antiquing is a technique that is commonly applied to furniture, in which case the wood is intentionally distressed. Antiquing type basically involves a similar process.

Begin the process by selecting a typeface that is reminiscent of the period. In the example shown on page 118, Caslon, a common English typeface from the period, is used. After kerning the type and converting it to outlines, it is given a weathered feel by applying the Roughen filter to it. Apply the filter in a very subtle manner. If you apply the effect too strongly, the type will lose its original look. This method will be effective only with type styles reflective of the period. No matter how much you roughen up a Helvetica or Futura, because their designs are relatively modern, they will never appear antiqued.

A Word About Filters

Once type has been converted to outlines, any of Illustrator's filters that apply to vector shapes can be applied. As with any filter you apply, use them with restraint. It doesn't take much to overapply the Roughen filter. Young designers are

Keepin' It Real: Staying True to the Original Typeface

One pitfall of converting type to outlines is that it becomes easy to distort the type and unnaturally change its character outlines. Here are a few ways to alter type while maintaining the original look of the font.

EXTENDING SERIFS Before converting type to curves it's a good practice to make a copy of the type. This way if changes need to be made later, you have a copy at hand.

MAINTAINING TYPEFACE Type outlines can be adjusted without distorting the typeface. One criteria to use in judging distortion is whether you can still recognize the original typeface. If you can't, it's distorted.

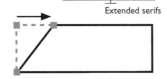

Ligature created using Unite

Extended serifs

Custom serifs created by editing points with the Direct Selection Tool

← All points at the top of the characters selected and moved up as one

EXTENDING ASCENDERS In the type to the right its ascenders have been altered and extended higher than the typeface's original design. This manipulation helps emphasize the literal meaning of the words.

Initial characters resized and repositioned

Descender extended by selecting and moving specific points

RESTYLING TYPE Multiple points are selected to reshape the type. This works well with italic typefaces.

Here the size of some characters is reduced. Avoid distorting the type by holding down the Shift key to maintain the type's original proportions.

Characters are connected by extending the serifs of the word's first and last letters so that they overlap.

Once the extended serifs overlap the two letter forms can be converted into one shape by selecting both and applying the Pathfinder Unite filter.

Letter *I* is scaled down and the serif of the *R* is extended

Adjust sections of a letter by selecting and moving multiple points. Use the arrow keys to move points to the left without changing baseline position.

Consistent vertical and horizontal spacing

Equal spaces should be found consistently throughout the type design.

Applying Filters: The Good, the Bad, & the Ugly

Filters offer powerful ways to handle type, but they can also result in type being distorted beyond recognition. Let's look at some filters and how they can be applied to type effectively.

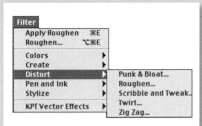

ROUGHEN FILTER This filter adds random points to an object's edge to give it a rough look. Since filters affect only vector shapes, the type must be converted to curves before the filter is applied.

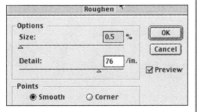

APPLY SUBTLY It's easy to apply a filter's effects too heavily. When applying a filter to text, it's best to keep the size setting low and the level of detail high. This filter can add either smooth or corner points.

We the people

ANTIQUING TYPE The Roughen filter can be used to give type an antique feel, as if it has been printed on rough paper. Some font families like Caslon actually offer antique variations. In the example above, the Roughen filter is applied very lightly but with a high level of detail. While the type has been technically distorted, the original typeface used is still recognizable.

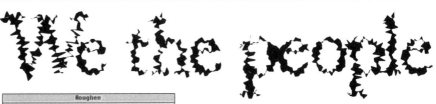

OVER THE TOP It's easy to overdo a filter's effects. In the type above, the Roughen filter has been applied in a heavy-handed manner. The original typeface used has become indiscernible. This type of manipulation is unattractive and should be avoided.

understandably intrigued with the results that such filters can have on type, but it's easy to filter the typeface beyond recognition. One criterion that can be helpful when you're manipulating type is to ask yourself if you can determine what the original font was. If the original typeface

is rendered unrecognizable, you probably have applied the filter too strongly.

Shattering Type
You may run into designs that call for type to be sliced up or shattered to give a broken-glass feel. This

approach is common and can give a feeling of psychological imbalance to the type. Like antiquing, it is a simple process and there are a few ways to achieve it.

Perhaps the most direct way to shatter type is to use the Knife tool. Once the type is styled and convert-

Twirl filter creates awkward type shapes

Type on path doesn't distort type

Zig Zag filter applied to an entire word

Zig Zag filter applied to a single letter

TWIRLING TYPE The Twirl filter affects the type in the same way that the Twirl tool does. One benefit of the Twirl tool (as opposed to the filter) is that it allows you to see its effects as they are applied. Twirling is fine for shapes, but it adds awkward edge artifacts to type.

A BETTER APPROACH Placing type on a curve will not distort the characters' shapes, as the typeface remains an editable font.

ZIG ZAG FILTER will add equally spaced points to the selected type outline and give its edge a zigzag feel. It can be effective if used subtly. The top version has a retro sixties feel, while the bottom variation is subtler.

HATCH EFFECTS allow shapes to be filled with preset patterns. These patterns can be highly detailed and create complex files. Hatch effects work by using the original shape as a mask. It's best to simplify the hatch effects after they are applied.

After Hatch applied

Release mask to see the file's construction. Simplify by deleting unseen outer lines.

Hatch allows you to select and set a density for the hatch pattern and control how the pattern is dispersed.

ed to outlines, the Knife tool can be dragged over the selected type to cut it into separate pieces. To emulate broken glass, select a point to act as a center from which the shattering emanates. Then drag the Knife tool outward from the designated center. Continue to cre-

ate broken lines in different directions. This divides the type into separate pieces or shards that can be moved away from each other to give a sense of space between the pieces.

Another method for shattering type is to apply the KPT Shatterbox

effect. It will give you a wide range of stylized shattering effects that can be accurately manipulated. KPT Vector Effects are a separate set of third-party filters that are designed to work in conjunction with Illustrator's standard tools. This set of filters can be incredibly

Shattering Type

Shattering is one way to give type an edgy and nervous feel. Here are two methods to get a shattered look.

 KNIFE TOOL

The Knife tool can be used to cut up and divide type outlines. This tool is located in the tool box with the Scissor tool. Using the Knife tool is the most intuitive way to shatter type. Convert the type to outlines before applying the Knife tool.

Drag the knife tool over the type outlines. Shapes do not have to be selected when applying the knife tool.

To emulate a shattered glass, you need to decide on a point of impact and then draw lines with the knife that emanate outward from that point.

 DIVIDE FILTER

Shattering type using the Divide filter offers more control. Draw a series of lines with the pen tool over the type. The lines should be created with corner points to get a hard-edged quality. Then select the lines and the type and apply the Divide filter to create separate pieces.

Using lines to divide the type into separate pieces offers more control than using the knife tool and produces sharper-looking edges. Shapes must be ungrouped after applying the Divide filter.

KPT SHATTERBOX offers a much less manual approach to shattering type.

Preview displays how filter breaks up the type and how its shards are displaced. Move preview shape to control the point of impact

Radial Shatter controls the number of fragment lines used to shatter the shape.

Give the shattered effect a less controlled feel by increasing the random lines and curves settings.

Control the direction in which the fragments are placed by setting Dispersion.

Soft drop shadows can also be added to the design.

useful and in some cases provide the only way to achieve complex manipulations. While some of the filters included within the package are unnecessary, its 3D Transform, Warp Frame, and Vector Distort features are invaluable to type designers and illustrators. Effects that would have you racking your brain trying to figure out a way to achieve them become easy as a result of these filters.

Drop Shadows

Adding a drop shadow is one of the most common ways to style type. While drop shadows are often used to increase readability, they may also be employed solely for design reasons. Drop shadows effectively increase type legibility by creating a sense of space between the type and the background it sits upon. They also help to define the character edges, which increases readability.

The simplest way to create a drop shadow is to place a darker copy of the type behind the original text. Positioning of the drop shadow is largely a matter of personal taste. While some designers will place their shadows down and to the right, others prefer them placed down and to the left. Most agree on positioning the shadows lower

◄ **PHOTOCOPY TYPE** The original type design was created in Illustrator using Friz Quadrata. The outlines were manipulated to create the logotype. The design was then printed and photocopied. To get the distressed look, masking tape was used to remove toner from the photocopy. This technique will not work with laser printouts. The type was then scanned, selected, and colorized in Photoshop.

> *Advanced type design is covered in Chapter 4.*

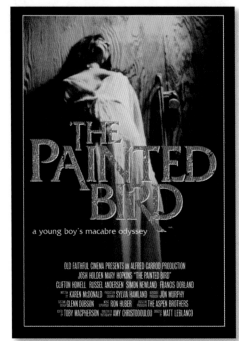

Movie Posters / The Painted Bird

These three poster designs were created around a series of photographic images created by Alli Rufrano. The original type design was created in Illustrator and then given a distressed look by using photocopy type methods.

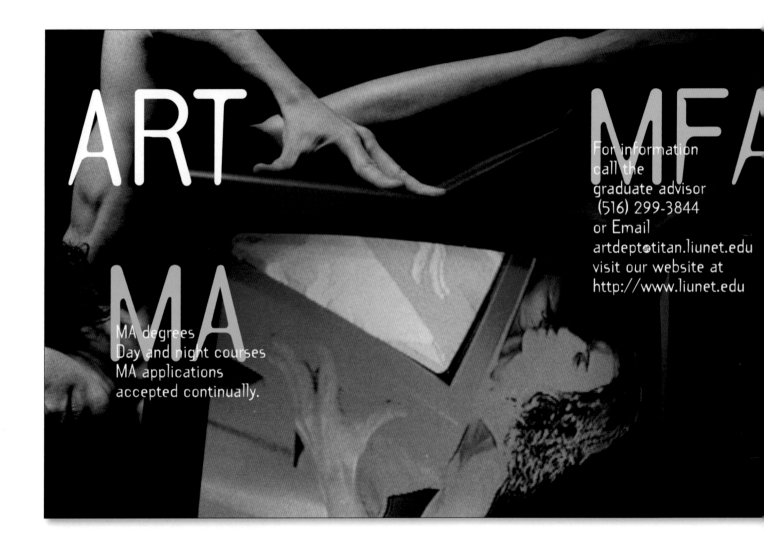

ART

MFA

For information
call the
graduate advisor
(516) 299-3844
or Email
artdept●titan.liunet.edu
visit our website at
http://www.liunet.edu

MA

MA degrees
Day and night courses
MA applications
accepted continually.

Poster Design / Long Island University

This poster was designed to promote the Graduate Art Program at Long Island University. The project's budget called for a two-color design. The original photo was taken by Alli Rufrano and is used here as a duotone. The fonts used are Template Gothic and Copperplate.

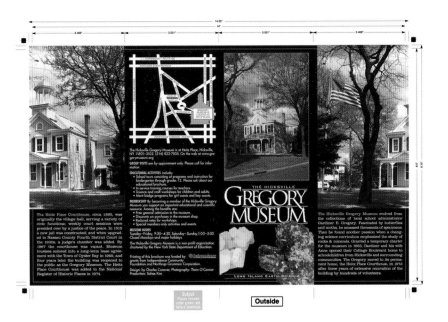

MECHANICAL includes crop, trim, and fold marks as well as the dimensions for each panel. The images and tints that bleed off the page edge are extended beyond the trim marks.

> *Building Mechanicals is covered in Chapter 1.*

GATEFOLD IMAGES are placed on the outside panels on the mechanical. The width of the outside panels is slightly narrower than the inside panels. This space ensures that the brochure will fold correctly.

LOGO DEVELOPMENT Besides designing the brochure, a logotype also needed to be created. The process began with a survey of possible typefaces. Once the font choices were narrowed down, the logo design was started. Above is a series of logotype variations. These designs experiment using knockout type, small caps, and rules. The final logotype was designed using Trajan and Bank Gothic as its typefaces. These typefaces were also used throughout the brochure to give the design a sense of consistency.

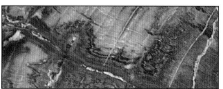

Original Image 100%

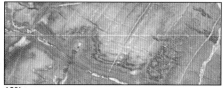

60% transparency

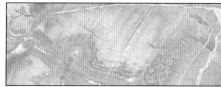

35% transparency

25% transparency

15% transparency

CLIPPING PATHS The images were shot digitally and then silhouetted using clipping paths in Photoshop. Some of these paths were very complex, and in the case of the baby carriage the path was too complex to be output to film. The silhouetted carriage was copied onto a black background that was sized to fit the Quark document.

> *Clipping paths are covered in Chapter 5.*

WORKING GRID The layout for the brochure follows a working grid of column guides and baselines. The green infographics are positioned so that one falls on each panel. The black sidebar fits within the two middle panels. Most of the images are placed so that they do not fall over the folds. The larger images such as the dinosaur skull help to break up the grid.

BACKGROUND IMAGE A background image of petrified wood was used to give texture to the inside of the brochure. The images above show the same texture at different transparency settings. These image variations helped to determine how densely the image could be used without interfering with the readability of the type.

> *Creating textures is covered in Chapter 5.*

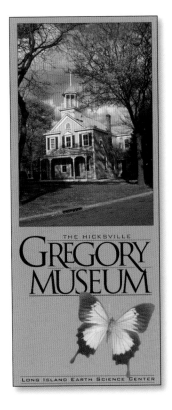

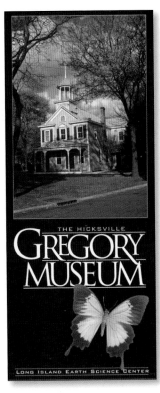

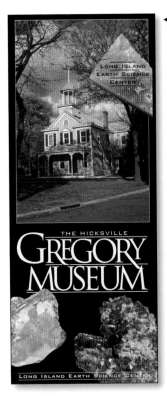

◀ **COVER VARIATIONS** Numerous versions of the brochure were developed for the project. In these samples the colors as well as the images used are varied.

EMPHASIS Because the museum's most extensive and important collection is its rocks and minerals, it was decided that representative samples from that collection should be featured on the cover of the brochure.

VARNISH This is actually a five-color job. The fifth color is a clear varnish that was printed over the front cover. Varnishes can be especially effective when black is a dominant color. It gives the black a gloss. Fingerprints are also less visible when a varnish is used.

THE BUTTERFLY COLLECTION

▶ The Butterfly and Moth collection takes us back to the museum's origins as a natural history collection. Exotic butterflies from all over the world are on display along with many local specimens. All but the local specimens were were raised in captivity. We need to add text here and here.

FOSSIL COLLECTION

The Museum's collection of fossils may be small, but it is impressive representing most of the major plant and animal groups. Our most recent addition as a four-and-a-half foot sauropod leg bone. Other earth science exhibits explain the geologic history of Long Island and its groundwater resources.

BUTTERFLY COLLECTION

▶ The Butterfly and Moth collection takes us back to the museum's origins as a natural history collection. Exotic butterflies from all over the world are on display along with many local specimens. All but the local specimens were were raised in captivity.

◀ **GRAPHIC VARIATIONS** Small graphics were created to give a brief overview of each of the museum's collections. Here are a few variations that were created during the design process. Tabbed shapes give the brochure a contemporary feel. These graphics were created in QuarkXpress using its Merge tools to create the customized shapes.

> *Merge tool techniques are covered in Chapter 3.*

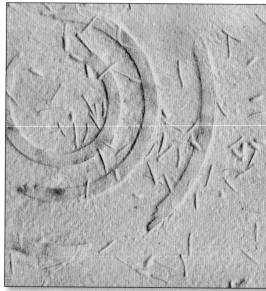

CD Design / Bubble

This music CD was designed for an album entitled "Bash Bish" by the pop rock group Bubble. The project involved creating an original piece of artwork for the cover and designing the booklet, tray card, and compact disc. Hand drawn lettering was created by David Foster.

▲
ORIGINAL ARTWORK was created using layers and montaging techniques. The images used in the artwork were collected from diverse sources. Many of the small illustrations used were rough sketches that were scanned in as bitmap images.

> Scanning bitmap images is covered in Chapter 5.

HANDMADE PAPER was used in the booklet and back cover design. It was scanned in and tinted in Photoshop. The torn paper edge was created using another piece of paper and then merged with the original handmade paper to give realistic effect.

> *Torn paper techniques are covered in Chapter 5.*

ACCORDION FOLD The CD booklet uses an accordion fold format for its layout. Accordion folds are commonly used for CD booklets. The placement of the objects in the illustration is partly determined by the folds.

> *Formatting options are covered in Chapter 1.*

SCAN 3D OBJECTS Actual three-dimensional objects such as guitar strings and picks were scanned in on a flatbed scanner and used in the illustration. Clipping paths were created and these objects were pasted into the illustration as layers.

> *Scanning 3D objects is covered in Chapter 5.*

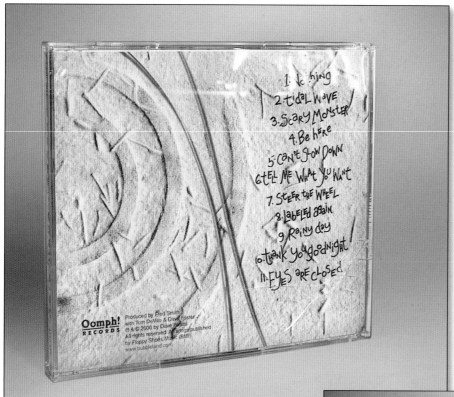

1. Nothing
2. tidaL Wave
3. Scary MonsteR
4. Be hEre
5. Can't Slow Down
6. tELL ME WhAt YoU WANt
7. Steer the WHeeL
8. LabeLed again
9. Rainy day
10. thank You goodnight
11. EYes are cLosed

▲ **HAND-DRAWN TYPE** was used for the list of song titles on the back cover. This design decision was determined by the use of the hand-drawn logo on the front cover. Type was scanned in as a bitmap image.

> *Scanning bitmap images is covered in Chapter 5.*

▲ **LOGO DESIGN** was based on a rough black and white sketch that was used for another band project. The CD title, "Bash Bish," was created later to match the original type, scanned in as a bitmap, and positioned using layers.

> *Working with layers is covered in Chapter 5.*

FOLDING:
1st fold in half
2nd fold in half

Vertical solid lines are fold lines.
Inside dotted lines are safety areas.
Outside solid lines are trim line.
Outside dotted lines are bleed lines.

QUEENS
TITLE: Compact Disc - Inline F8 (8 page Folder)
18-15/16 x 4-23/32 (18.9375 x 4.719)
DATE: 2/24/95 DL   DIE NUMBER: K-405

▲ **MECHANICAL** includes standard crop and trim marks as well as a small illustration of how the booklet folds. While including detailed instructions is helpful, it's a good idea to also submit a folded prototype to the printer. Because the design includes multiple columns of linked text, a baseline grid is used.

> Creating baseline grids is covered in Chapter 2.

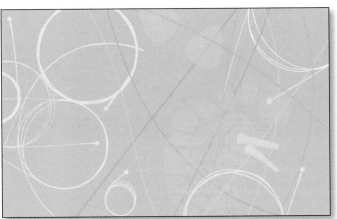

▲ **REPURPOSING PATHS** To create a textural background for the inside of the booklet, many of the paths that were built to create the front cover illustration were repurposed and used to tint sections of the background.

> Using Photoshop paths is covered in Chapter 5.

◀ **THREE-COLOR DESIGN** Because of its surface, printing onto compact disks is usually done with a line screen of 85 to 100 lpi. This design is created using three Pantone colors. The background yellow texture uses shades of the Pantone color to get tint variations.

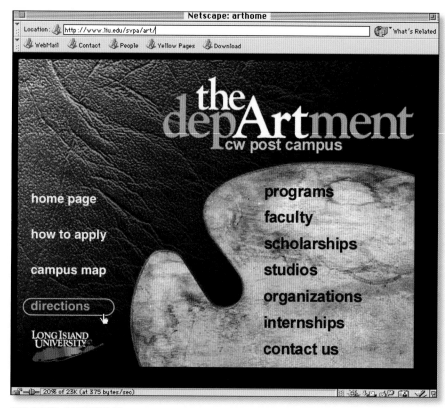

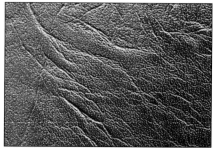

Original Background Texture

▲
VIGNETTING A leather portfolio was scanned in on a flatbed scanner and used as a background texture for the site. The image has been vignetted to black.

> *Vignetting techniques are covered in Chapter 6.*

RELATED OBJECTS There are numerous objects that can be scanned in and used as original art. Here a series of art-related objects are scanned and clipped into their own layers. The drop shadows are created in Photoshop. ▶

> *Photoshop drop shadows are covered in Chapter 6.*

Scanning 3D Objects / Web Site Design

This Web site was designed for the Art Department of Long Island University. While this book is geared for print design, this site provides a good example of how to use a scanner to capture 3D objects and shows consistent formatting.

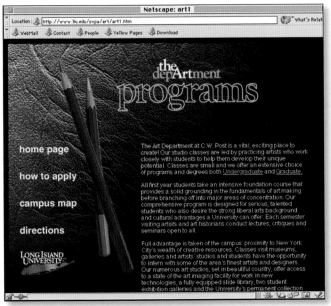

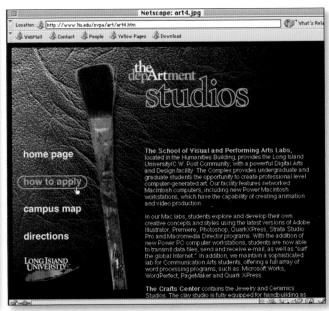

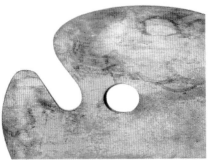

▲ BEFORE AND AFTER
The palette was scanned in on a flatbed scanner. The original palette had a finger hole that interfered with placement of type. It was removed using the Rubber Stamp tool in Photoshop.

> Rubber stamp tool is covered in Chapter 6.

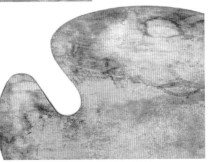

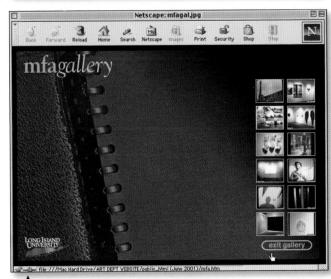

▲ SCANNING 3D OBJECTS For the gallery section of the Web site an open portfolio was sanned in on a flatbed scanner and used as a background.

> Scanning three-dimensional objects is covered in Chapter 6.

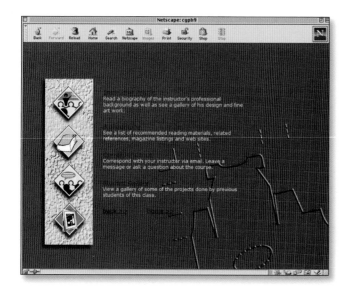

▲ **PAGE BACKGROUNDS** were created using Painter, Illustrator, and Photoshop. Icons in the bottom right-hand corner of the pages were created in Illustrator and then pasted in Photoshop as paths.

> *Copying paths is covered in Chapter 5.*

Icon Design / Virtual Classrooms

These icons were created for a series of virtual classrooms for courses taught at Long Island University. The icons were designed in Illustrator as buttons to link to specific areas. Whether a project is destined for print or the Web, the design process is the same.

◄ **SET OF ICONS** was designed to serve as buttons to link the user to related areas.
A Icon for gallery section that displays student work. Frame and image were created flat and then rotated using KPT 3D Transform.
B Icon for bibliography section, which includes required reading lists and related materials.
C Icon for instructor profile, which includes professional and academic biography.
D Icon for correspondence to contact professor via e-mail link.

> *Illustration techniques are covered in Chapter 6.*

Creating Hard-Edged Drop Shadows

While drop shadows can be used with type to help increase its readability, they can also be used for more purely aesthetic reasons.

KNOCKOUT SHADOWS
With certain typefaces drop shadows can be used as the type itself. Begin by converting the type to outlines. Then select the type and make it a compound path. Copy the type and place it over the original type in an offset manner. Select both and apply the Minus Front filter. This filter uses the type in front to crop away from the type in back and results in a shadow that reads as type.

Before Minus Front filter is applied

After Minus Front filter is applied

Shadow is offset both horizontally and vertically equidistant from the original type. Bold faces with even stroke widths work best with this drop shadow treatment.

◄ Create a drop shadow that has a white space between it and the letter form.
1 Create a slightly larger character outline by using the Offset Path tool.
2 Copy and paste the larger letter and place them so that they are offset.
3 Select letters and apply Minus Front. The cropped shadow shape should fit around the original smaller type.

1 **2** **3**

LINEAR DROP SHADOWS
are created by using lines instead of solid shapes for shadows. This technique uses the Pathfinder filters and the Offset Path Function.

Create a series of lines using the Transform menu. Create a line and select Transform: Move under the Object pulldown menu. Enter a position for the new line to be placed and select copy. If this distance is good, create another line by repeating the transformation.

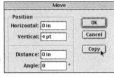

◄ Transformations can be repeated by using ⌘ + D. This is a quick way to create a series of lines.

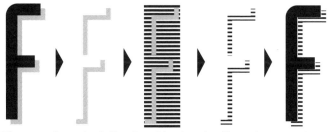

Offset type outlines and apply Minus Front. Select the series of lines and convert to shapes using Outline Path. Select the lines and make them a compound path. Place drop shadow shape over the lines and apply Crop filter. Place original letter next to linear drop shadow.

than the text they sit behind. Experiment with drop shadows in different relationships to the type and eventually you'll develop your own preference. While this is the most basic way of creating drop shadows, let's take a look at a few advanced techniques.

Soft Blurred Shadows
One of the most common drop shadow treatments today for type or images is the soft blurred drop shadow. Part of the reasoning behind this popularity is that they are easy to create, particularly in a program like Photoshop. While cre-

ating shadows for images is an appropriate task for a program like Photoshop, you generally want to avoid using it to style type. A better method for creating soft drop shadows for type is to create blends in Illustrator. This method keeps the text in a vector format (object-

Creating Soft Drop Shadows Using Blends and Filters

Soft blurred drop shadows can be created by blending shapes or using raster filters. Either method produces realistic shadows that give the appearance of a true light source.

OFFSET PATH Begin by converting the letter to outlines and then create a slightly larger copy of the letter by applying Offset Path.

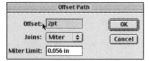

1 Offset Path creates a resized copy of the original outline. Enter in the distance, smaller or larger, that you want the new outline to fall from the original shape.

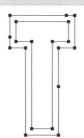

2 Sometimes the paths that Offset Path creates have more points than the original shape. The Blend tool works best when the two paths have an identical number of points.

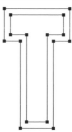

3 Use the Direct Selection tool to delete any additional points on the newly created shape until both paths have an identical number of points.

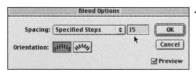

USING BLENDS is a powerful way to create a variety of effects. Blends can be used to create a series of repeating shapes or soft drop shadows. Here they are used to blend a series of shapes between two letter forms.

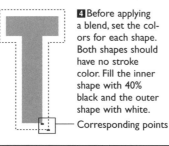

4 Before applying a blend, set the colors for each shape. Both shapes should have no stroke color. Fill the inner shape with 40% black and the outer shape with white.

Corresponding points

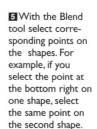

5 With the Blend tool select corresponding points on the shapes. For example, if you select the point at the bottom right on one shape, select the same point on the second shape.

6 Double-click on the Blend tool to access its settings. Reduce the number of steps as low as possible. Expanding the Blend expands the shapes that create the blend into separate shapes.

◄ **TOO MANY STEPS** The Blend tool often uses more steps than are necessary. Too many shapes create very complex files. Reduce the number of steps when possible. Here the blend was built using 100 steps, where 10 steps would suffice.

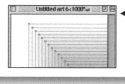

◄ **BLEND SHAPES** Once the blend has been expanded, you can access the stepped shapes and see the blend's complexity.

based) rather than a raster format (pixel-based). Vector formats will usually give type a sharper, more defined edge. To create this kind of shadow you must be familiar with how to use the Blend tool and manipulate and expand the blend. While there are a few ways to create

soft shadows, this method can be both visually effective and economical when used properly.

Blending is a very powerful tool that can be used to create any number of desired effects. It can also create unnecessarily complex files. To illustrate this point let's

create a simple blend. Start by creating two shapes, one small enough to be positioned within the other. Style the smaller inside shape so that it is filled with gray and has no stroke. The smaller shape should be placed in front of the larger shape. Style the outer shape so that

Rasterizing Vector Objects

Rasterizing vector shapes is another way to create soft shadows. When an object is rasterized it is converted to an image file. Once it's converted to a raster image, raster filters can be applied to it.

Draw a bounding box around the type. The box should have no stroke or fill color.

LONE WOLF

Fill the shadow type with gray before rasterizing it.

MASTER SHAPES Once the type design is final, copy and paste it to use later as a master shape. Once you rasterize a file, it is no longer an editable shape.

RASTERIZE TYPE AND BOX As shown in the example above, draw an empty box around the gray type. This box will create white space around the type after it is rasterized and allow a blur to be properly applied. Select the type and the box and select Rasterize from the Object menu.

LONE WOLF

Once type has been rasterized it can have any of Illustrator's raster filters applied to it. Here a Gaussian Blur is applied to create soft drop shadow.

LONE WOLF

Place the master shape that was created earlier over the rasterized drop shadow.

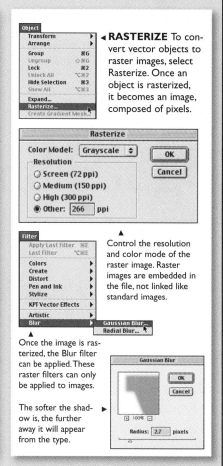

RASTERIZE To convert vector objects to raster images, select Rasterize. Once an object is rasterized, it becomes an image, composed of pixels.

Control the resolution and color mode of the raster image. Raster images are embedded in the file, not linked like standard images.

Once the image is rasterized, the Blur filter can be applied. These raster filters can only be applied to images.

The softer the shadow is, the further away it will appear from the type.

---

it is filled with white and has no stroke color. You are now ready to create the blend. With both shapes active, choose the Blend tool and select corresponding points on each shape. This should give the appearance of a soft blurred shape as the blend creates a series of stepped shapes between the original shapes.

Blending techniques depend on a few things to be successful. If your blend appears unsmooth, this may be caused by a different number of points on the corresponding shapes. For the blend to work optimally the two shapes that are used to create it need to have an equal number of points. If you are using Offset Path to create a resized version of a shape, this may result in the new shape having more points than the original shape. If this happens, the extra

Creating the Illusion of Transparency

By tinting overlapping sections appropriately, a type design can be given the illusion of being transparent.

The Divide filter creates unfilled shapes in the negative spaces between the letters.

◄ Use the group selection to select each shape without ungrouping.

TRANSPARENCY The top and bottom lines of type appear transparent. Overlapping areas are actually separate shapes filled with lighter tints to create the illusion of transparency.

MANUAL METHODS These take more time to create but offer more control and are less subject to output problems than using Illustrator's transparency features.

DIVIDE FILTER Create overlapping type and convert it to outlines. Apply the divide filter to create separate shapes. Manually apply color to these shapes to get transparency.

GROUP SELECTION All shapes are grouped after the Divide filter is applied. Use the Group Selection tool to select the separate shapes without ungrouping them.

Three sections of the shape share a transparency setting.

Ungroup the words to apply a transparency setting to each letter.

PLAY WITH COLOR Once you've created a type design, try applying the Adjust Colors filter to it. This filter adjusts the color profile of a design, enabling you to see it in alternative color palettes that you may not have considered. Playing with this filter is a good way to broaden your color sensibilities.

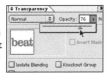

Recent versions of Illustrator offer a transparency palette that is easy to use. It applies transparency much in the same way that Photoshop does. Using transparency can result in output problems.

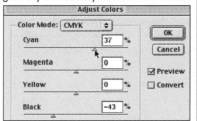

Here the amount of black in the objects is reduced, while the cyan values have been increased.

points will need to be deleted until the two shapes have an identical number of points.

The other thing to keep in mind is the complexity of the blend. Blends sometimes use an excessive number of shapes to create the illusion of a soft blur. The number of blend shapes can be checked by double-clicking on the Blend tool. This will allow you to access the Blend settings. Check the number of specified steps. By its default the Blend tool will typically use more steps (or shapes) than is necessary. This inordinate number of steps can make the file incredibly complex and cause output problems. It is not uncommon to find that a blend has been created using 150 steps where 20 steps would suffice. More steps will not result in a smoother blur; it will simply increase the file's output time.

Once the soft blend has been created and simplified, remember to expand the blend so that it is converted into separate shapes. It is also a good idea to then group these shapes so that they are easier to work with.

Drop Shadow Variations

There are many ways to use drop shadows. In some cases the shadow can be used by itself as a type

Separating Strokes and Fills

Once a type character's stroke and fill have been converted into separate shapes, they can be used to create fun and playful type designs.

OUTLINE PATH

This tool allows an object's stroke and fill to be converted into separate shapes. When it is applied to a line, the stroke is converted to its own shape.

WHITE FILLS Outline Path can create "invisible" white shapes when applied to line segments that have a fill color. Avoid this by making the fill color none before applying.

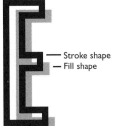

BEFORE Type has black stroke and gray fill. Convert to outlines before applying Outline Stroke.

AFTER Once Outline Stroke has been applied, the stroke and fill become separate shapes.

— Stroke shape
— Fill shape

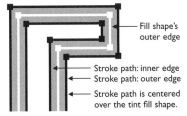

Fill shape's outer edge

Stroke path: inner edge
Stroke path: outer edge
Stroke path is centered over the tint fill shape.

When applied to a shape that has a fill and stroke color, Outline Path produces three paths. The inner and outer paths represent the edges of the stroke shape. The path placed between these two represents the outer edge of the fill shape.

STROKES AND FILLS can be manipulated separately to produce playful effects. Here both the stroke shapes and the tint fill shapes have been moved and offset from each other and rotated subtly to create a lightweight, fun feel. The tint colors have also been varied slightly.

The second stroke is white and thinner than the black stroke. The dashed line creates the custom border.

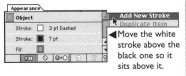

◄Move the white stroke above the black one so it sits above it.

CUSTOM BORDERS Multiple strokes can be applied to a shape. Select Add New Stroke from the Appearances palette and a second stroke is applied to the shape. Change this stroke's color and size to create a custom border.

design. In such cases the actual type is white and the drop shadow is placed in such a way that it defines the type in front of it. This technique involves knocking the white type out from the darker shadow behind it. It is an easy method to use, but it will work

effectively only with certain typefaces and its success depends upon the shadow's positioning. Because the type design depends upon the shadow to define its characters, the typeface you choose and the angle at which the drop shadow is placed are critical to the type's readability.

This method works best with typefaces that are relatively bold, whose characters don't include a wide range of thicks and thins. Extended bold fonts like Bank Gothic, Copperplate, or Eurostyle will work particularly well with this technique.

Overlapping Transparent Type

While transparency features have been added to recent versions of Illustrator, there are standard ways to achieve the illusion of transparency. One technique involves converting the overlapping area between two shapes into its own separate shape and then adjusting the color of the overlapping area to give the appearance of transparency.

Transparent type can be applied to designs in many ways. In the example provided here transparency is used to give the type design a light, fun feel. It is a simple technique that uses the Pathfinder filters to divide the type outlines. Once each overlapping area has been divided, each separate shape can be shaded accordingly to give the impression that the type can be seen through.

While more recent versions of Illustrator allow transparency to be applied to objects much in the same way that Photoshop handles layer opacity, these new features can be troublesome when it comes to final output. In order for Illustrator to apply transparency it has to treat the overlapping objects as it would a raster or image file. Because Illustrator is by its nature a vector-based package it has to convert this transparency information into vector information, or flatten the information into embedded image files. This can result in complex files that output inconsistently. While you can control how Illustrator handles transparent objects when it saves the file, it is probably best avoided. Creating shapes with shading that gives the illusion of transparency is generally a safer approach.

Separating Strokes and Fills

Separating a character's stroke from its fill color is an effective way to handle type designs. Once

3D Type: Beveling Type Outlines

Creating beveled type is an advanced technique that gives the typeface the appearance of being chiseled.

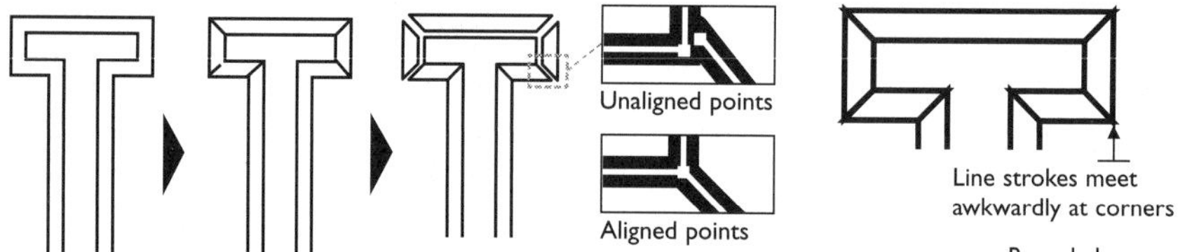

1 OFFSET PATH Convert the type to outlines and create a larger outline by using Offset Path.

2 BEVEL LINES Use the pen tool to draw lines between the corners of the two paths. Type V and P after drawing each segment to save time.

3 DIVIDE FILTER Once bevel lines are drawn, select the shapes and line and apply the Divide filter. This will create separate shapes.

4 FIXING SHAPES When bevel line endpoints aren't positioned exactly, they won't divide properly. Select the misaligned point and reposition. Then reapply the Divide filter to create separate shapes.

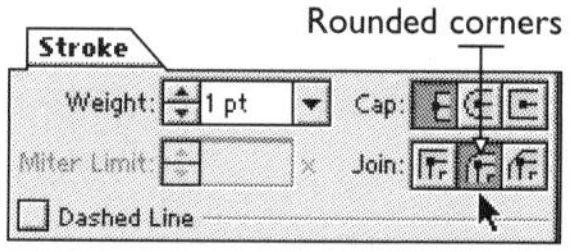

ENDPOINTS A common problem with beveled shapes is that the stroke can meet awkwardly at the corners. Fix this by selecting rounded endpoints on the Stroke menu.

IMPLIED LIGHT SOURCE
Once all of your bevel shapes have been separated, you can begin to apply tints to each section to give the impression of an implied light source. In this example the light source is emanating from the top down to the right.

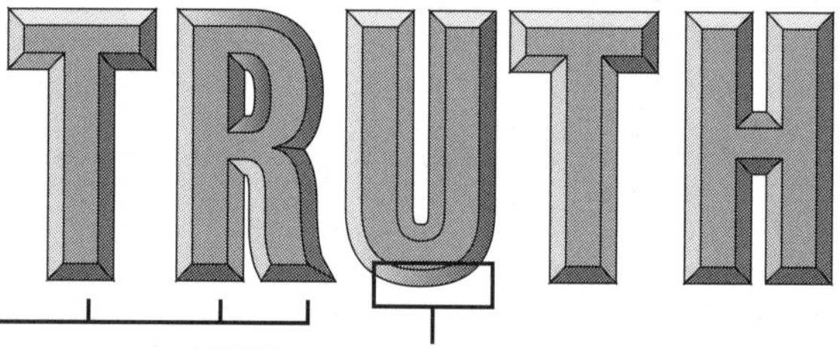

CONSISTENT TINT Select shapes that fall in similar positions and apply a consistent tint shade.

GRADIENT TOOL Gradients can be used to apply a realistic sense of light to rounded shapes.

Complex Beveling

INNER BEVEL Instead of having the bevel shapes appear around the outside of the letter form, you can create a faceted letter form in which the bevel shapes appear inside the letter. In this case the inner shapes were drawn manually with the pen tool, rather than by using Offset Path.

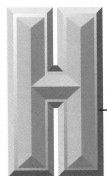

COMPLEX BEVELS You can build upon the original beveled letter by using the same methods to get complex, multi-faceted letter forms. Here inner and outer bevels are applied to the same letter form.

GRADIENT This technic is used on the face-plate of the letter form. Apply a gradient to the shapes and then use the gradient tool to control the direction of the gradient in each facet.

Beveling with KPTs

KPT Vector Effects offers the 3D Transform Filter, which has the capability to bevel text once it has been converted to outlines.

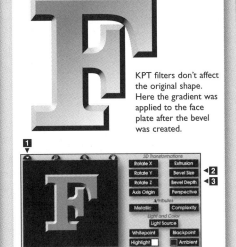

KPT filters don't affect the original shape. Here the gradient was applied to the face plate after the bevel was created.

1 PREVIEW the effects of the bevel by choosing the rough or full preview settings from the File pull-down menu.

2 BEVEL SETTINGS control how far the bevel extends beyond the original text outline.

3 OTHER SETTINGS like Rotating or Extruding Type can also be used.

you want to have a Pathfinder filter affect a line. Remember that the Pathfinders generally work best when applied to shapes. While a line may not appear to be visibly changed after Outline Path has been applied, the Pathfinder filter will treat the line as it would any shape. The simplest way to see the effects of Outline Path on a line is to compare the number of points that make up the line before and after it is applied. A line has two endpoints before it is converted to a shape and four corner points after Outline Path is applied.

Beveling Type

Another type technique that also makes use of the Offset Path and Divide filters, but with very different results, is beveling type. Beveling has a long history in type design, from the chiseled type found adorning ancient Roman temples to the History Channel's logo. Beveling type gives it facets that appear raised or recessed from the surface it sits upon. The illusion of being raised or recessed depends on how color is applied to the facets. Color can also be applied to the beveled type to create the sense of a directed light source.

Beveled type is most effective

the stroke and fill have been converted into separate objects, they can be moved, sized, and rotated individually. This method generally works best with bolder fonts with outlines that are relatively heavy.

To separate a character's stroke from its fill, the type must first be converted to outlines. When Outline Stroke is applied to the type it converts the stroke into a shape separate from the fill.

Outline Stroke can be used to convert any line into a shape. This method should be used anytime

Extruding and Creating Perspective

Realistic three-dimensional type that has a defined light source can be easily created by understanding a few basic rules concerning perspective.

FACEPLATE is inlaid by using Offset Path to create the inner shape.

GRADIENTS can be used to create a sense of volume and light.

RECEDING SIZE Objects appear smaller when they are placed in the distance. Apply this principle and make the background letter smaller than the one in front.

MASTER SHAPES These are the original shapes used to create a design. Copy the original letter and put aside. Because the type will be divided, this shape may be useful later on.

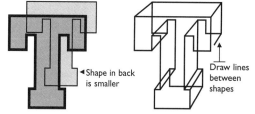

◄ Shape in back is smaller

Draw lines between shapes

1 TWO SHAPES Begin by converting type to outlines and placing the smaller copy behind the original shape.

2 DIVIDING LINES Draw lines connecting the two letters. These will form the planes of the extruded type.

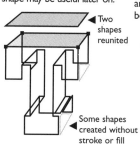

◄ Two shapes reunited

◄ Some shapes created without stroke or fill

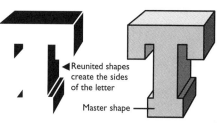

◄ Reunited shapes create the sides of the letter

Master shape ─

3 DIVIDE FILTER Select the letter forms and lines and apply the Divide filter to make each area a separate shape. Some shapes will not be visible because no fill or stroke is applied to them.

4 REUNITE SHAPES Select and ungroup the divided shapes and then reunite them using the Unite filter to create the sides of the letter. Delete extra shapes that are not needed.

5 FINISHING UP Once the extruded sides have been created, place the original letter (master shape) in front of these shapes. Then use flat tints or gradients to give the type a sense of volume.

when it is applied to bold typefaces whose characters are designed with straight vertical and horizontal lines. Because beveling involves the use of mitered corners, typefaces that include many curves do not work as successfully.

Beveling techniques are not limited to type and can be applied to any shape. They can be used on simple primary shapes or on complex shapes like polygons and stars to create three-dimensional forms. Once you understand these techniques, experiment and see how you can apply them in an original manner.

Begin the beveling process by creating a type design, perhaps a simple word, which uses a bolder typeface set in all uppercase. Depending on which direction you want to bevel to go, adjust your kerning accordingly. If you want your beveled edge to extend beyond the character's edge, in effect creating a beveled outline and a raised effect, you will need to allow for extra letterspacing. If your text is going to appear to be chiseled into the page surface, you can kern the type as you normally would, because no additional space outside the character outline is required.

To give the text a raised feel

begin by kerning the text loosely and then convert it to outlines. The loose kerning will allow room for a larger outline to be added around each character. This can be done by selecting the character outlines and offsetting the path.

Once you've created an outer path around the character, you can begin to create bevel lines, which will help divide the type into separate facets and achieve a chiseled look. It's not difficult to create bevel lines. Before you begin, select all of the outlines and give them no fill and a half-point black stroke. This will make it easier to properly position the bevel lines. Using the pen tool, draw lines that connect the corners of the larger letter to the corresponding corners of the smaller one. A quicker way to do this that doesn't involve reselecting the pen tool each time you want to draw a separate line is to type V after each segment is drawn (this will end the segment) and then type P to reselect the pen tool.

Once this process is complete, a wire frame of the beveled character will take shape. Make sure that each line's endpoints are positioned exactly over the corner points. This will ensure that your bevel shapes will separate and divide properly later.

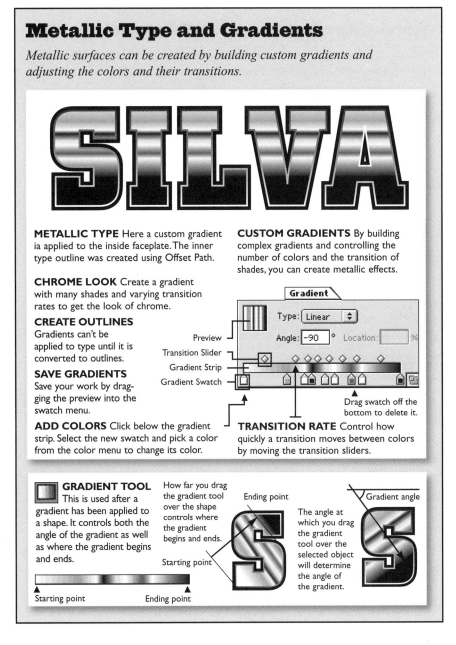

Metallic Type and Gradients

Metallic surfaces can be created by building custom gradients and adjusting the colors and their transitions.

METALLIC TYPE Here a custom gradient ia applied to the inside faceplate. The inner type outline was created using Offset Path.

CHROME LOOK Create a gradient with many shades and varying transition rates to get the look of chrome.

CREATE OUTLINES Gradients can't be applied to type until it is converted to outlines.

SAVE GRADIENTS Save your work by dragging the preview into the swatch menu.

ADD COLORS Click below the gradient strip. Select the new swatch and pick a color from the color menu to change its color.

CUSTOM GRADIENTS By building complex gradients and controlling the number of colors and the transition of shades, you can create metallic effects.

Gradient

Type: Linear
Angle: -90 ° Location: %

Preview
Transition Slider
Gradient Strip
Gradient Swatch

Drag swatch off the bottom to delete it.

TRANSITION RATE Control how quickly a transition moves between colors by moving the transition sliders.

GRADIENT TOOL This is used after a gradient has been applied to a shape. It controls both the angle of the gradient as well as where the gradient begins and ends.

Starting point   Ending point

How far you drag the gradient tool over the shape controls where the gradient begins and ends.

Starting point

Ending point

The angle at which you drag the gradient tool over the selected object will determine the angle of the gradient.

Gradient angle

Receding Type into the Distance

A sense of depth and space can be given to paragraph type by rotating it so that it appears to recede into the distance.

Move points in equal increments to get the proper effect.

RECEDING TYPE There are a few methods to make type appear as if it recedes into the distance. This effect is associated with the opening sequences of the Star Wars movies. Some versions of Illustrator (7, 9, 10) include a Free Transform filter that can be used to create this effect. KPT Vector Effects offers a 3D Transform filter, which allows type to be truly rotated.

By the dawn of the twentieth century industrialism had swept its way across the country, leaving nothing untouched in its wake. Seemingly overnight industrialization profoundly changed the face of the nation, influencing every aspect of life. The events that took place between 1885 and 1910 represent the metamorphosis of the country from a society relatively untouched by industrialism to one almost transformed by it. Emphasizing

By the dawn of the twentieth century industrialism had swept its way across the country, leaving nothing untouched in its wake. Seemingly overnight industrialization profoundly changed the face of the nation, influencing every aspect of life. The events that took place between 1885 and 1910 represent the metamorphosis of the country from a society relatively untouched by industrialism to one almost transformed by it. Emphasizing

SET TEXT Justified text, because of its right and left alignment, works best with this technique. Once type is set, convert it to outlines.

FREE TRANSFORM This filter creates the illusion that type is rotating back into the distance. This can also be done using the Free Transform tool.

USING FILTER A bounding box appears around the text. Select the corner points and move them to change box shape and create an illusion.

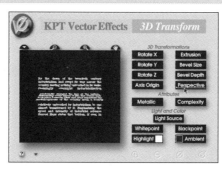

SELECT TEXT Create paragraph text and convert the type to outlines. Ungroup the text and with the selection tool select and group all of the characters included in the middle four lines.

KPT 3D TRANSFORM This filter allows the text shapes to be rotated on any axis. Here the type is rotated on the y axis. Use Show Unselected Art to see the rest of the paragraph.

By the dawn of the twentieth century industrialism had swept its way across the country, leaving nothing untouched in its wake. Seemingly overnight industrialization

profoundly changed the face of the nation, influencing every aspect of life. The events that took place between 1885 and 1910 represent the metamorphosis of the country from a society

relatively untouched by industrialism to one almost transformed by it. Emphasizing the speed and intensity of industrial advance Samuel Hays states that "seldom, if ever, in

TYPE BLOCKS that appear above and below the rotated text have to be manually resized and positioned after KPT 3D Transform filter has been used to rotate the text in the middle.

Once all the bevel lines are drawn, the character is ready to be divided into separate shapes. Select the bevel lines and inner and outer character outlines and apply the Divide filter. The Divide filter will create a separate shape for each overlapping section. If some sections have not divided properly, zoom into that area and inspect the positioning of the points on your bevel line. Chances are the line's endpoints don't align perfectly with the corner. Reposition the line's endpoints and reapply the Divide filter.

Once the separate bevel shapes have been created, color can then be added. The way in which color is applied will bring a sense of depth to the type as well as imply a light source with a direction. Since the

◀ Empty box creates buffer space and without it the blur will be cropped by the image edge.

CREATE SHADOW Copy the rotated text and fill it with gray. Before rasterizing this type, draw a box around the type that has no stroke or fill. This box provides a buffer space around the image so that the blur will work when it is applied.

Select the type and box and rasterize them. Since it will be used as a shadow, choose grayscale and 266 dpi.

BLUR RASTER IMAGE Once type is rasterized, any of Illustrator's raster filters can be applied. To get a soft drop shadow apply the Gaussian Blur filter. Once the blur is applied, drag the original type over shadow.

When applying Gaussian Blur, the more you apply it, the softer and less defined the shadow will be. The softer the shadow, the further the type will appear from the page.

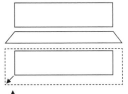

▲ **RESIZE** Adjust the size of the text on the bottom so that its width matches the width of the last line of the rotated text.

CONSTRAIN Make sure to constrain the proportions of the type by holding down the Shift key when scaling.

By the dawn of the twentieth century industrialism had swept its way across the country, leaving nothing untouched in its wake. Seemingly overnight industrialization *profoundly changed the face of the nation, influencing every aspect of life. The events that took place between 1885 and 1910 represent the metamorphosis of the country from a society* relatively untouched by industrialism to one almost transformed by it. Emphasizing the speed and intensity of industrial advance Samuel Hays states that "seldom, if ever, in

STEPPED TYPE Once the copy blocks above and below the rotated text have been resized, you should get stepped type that appears to move back into the distance.

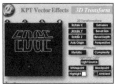

Create type and convert it to outlines. Place a box over the type shapes and apply the Divide filter.

Ungroup shapes after dividing them. Delete any unfilled shapes created by the Divide Filter. Select the top half of the word.

Select the KPT 3D Transform filter and rotate the top half of the word so that it recedes into the distance. Here the type is rotated on its y axis.

Resize the bottom half of the letters so that their width matches the rotated half of the type. These shapes can then be united.

Divide filter groups all of the elements that it affects, the shapes must be ungrouped before applying color.

3D Type: Extruding Type

The same methods used to bevel type—creating bevel lines and dividing—have many applications. Creating type that appears three-dimensional involves similar techniques. Because it does not appear flat, three-dimensional type sits much differently on a page and can be bold and dramatic.

Like beveling, a copy of the type outline is required. This copy should be scaled down slightly and placed offset behind the original type. This smaller copy will create the back plane of the type. Then, just as was done with beveling,

KPT 3D Transform: Extruding & Beveling

While it's helpful to know how to extrude and bevel shapes manually, KPT Vector Effects offers two filters that can create similar effects quickly.

CREATING 3D TYPE Using KPT filters to bevel and extrude type is easier than creating the effects manually, but its files can be overly complex.

1 ROTATE Begin by converting the type to curves and then applying KPT 3D Transform. Here the letter is rotated only on its x axis, but rotation can be done on all three axes.

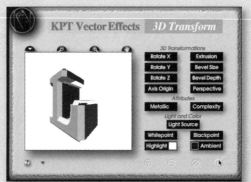

2 BEVELING Set the bevel size and depth. Bevel Size controls the size of the bevel shape. Bevel Depth handles how deep or far away from the faceplate the bevel appears.

X Axis   Y Axis   Z axis

UNDERSTANDING ROTATIONS It's important to have a basic understanding of the effect that rotating on each of the three axes has. The z axis is the third dimension and gives depth to flat objects. It's what makes a circle into a sphere, or a square into a cube. When initially working with rotations, start by rotating an object on each axis separately until you understand how each works.

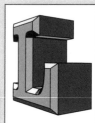

3 EXTRUDE will create a three-dimensional shape behind the original shape. In this case the extrusion is placed behind the letter's face plate and its bevel shapes.

4 PERSPECTIVE settings create a forced perspective rather than an orthogonal view and gives the sense that the object is being viewed from an extreme angle.

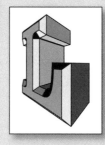

5 LIGHTING effects allow you to control the direction, color, and strength of the light source. Lighting is not applied to the original shape, only to the shapes that are created by the KPT filter.

---

draw lines between the shapes' corresponding points. The Divide filter is then applied to create separate shapes.

There is one procedural difference between the beveling and 3D extrusion methods covered. While both of these illustration techniques require dividing sections into separate shapes, extruding type requires some of these separate shapes to be reunited to create the sides of the 3D type. This can be done by applying the Unite filter. One way to avoid too much reuniting is to make copies of the original letter outlines before dividing. This process of division and reuniting is common in technical illustration.

Once the proper shapes have been created, color can be applied to them to give the beveled type a sense of volume. Color should be handled in the same manner as beveling. One way to build upon this method is to apply gradients to the individual shapes.

Applying Gradients to 3D Type

Gradients can be a great way to get a sense of volume and light. Unlike flat color, gradients can be controlled to achieve a more dramatic sense of light. Before applying the gradient, decide from which direction the light source will emanate.

To apply a gradient to your 3D extruded type, begin by selecting all of the shapes and apply the same gradient to them. The gradient tool can then be used to control the gradient's direction and the rate of transition on each individual shape. To attain a consistent sense of light, try selecting multiple corresponding planes—the sides of the word's characters—and applying the gradient in the exact same way.

Metallic Effects and 3D Type

Gradients can be used to give a sense of surface quality. They are especially good at emulating highly polished or metallic surfaces. By building complex, high contrast gradients, the look of a metallic surface like chrome can be achieved. Complex gradients can be built using numerous colors. The rate of transition from one color to another can also be controlled.

Receding Type

Type can also be made to appear as if it recedes into the distance. This technique is similar to extruding type in that it tilts paragraph text so that it fades back into the distance and takes on a three-dimensional feel. While the characters themselves appear flat, the paragraph appears as a flat plane that has been rotated. This treatment has become associated with the opening sequences of the Star Wars movies. There are two ways to get this effect. One method uses the Free Transform filter, and the other requires KPT's 3D Transform filter.

The easiest and most direct way to create receding type is to use KPT's 3D Transform filter. Begin by styling a paragraph of justified text. Choose an appropriate face for your body copy, one that will remain relatively readable at small sizes. This is important because the more the type recedes the smaller it will appear.

Once you've styled the paragraph, convert the type to outlines. KPT filters are designed to work with shapes and will have no effect on type until it is converted. Select the paragraph and then apply the 3D Transform filter. The 3D Transform filter allows the selected shape to be rotated on the x, y,

or z axis. For these purposes the type needs only to be rotated on the y axis to make it recede.

The same effect can be created by using the Free Distort filter offered in Illustrator. While this filter is more limited than its KPT counterpart, it will get the job done. (Free Distort is available in most Illustrator versions but was not included in version 8.) Select the paragraph and choose the Free Distort filter. Free Distort provides a bounding box that represents the edges of the selection. The handles on the bounding box can be positioned so that the text appears to be rotated back. While this method requires a little more effort than using the KPT 3D Transform filter, its overall effect will be the same.

Inlaid Type

Inlaying refers to placing elements into character outlines. Any number of elements, such as lines, shapes, patterns, and even photos, can be inlaid into type. Depending on what you want to place inside the type, inlaying can be a complex method that demands an understanding of offsetting and outlining paths, compound shapes, and various Pathfinder filters. Despite this, it can be an extreme-

Inlaid Text: Cropping Objects into Type

Many design elements, such as shapes, lines, or even type, can by inlaid into a character's outlines by using compound paths and the Pathfinder filters.

Inlaying Straight Lines into Text

Inlaying a series of straight lines into a type is a relatively simple process except for a few steps that involve expanding blends, applying compound paths, and outlining strokes.

COMPOUND PATHS Before cropping lines into the type, select all the lines and convert them to a compound path. This allows the Pathfinder filters to treat the lines as one object.

Select the type and make it a compound path.

Select the lines and make them a → compound path.

 PREPARING BLENDS Create a blend of lines and adjust its setting by double-clicking on the tool. When the blend is finished expand it so that the lines become separate elements. Convert the lines to shapes using Outline Path before applying any Pathfinder filters.

EXTRA PIECES Some Pathfinder filters, like Crop, place unfilled shapes in the negative spaces. Here white shapes appear between the black lines.

CROP FILTER Place the type above the lines, select all, and apply Crop.

APPLY FILTER Both the type outlines and the set of lines need to be separate compound paths. This allows Pathfinder to treat them as two shapes. Select the text and the lines and apply the Crop filter.

Inlaying Wavy Lines into Text

Cropping curved lines into text involves a process similar to that above. Undulating lines are created by using a guideline grid with snap to guides. Create a blend of wavy lines and then reshape one of the original blend lines to create interesting linear effects.

PREPARING BLENDS Begin by creating a uniform blend between two identical curved lines. Then experiment by manually adjusting the points on the original curved blend lines. The two lines that make up the blend can be selected using the Group Selection tool.

Grid of guidelines

Pen tool snaps to the grid, placing points at intersecting guides.

Place smooth points so handles are flat and evenly spaced.

Copy the wavy line and create a uniform blend of wavy lines. ▶

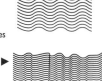 The Group Selection tool selects the shapes while the blend is active.

Create a "folding blend" by adjusting the top and bottom lines while the blend is still active. ▶

Expand the blend and place the type outlines over wavy lines. Both the type and lines should be separate compound paths. Select both and apply the Crop filter.

Before cropping the lines into the type, create a slightly larger type outline by using Offset Path. After applying crop filter place this outline so it surrounds the lines.

Creating Concentric Shapes

Create a series of concentric circles. Draw a small circle and then create a larger one around it by using Offset Path. Repeat this process to create the circular pattern.

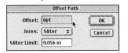

Select original circle and apply Offset Path. This creates a copy of the original shape at a new size.

Convert the lines to shapes using Outline Path and then select all the lines and make them a compound path.

Place type outline over the circles. Type should also be a compound path. Apply Crop filter to the type and the lines.

Building Concentric Patterns

Many shapes can be used to form concentric patterns. Here are some samples that use the method shown above.

Outline Path converts lines into shapes. Make sure the line has no fill color, otherwise a second shape for the fill is created.

Before Outline Path

After Outline Path

A
One shape

B
Fill shape
Stroke shape

Line A had no fill before Outline Path was applied. Shape B had a white fill.

Star settings are accessed by double-clicking with the Star tool in the document.

Scalloped shape is created by applying the Zig Zag filter to a circle.

Original shape is drawn with the pen tool. The medium-sized shape was created first and then the larger and smaller surrounding shapes were created using Offset Path.

ly effective way to handle type and can be applied to diverse type designs. Just about anything you create in Illustrator can be inlaid into a typeface.

One way to vary the inlaying process is to allow a series of lines, shapes, or patterns to form the actual type without using the character outlines. A good example of type that relies on lines to create its letter forms is the IBM logo. This is a simpler method than creating inlaid type and basically involves using the Blend tool and the Crop filter. This method crops with the type's outlines, so that the cropped pattern appears to form the letters. It generally works best with lines that have heavier strokes or with thinner lines that are closely set. Start by simply cropping a series of straight lines into a single letter form and then move on to cropping more complex patterns into entire words.

Begin to create a pattern by drawing a straight line with the pen tool. Copy and place a second line directly below the first line, allowing some space between the two. With the Blend tool, select corresponding points to create a series of lines. Set the number of steps in the blend so that the lines are close enough to define the type once they

Type on a Path: Curves, Spirals, & Circles

Type can be placed along any number of shapes, from basic curved lines to complex spirals, creating a sense of movement and motion.

slowly heading homeward

TYPE ON A CURVE To get type to move along a path, create a curved line using the pen tool. Then select the Type on a Curve tool and click on the line. The line is converted to a text path and a blinking cursor appears. Enter text on the path and style it. Smooth curves work best. Kerning should be adjusted so that the type moves smoothly across the path.

MOVING TEXT To move text along a path select the text cursor with the selection tool and move it along the path. Drag the cursor underneath the path and the text will wrap along the bottom of the line.

BASELINE SHIFT controls how the type is positioned along the path. Here the type is placed above the path by a using positive baseline shift setting.

▲ Baseline shift

slowly hea

Drag cursor along the path to reposition the type or drag it below the line and the type will appear below the text path.

Move cursor inside the circle and the type will run along the inside of the circle.

All caps works very nicely with Type on a Path.

TYPE ON A CIRCLE Select a circle with the Type on a Curve tool. Text is moved the same way as on a simple path. Type runs clockwise when it is placed on the outside, counterclockwise on the inside.

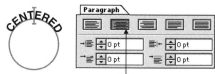

TO CENTER TYPE on a circle, click on the top center of the circle with the Type on a Path tool and select Center Align from the Paragraph Menu.

TYPE ON A SPIRAL Spirals can also be used effectively as text paths. Depending on the tightness of the spiral and how much type is being used, the type size may have to be reduced as the spiral gets tighter.

83% decay   90% decay

SPIRAL SETTINGS To access the spiral settings click in the document with the Spiral tool. To get a tighter spiral the decay should be set high (90%). The more segments used, the longer the path will be.

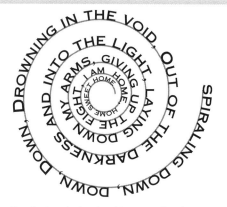

Here the type size is reduced incrementally as it moves toward the center of the tightening spiral.

SKEWING TYPE One way to get type to feel as if it is moving in an orbital fashion is to skew the type on a spiral. This works best when the type is first converted to curves.

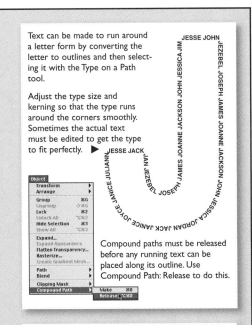

Text can be made to run around a letter form by converting the letter to outlines and then selecting it with the Type on a Path tool.

Adjust the type size and kerning so that the type runs around the corners smoothly. Sometimes the actual text must be edited to get the type to fit perfectly. ▶

Compound paths must be released before any running text can be placed along its outline. Use Compound Path: Release to do this.

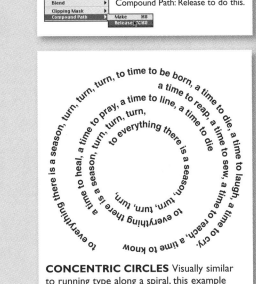

CONCENTRIC CIRCLES Visually similar to running type along a spiral, this example places text along a series of concentric circles. Each line of text needs to be selected separately with the Type on a Path tool.

are cropped.

Once the blend of lines is done, it can be prepared for cropping. Since a Pathfinder filter will be applied to these lines, there are two things that need to be done before applying the filter. In order for Pathfinder to properly affect the lines, the blend must first be expanded so that the lines are converted into separate elements. These lines must then be converted into shapes by outlining the stroke. Before converting the lines to shapes make sure there is no fill color applied to the lines. A fill color, even though it is not visible, can create unnecessary shapes when line strokes are outlined. Pathfinder filters have no effect when applied to objects that include blends, and they work better when they are applied to shapes. Once the blend is released and the strokes are outlined, they can be cropped into any shape.

Place a type outline over the series of lines. Select both the series of lines and the type and then apply the Pathfinder: Crop filter. The lines should appear to be cropped by the type's outlines. To use the Crop filter, you must place the shape used for cropping in front of the object(s) that it is cropping into.

Cropping and Compound Paths

If you want to crop a pattern of lines into an entire word, compound paths must be created first. Compound Paths essentially allow holes to be placed in objects. Shapes that are built with compound paths are composed of more than one path. Type forms are commonly composed of two or more paths. An uppercase *B*, for example, is composed of three paths: one outer path and two inner paths. To see the effect of a compound path, simply draw a smaller shape over a larger one, select both, and apply Compound Path. The smaller shape will act as if it has been cut away from the larger shape.

In order for the Pathfinder filters to treat multiple shapes as one shape they need to be converted to compound paths first. In the case of cropping a series of lines into a word, both the word and the lines are composed of multiple elements. In order for Pathfinder to crop all the lines into all the word's characters, each group must first be converted to a compound path.

Cropping Background Patterns

There are any number of ways to create background patterns for type.

Vertical Type: Cheap Motels & Drive-ins

While most graphics programs allow designers to create vertical type, more often than not it can be awkward and difficult to read.

VERTICAL TYPE To run type vertically on a path, create a line with the pen tool and then select that line with the Vertical Type tool.

UPPERCASE type works much better in a vertical format, because the letter forms are generally similar in width.

LOWERCASE characters generally vary more in width than uppercase settings do.

KERNING TYPE is controlled by using the standard kern settings in the paragraph menu. In this case leading will not affect the vertical space between the letters.

A **B** **C**

READABILITY One reason that vertical type is difficult to read is because our eyes don't naturally read this way. Overall consistency in letter shapes contributes to readability. Sample A has much less variance in letter width than B. Placing a series of shapes behind each letter like in sample C helps make each letter appear to be of similar width.

CUSTOM SHAPES can be used to help readability and give the design a retro feel. This series of shapes is skewed and placed behind the type.

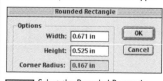

Select the Rounded Rectangle tool and click once in the document to set the shape's corner radius. Then create a series of evenly spaced rounded rectangles using Align to distribute them evenly.

 SKEW Select the rectangles and skew them as a group.

Amount controls how far the blended neon line comes from text edge.

◄**KPT NEON** filter is applied to the type outlines and then placed on a black background.

Background patterns can be based on a simple repetition of basic shapes or can be composed from complex arrangements of overlapping lines and ornate shapes. Repeating shapes can be scaled, sized, skewed, and rotated in any number of ways to create a background with a sense of rhythm.

Guideline Grids and Wavy Lines

A series of undulating wavy lines can be effective when cropped into type. Lines that undulate in a consistent manner could be drawn freehand, or they could be created using the pen tool by placing points and adjusting the handles by eye,

but using a grid of guidelines can greatly simplify the task.

Begin by creating a grid of evenly spaced guidelines. This grid is used to position the line's points at precise increments to create a line that undulates evenly. By using Snap to Guides, the line's smooth points can be positioned

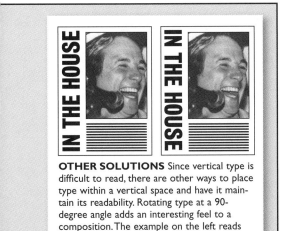

OTHER SOLUTIONS Since vertical type is difficult to read, there are other ways to place type within a vertical space and have it maintain its readability. Rotating type at a 90-degree angle adds an interesting feel to a composition. The example on the left reads into the page, whereas the design on the right leads the reader's eye off the page.

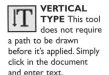

VERTICAL TYPE This tool does not require a path to be drawn before it's applied. Simply click in the document and enter text.

TEXT IN BOX Vertical type can be placed in a text box to run in a paragraph format. Use this tool when setting type in other languages that read in this manner.

```
i
t m v t t
o p i h e
 o r i x
r s t s t
 s u
re i a  b  s
a b l  w  e
d l l  a  t
 e y  y
```

Vertical type set in box

along the grid. The handles can also be manipulated to snap to the grid, and this ensures that each curve on the line is identical. This method can be used in either QuarkXpress or Illustrator. You can also experiment with building irregular grids by using this method.

Using Vertical Type

While many graphics software programs allow designers to set type vertically, a few factors need to be considered before doing so. First of all, type is generally difficult to read when set vertically because, at least in Western cultures, our eyes are not trained to read in this direction. For this reason alone, it's best to limit your vertical type to a few words. A general recommendation would be to find other ways to set the type if possible.

There are certain situations where vertical type may be effective, and in that case you need to consider a few things. Vertical type is most awkward when there is a great disparity in the widths of its character forms. For instance, a word that includes both a *W* and an *I* will create an awkward overall shape because of the differences in the width of these letters. Vertical type will work best when the letters that make up the word have relatively consistent widths.

Vertical type is often used as a means to get type to fit within a specific space. One effective and attractive way to get type to fit within a vertical space is to rotate it at a 90-degree angle. The type will be more readable and the

design more interesting using this approach.

Type on a Curve

Type on a curve can bring a sense of motion and freedom to a type design. Type on a curve breaks away from the formal confines of perfectly horizontal type. Type can be placed along many different path types, including shapes and spirals. It is a fun way to handle type, but it poses its own set of typographical problems that must be solved in order for the type to work successfully.

The simplest way to begin is to create a curved line with the pen tool. Then, with the Type on a Curve tool, select the line. A type cursor will appear on the line and you can enter type along the line. Note that any stroke and fill information that the line had is lost when it is converted to a type path.

Type on a curve will generally work best when it's placed along paths that curve smoothly. One of the pitfalls of type on a curve is that awkward spaces between letters can occur, especially when the path twists abruptly. In some cases characters will start to butt into each other as they move along the path. Generally the smoother the path, the less awkward the spaces

Filling Shapes with Body Copy

Any shape that you can create can be used as a type box. This allows the paragraph text to take on a more visual role within a design.

TEXT SHAPES Convert any shape to a text box by clicking on the shape's edge with the Area Type tool. When the blinking cursor appears, enter the text. Getting paragraph text to work within the shape involves adjusting type size, leading, and kerning. Justified text is best used to follow the shape's outline.

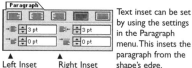

Text inset can be set by using the settings in the Paragraph menu. This insets the paragraph from the shape's edge.

Left Inset   Right Inset

By the dawn of the century industrialism had swept its way across the country, leaving nothing untouched in its wake. Seemingly overnight industrialization profoundly changed the face of the nation, influencing every aspect of life. The events that took place between 1885 and 1910 represent the metamorphosis of the country from a society relatively untouched by industrialism to one almost transformed by it. Emphasizing the speed and intensity of industrial advance Samuel Hays states that "seldom, if ever, in American history had so much been altered within the lifetime of a single man." The accelerated rate of technological progress quickly rendered obsolete everything that had provided meaning for members of preindustrial America. These sudden and unprecedented changes left people disoriented and unable to call on previous experience to help understand their changing surroundings. Religious beliefs were challenged by science and by the dominance of the Protestant

To apply color to the original shape outline, select the shape with the Direct Selection tool and apply a fill or stroke color.

Create line breaks by entering hard returns at the end of lines to reduce bad word spacing. Since the text is subject to reflowing should it be resized or edited, it's best to create the line breaks when type is finalized and will not change.

Here the letter *O* is filled with text. Convert the letter *O* to outlines, then release the compound path and delete its inner shape. The outer shape can now be filled with text by selecting it with the Area Type tool.

TYPE IN TYPE Here a letter form is used as a type container. Convert the letter to outlines and release its compound path. When designing type in this manner, bolder letter forms will better accommodate body copy.

By the dawn of the twentieth century industrialism had swept its way across the country, leaving nothing untouched in its wake. Seemingly overnight industrialization profoundly changed the face of the nation, influencing every aspect of life. The events that took place between 1885 and 1910 represent the metamorphosis of the country from a society relatively untouched by industrialism to one almost transformed by it. Emphasizing the speed and intensity of industrial advance Samuel Hays states that "seldom, if ever, in American history had so much been altered within the lifetime of a single man." The accelerated rate of technological progress quickly rendered obsolete everything that had provided meaning for members of preindustrial America. These sudden and unprecedented changes left people disoriented and unable to call on previous experience to help understand their changing surroundings. Religious

Text runs along the side of the letter *N*, which is beveled and extruded using KPT 3D Transform.

NOT SINCE ELVIS HAS ONE MAN SO SHAKEN THE HEARTS OF YOUNG WOMEN AND MUSIC EXECS. NEO THE MAN BEHIND THE RUMBLE HIS MUSIC IS GROUNDED IN CLASSIC R&B YET BORN ON THE STREET

NOT SINCE ELVIS HAS ONE MAN SO SHAKEN THE HEARTS OF YOUNG WOMEN AND MUSIC EXECS. NEO, THE MAN BEHIND THE RUMBLE. HIS MUSIC IS GROUNDED IN CLASSIC R&B YET BORN ON THE STREET

Using KPT Warp Frame, adjust the bounding box so that the text's perspective matches the side of the letter.

Once the text is styled, convert it to outlines and apply KPT Warp Frame to change its perspective.

Rectangular text box is placed over the shape and then the text is converted to outlines.

Side of letter *N*

---

between the type will be. These spaces can sometimes be fixed by manually kerning the type. Type size also contributes to how even the letter and word spacing is. Like all design, getting your type to move gracefully along a path is a matter of finding a balance between

typeface, type size, and the nature of the curve.

Type on a Closed Shape

Just as type can be applied to a line, it can also be made to move along the outside of any closed shape. Many of the same guidelines used

for running type along a path apply to this technique. Some shapes are more conducive to running type than others. As a general rule, simple curvilinear shapes work better than rectilinear shapes. For example, shapes like circles and ovals accommodate type well, whereas

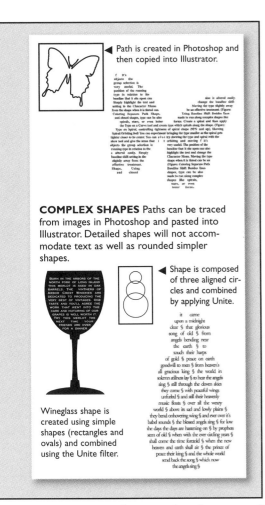

Path is created in Photoshop and then copied into Illustrator.

COMPLEX SHAPES Paths can be traced from images in Photoshop and pasted into Illustrator. Detailed shapes will not accommodate text as well as rounded simpler shapes.

Shape is composed of three aligned circles and combined by applying Unite.

Wineglass shape is created using simple shapes (rectangles and ovals) and combined using the Unite filter.

squares and rectangles, because of their corners, tend to be more difficult to run type around.

Creating type that runs along a closed shape is simple to do in Illustrator. While this can be done in QuarkXpress, Illustrator's tools offer a higher level of control. The simplest way to do this is to create a circle and then click on it with the Type on a Shape tool. When you click on the circle make sure that you click the cursor on the circle's path. Like Type on a Curve, a blinking text cursor appears after it is selected and text can then be entered. The type can be positioned along the path by selecting and moving the cursor.

Alignment settings can be helpful to place the text along the path accurately. For example, let's say you want to have your text centered along the top of the circle. When you select the circle, click at the top center of the circle's path. Then by selecting a centered alignment in the Paragraph menu the type will be perfectly centered along the top of the circle.

Adjusting Text on a Shape

There are many options for positioning your text along a closed shape. Type may be moved around the shape, but it can also be positioned to run inside the shape as well. This can be done by simply dragging the cursor inside the shape. When the text runs along the outside it moves in a clockwise direction, and when it runs on the inside of the shape it moves in a counterclockwise fashion. Running the type in a counter-clockwise fashion along the outside of a shape involves more complex manipulation.

Once you've got the type running along a shape, there are a few ways to style it. The shape's path can be assigned a color by selecting the shape with the Group Selection tool. If you want to keep a group intact but need to change one of its objects, Group Selection is very useful. The type can also be moved away from the path by adjusting its baseline shift. The baseline shift setting is found in the Character menu. By highlighting the text and adjusting the baseline shift, the text can be moved away from the shape or positioned inside of it.

Type Along Complex Paths

Besides lines and closed shapes, type can be also made to run along complex shapes such as spirals, stars, or even letter forms. Spirals can be very effective. Use the same methods you would for placing any type along a path. You can experiment with reducing the type size as it moves closer to the center of the spiral. This will give the type a sense of movement and three-dimensionality. Spiral type can also be skewed to give it the sense that it is moving in an orbital fashion. To do this simply select the

Bubbles and Balls: KPT Vector Distort

Getting type to appear rounded, as if it has been placed on a curved surface, is an easy task using KPT's Vector Distort filter.

VECTOR DISTORT allows any shape, including type, to appear as if it is on a rounded surface. In KPT Vector Distort's preview window a circular bounding box appears. This circle determines how the effect will be applied to the shape. Convert type to outlines before applying the filter.

The circle in the preview window determines the placement of the effect. It can be moved or sized and remains active, so its effect can be seen as it is changed.

Spherize controls produce a "bubble" effect. Convex or concave effects can be created.

Move the circle to a new position over the shape to see the new effect. Hold down the Shift key when resizing it to keep the circle perfectly round.

WRAP TEXT so that it appears to run around the sphere. Start by creating a round text box. Special attention to word placement and kerning must be given for this to work well.

Maintain readability throughout design. The type on the edges should remain legible.

Word placement is integral to the success of this technique. Small names are used on the shorter top and bottom lines.

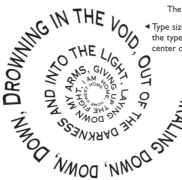

The type is set at the same size throughout.

Type sizes decrease as the type moves to the center of the spiral.

SPIRAL TYPE In the example on the left the type is spherized to create the illusion that it is spinning in a downward motion. Above, the type moves oppositely.

text and shape with the Skew tool. The technique has a similar effect on type that runs along a circle.

Type Inside a Shape

While type can be made to run along the path of any closed shape, these shapes can also be used as text containers, in which paragraph text is placed within the shape. This is a great way to introduce shapes into a design and get body copy to take on illustrative qualities. Because of the nature of

body copy, different shapes will accommodate text better than others. Detailed shapes that include extensions and vestiges, such as stars, are not well suited for paragraph text. Since type flows in a downward fashion, the shapes you

SPHERIZE can be used effectively by applying it only to certain sections of a shape. Here the circle is sized smaller than the type so that it affects only a portion of the type.

While Spherize can be used to fit rounded type within a specific shape, it can also be used to affect the shape and and the type simultaneously.

Original shapes before ▶ Vector Distort filter is applied

COMPLEX TYPE DESIGNS can mix spherized type with standard type. Avoid overusing filtered type. Here the word *Probowl* implies the round shape of the football, while the smaller words are flat.

Select similar points with the Blend tool.

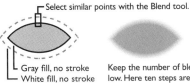

Gray fill, no stroke
White fill, no stroke

Keep the number of blend steps low. Here ten steps are used.

The blurred shadow is created using a blend between two shapes. Create the larger football shape using Offset Path.

Once the drop shadow is created, expand the blend into separate shapes and group them. Then place the shadow behind the logo design.

Symmetrical shapes, as long as they don't contain overly narrow sections, work well. Try illustrating the shape of an apple or a car and then running type into it.

Handle the type within these shapes as you would any paragraph text. Don't let the fancy text shape fool you; it's still body copy, and all the previous rules continue to apply. This means being sensitive to type size, leading, readability, and its relationship to the shape. Watch out for awkward spaces that often crop up when justified text is being used. Getting type to work well in complex shapes requires a lot of fine-tuning.

Creating Logotypes

KPT's Vector Distort filter is incredibly powerful and an invaluable tool for any designer who creates logotypes. The standard tools offered in Illustrator provide no way to manipulate type outlines in this manner. The Vector Distort filter allows you to affect multiple shapes as if they were one overall shape. This filter is especially powerful when applied to text. Vector Distort creates a bounding box around the selected text much in the same way Illustrator's Free Transform does. The big difference here is that the bounding box

select for this technique must be able to accommodate the running text without creating any awkward gaps. Because of the way in which the type fills the shape, justified text alignments most successfully define the shape.

Besides flowing text into primary shapes such as circles and squares, you can also use representational shapes as type containers. Any shape that you can draw or trace can be used to hold paragraph text as long as the path is closed.

in Vector Distort has Bézier points and handles applied to its corners. Manipulating these handles and changing the shape of the bounding box directly affects the type. Because of its unique approach to handling type it can create results that would be virtually impossible to attain using Illustrator's standard tools.

It's easy to get carried away with how you use the Vector Distort filter.

Its effectiveness depends on how you use it and on the font you originally selected to use with it. Some fonts adapt well to being manipulated in this manner, while others don't.

KPT Warp Frame

Like the Vector Distort filter, KPT's Warp Frame also offers a unique approach to affecting type. Warp Frame offers a wide range of settings, but the one that is most

applicable to type is its Spherize effect. Spherize makes the selected object appear as if it is sitting on a rounded surface, like a balloon. The circle displayed in the filter's preview window represents which part of the object will be affected. This circle can be moved or resized and shaped by selecting its points and adjusting them. Once you've got the circle sized and positioned, you can start to apply the Spherize

Creating Logotypes: KPT Warp Frame

KPT's Warp Frame filter allows type outlines to be reshaped as an entire unit and is an invaluable tool for creating logotypes.

WARP FRAME creates a bounding box around the vector shape, which allows it to be affected as a whole unit. By adjusting the points and handles of the bounding box in the preview window, the shape can be adjusted in complex ways not possible with Illustrator's standard tools.

Label shape is created by overlapping triangles and rectangles and applying the Unite filter.

Outer border is made by applying Offset Path to smaller inner shapes.

Keep the type's vertical lines straight by holding down the Shift key when moving the handles in KPT filter.

Create new settings by selecting Reset All from the File menu.

Rather than manipulate single handles separately, select both handles on the bottom and move together. Hold down the Shift key so that the type's vertical lines remain straight.

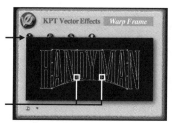

Only the middle letters are selected and affected by filters. First and last letters are visible by selecting Show Unselected Art.

Type can be affected in any number of ways. Instead of adding curves to the bottom of the text, select all four handles and move up together to get type to move on an arc.

Double Bézier curves allows more points to be used when affecting the shape.

Type is skewed upward to match the box shape using 3D Transform. Background box is made visible by selecting Show Unselected Art.

effect. To quickly see the power of Warp Frame, create a circle that is filled with text and convert the text to outlines, then try applying the Spherize filter. Like Vector Distort, there is no way to affect type or objects in such a way using standard illustration tools.

Type as Texture

While the primary purpose of type is to inform and communicate, type always plays some role as a design element. In some cases type can be used purely as a design element, such as when it becomes a textural element on a page. In this case the type is asked not to communicate information but rather to enhance a design. Very often in contemporary design type will be used within design projects for purely aesthetic reasons. For example, large, softly tinted character forms are often incorporated into the background of designs to bring color and texture to the page. David Carson, one of the most well known contemporary designers, often uses type in a textural fashion.

When type is used as a textural element, certain words or phrases might retain their readability, but the text itself is not intended to be read or to communicate specific information, only to give texture

Warp Frame is ideal for creating complex logotypes. This logo combines filtered and standard type. White space between the type and drop shadow is created by a white stroke on the type. The initial letter has been resized larger.

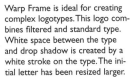

Locked point

Set an anchor point to scale off by clicking on the corner of the A before scaling. This will maintain the original position of the letter.

Lower handles are used to create a wave at the bottom of the type. Handles are moved separately with the Shift key held down to keep the vertical strokes straight.

Complex designs that involve a lot of type must be finalized completely before any filter is applied. The bulk of the design work is done before Warp Frame is applied. Getting all the text to fit comfortably is difficult and demands great attention to kerning and word placement

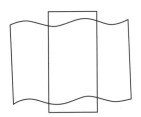

To create separate folds in the flag, place a rectangle overlapping the flag shape and apply Divide.

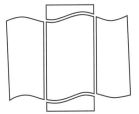

The Divide filter divides overlapping areas into separate shapes. Ungroup and delete any unnecessary shapes.

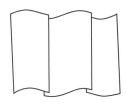

Place shapes so that they overlap. Draw connecting shapes between the folds with the Pen tool.

Using Type as Texture

While type's primary function is to communicate information, it can also be used as a pure design element in the form of texture.

TRANSPARENCY In this sample large overlapping type appears to be transparent. The numbers' shapes are discernible, while the overall background remains light enough to place text upon.

  Text pattern is designed and grouped. A rectangle is placed over the text and acts as a crop shape. Select all and apply Crop.

TYPE AS TEXTURE Running copy or support text can be used texturally. In this poster, tour dates and venues are treated as a background texture. Sans serif faces will hold up better at smaller sizes. Type is tilted to make the design less static.

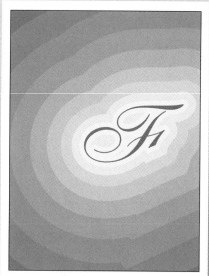

CONCENTRIC TYPE Once type is converted to outlines its shape can be made to move concentrically outward, creating a texture and a sense of movement The lighter area acts as the focal point.

 Apply Offset Path to the type outline to create concentric shapes. Place a rectangle over the shapes and apply the Crop filter.

and tone to the design. There are countless ways to approach type as texture. The examples included in this book provide good exercises in cropping type into complex compound paths.

In many ways the techniques for creating textures are related to the methods for creating inlaid type in that they both require sets of objects to be cropped into shapes. Instead of cropping wavy lines into character outlines, type is cropped into shapes.

Images, Masks, and Type

The last method covered in this chapter involves placing imagery within type by using masks. Masks are simple to create and can be altered and released at any time. There are a few things to consider when placing images within type. Readability is always an issue, and you don't want the image to inter-

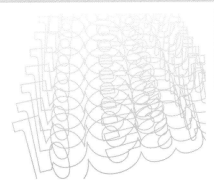

LINEAR TYPE TEXTURE Besides using filled type for texture, type strokes can also be used to create a linear textural pattern.

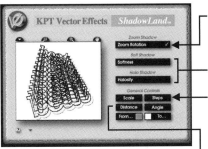

KPT SHADOWLAND This filter is generally used to create soft drop shadows, but it can also be applied to create interesting motion effects.

After applying the KPT Shadowland filter to the type, the type needs to be cropped to fit onto the page. Select the type and convert the strokes to shapes by applying Outline Path. Then select all and apply the Unite filter to combine the shapes. Then place a rectangle over the text and apply Crop.

Zoom Rotation controls how the added shapes emanate from the original shape.

Softness and Halosity are used when creating soft drop shadows.

Scale and Steps Steps sets the number of transition shapes. High settings make the separate shapes less discernable. Scale controls the size of the stepped shapes.

Distance controls the space between the original shape and new shapes.

Create an internal grid to position the type in a consistent manner. Decide on a fixed spacing between the words and apply equal spacing throughout.

Separate letters are scaled to create interesting spaces and to accommodate smaller blocks of type. Make sure to scale the type proportionately.

Keep the type consistent to get continuity. This design uses one typeface, and the number of sizes used within it is limited to four. All the dates are treated consistently.

This design involves deleting type shapes from a black background. Create the type design and convert the type outlines to a compound path. Draw a box over the text and apply the Minus Back filter. This essentially uses the type to cut a hole through the black background.

Create a simple drop shadow by copying the shape and placing it behind the darker version.

fere with it. Masking images into type is generally reserved for display type. The typeface that you select will greatly determine how decipherable the image will be. Because the entire image will not be visible when it is placed within the type, the image needs to be positioned so that its pertinent information is seen. Bold typefaces set at larger sizes will obviously accommodate more of the image area. Because of their varying stroke widths, serif faces usually don't work well with this technique. To help maximize the amount of viewable image you might try kerning the type closely so that the characters actually touch.

Creating masks is a relatively easy task. Start by styling the text and then place it so it overlaps an image. Select both and then apply a mask. The image will appear as

Masking Images Into Type

Using masks to place images within type outlines allows the type to convey both literal and visual information.

1 CREATING MASKS Any shape can be used to act as a mask. The image that is used stays linked to the Illustrator file, and that link must remain intact. The image status can be checked using the Links palette.

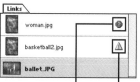

Missing Link   Modified Link

TYPE DESIGN Images should remain recognizable when they are placed in type. The more visible the image area, the better. Bold, tightly kerned type works well. Once designed, convert the type to curves and apply Unite Filter.

IMAGE LINK STATUS The first image on the list is missing and its link is broken. The second image has been modified since it was originally placed in Illustrator. The last image link remains active.

2 PLACING IMAGES To place an image into Illustrator, select Place from the File menu.

COMPOUND PATHS Before creating a mask, select the type outlines and make them a compound path. This allows the image to appear in all the letters.

Original placed Image

CREATE MASK Place the type design over the image. Select both the image and type and apply the mask.

Place type design over image

3 ADJUST MASK Once the mask is created, the positioning of either image or type can be changed. Use the Direct Selection tool to select either the type or the image to change its placement.

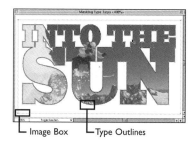

Image Box   Type Outlines

4 FINE-TUNE For this method to work, the image must maintain recognizability. Highly detailed images won't work as well as simple images with clear focal points.

The image of the snowboarder remains recognizable.

if it is pasted into the character outlines.

Bells and Whistles

While this chapter focuses on the many techniques you can use to style your type, these techniques will not guarantee an attractive and effective end product. They need to be applied to appropriate projects. Some of the techniques are limited in how they can be used. They are meant to introduce you to ways of approaching type design. In order for these effects to work properly, you need to begin with a strong overall type layout.

Chapter Five
Preparing Your Images

Working with photography is an integral part of design, and knowing the proper way to prepare and optimize your images for print can make or break a design project. With the proper manipulation a designer can transform an average photograph into a strong image by emphasizing the image's strengths. Conversely, a beautiful photo that is formatted and handled improperly can fall flat when printed. Photographic images are often greatly responsible for the visual impact a design has, and being able to maximize that impact is an essential skill for designers. This chapter will address many of the basic image preparation methods such as scanning techniques, color correction, and formatting, as well as introducing many of the most common techniques for styling images.

For Position Only
All designers scan images for use in their designs. Sometimes these scans will end up used as final art, but more often they are used for sizing purposes and as placeholders within a design. When scans are used this way they are referred to as "for position only," or FPO art. Working with FPO art is a common practice among designers who send their original photo transparencies out to a service bureau for high-end drum scans. FPO art is usually a lower-quality version of the image that can be used to temporarily design with until the final high-quality scan is done. When designing with very large images, it is sometimes advantageous to use a low-resolution version of the image. The smaller image file will take less time to print as well as speed up the software's performance. Once the design is finalized, the FPO art can be replaced with the high-resolution version of the image.

Whether you end up using the scans produced on your flatbed scanner as your final artwork or as a simple placeholder, you need to understand the scanning process and know how to optimize your images.

Know Your Final Destination
The most important thing you need to know before you scan an image is how is it going to be used. Is the image intended to be used for a Web site, a print project, or possibly both? Knowing this before you scan will help you determine how to format the image appropriately. Proper formatting involves selecting the correct color model, resolution, and file format in Photoshop.

Choosing the Right Format
Properly formatting the scan depends on what your image's final destination will be. Image formats for print or Web require very different color and resolution settings. These formats are not interchangeable. Using images that are not formatted properly for their intended use can have disastrous effects.

The output device for each medium determines the format settings—the computer screen display determines how a Web image should be formatted, and the four-color print process determines the print image's formats. Because they use the RGB color model and require a lower resolution, Web images will appear pixellated and in grayscale if used for print. Conversely, a high-resolution four-color print image will load extremely slowly and be subject to wide color shifts if used on a Web site.

Using the appropriate format is essential to successfully designing. Setting up proper formats is not that difficult once you understand the differences and requirements of each medium.

Setting Color Models

Because Web-based images are destined to be output to a monitor, they need to be formatted in the RGB color model. While a CMYK image could technically be used on a Web site, its color information would have to be translated by the screen to emulate the RGB color space, and the image would be subject to color shifts.

The RGB color space can emulate a wider range of colors than the CMYK model. Whereas a color monitor can display up to 16 million colors, a high-quality CMYK print can only emulate around 4,000 colors. This wider range is evident when an image's color model is changed from the RGB to CMYK. The translation to CMYK causes a reduction in the overall color palette, and this produces an

Destination Please? Formatting Images

How you plan on using an image will determine its color mode, resolution, and file format. Knowing this before scanning will guarantee that the image outputs properly.

Choosing the Proper Format

Proper image formatting maximizes the visual impact an image has. Incorrectly formatted print images will output poorly. Choosing the wrong format for Web images makes them download slowly with inconsistent color. This decision guide should simplify the process.

What is the final destination of your image? Print or Web?

PRINT → ← WEB

	RESOLUTION	
Print media require images to be high-resolution, usually 300 dpi. Resolution is determined by the line screen that your file is being output at. The rule of thumb is to double the line screen to get proper resolution.		Images intended for Web sites are formatted for screen output. Resolution is determined by the screen resolution, which is typically 72 dpi. This helps images to load quickly. Higher-resolutions will not enhance image quality.

	COLOR MODE	
Color mode for print projects can vary depending on the number of colors being printed. For black and white projects the image should be in grayscale mode. For four-color projects images must be specified in CMYK.		Because Web images are displayed on-screen their color model is RGB, the same colors that make up the screen display. "Web-safe" palettes that limit the color palette to 256 colors are often used to ensure color consistency.

	FILE FORMAT	
The two most commonly used formats for print are .EPS and .TIF. Make sure not to apply file compression to the files.		Typical file formats used for Web output are the .JPG and .GIF formats. JPG formats are best used for photographic images, while .GIF formats are best used for hard-edged graphic images. Both use file compression so that images load quickly on the Web site.

	OTHER INFO	
• Images links must be maintained in Quark for proper output. Check links in Utilities: Usage in Quark. • Make sure to initially scan at a high resolution, as resolution can't later be increased in Photoshop. • Many print projects are limited to two or three colors. In this case spot colors are used. These colors are typically specified as Pantone colors.		• Lossy compression allows images to be compressed when not in use and then expanded when called upon. Images using this type of compression are subject to having their image quality decline. Each time the image is recompressed it loses some quality.

Adjusting Resolution and Image Size

All images used for print must be high-resolution.

SCAN IMAGES Make sure to scan images at a high resolution and generally larger than you need. This allows for rescaling an image to a larger size if needed.

IMAGE QUALITY Images can be sized down if necessary, but increasing an image's size in Photoshop will result in a loss of quality. If the image needs to be larger than the size it was initially scanned at, it must be rescanned.

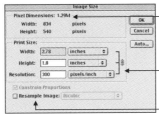

FILE SIZES are large for print images because of their high resolution. File size should not get larger when you resize an image.

PRINT SIZE and resolution are directly linked when Resample Image is selected.

RESAMPLE IMAGE will extrapolate the image and add approximated pixels to increase its size. This will result in loss of image quality. Resizing an image will not change the file size if Resample Image is not selected.

DOWNSIZING Images should be scaled down in Photoshop so that their size in Quark is close to 100 percent. To scale down an image select Resample Image and enter the percentage in Print Size. This will maintain resolution.

Color Models

The color model you select will be determined by the number of colors the design requires. The most common color models for print images are grayscale and CMYK.

Grayscale images contain 256 shades of gray.

CMYK is the standard format for full-color images.

RGB images are used for screen and Web output

EXCEPTIONS TO THE RULE Some designs require the use of spot color, usually specified in Pantone colors. Pantones are a system of premixed inks that are commonly used in two- and three-color jobs. Duotone images make use of Pantone colors and need to be saved as duotone .EPS files. If a project calls only for Pantones, none of the colors, except black, should be specified in CMYK.

File Formats

The two most commonly used formats for images used in print projects are .EPS and .TIF files. There are many file formats, and designers need a basic understanding of them.

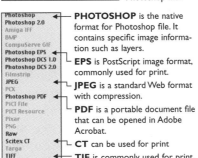

If other formats aren't available, the file probably needs to flattened. To retain layer info, save first as a Photoshop file.

PHOTOSHOP is the native format for Photoshop file. It contains specific image information such as layers.

EPS is PostScript image format, commonly used for print.

JPEG is a standard Web format with compression.

PDF is a portable document file that can be opened in Adobe Acrobat.

CT can be used for print

TIF is commonly used for print.

image that is grayer and less vibrant. This is a major reason why images tend to look better on the screen than in print.

When scanning images for print projects, the final color palette must be set in the CMYK mode. While it's appropriate to scan in the RGB mode, as many flatbed scanners do, the image's color model should be adjusted before final output. While most lower-end color printers can output RGB color, many high-end image setters cannot translate a RGB image into CMYK. This will result in the color image being output as grayscale. Remembering the proper color models is pretty simple: RGB for Web, and CMYK for print.

Setting Image Resolution

The resolution of an image is also determined by its final destination. Since the output device for Web images is a color monitor screen, the resolution is set much lower than for print images. Typical screen resolution for most monitors is 72 dots per inch, and the resolution of Web images needs to be set to match. Using a higher-resolution image for screen output will not improve the quality of the image because the highest amount of information that a screen can

Sizing, Scaling, & Setting Resolution

Optimizing resolution and size helps maximize an image's visual impact and ensures that it prints accurately.

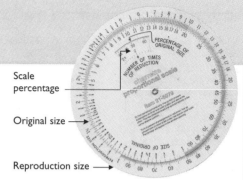

Scale percentage

Original size

Reproduction size

Scanning and Scaling Images

The percentage used to scale an image is determined by its final printed size. There are a few ways to calculate this percentage.

Before scanning an image, you need to know both its original size and its final reproduction size. You can mathematically calculate this proportion or use a proportion wheel.

RULE OF THUMB Images can always be scaled down after they've been scanned. But an image's size cannot be increased without some loss in quality. The general rule is to scan the image at a larger size than you expect to use. This will allow a wider range of options in how you use the image within the design.

SCAN LARGE Often the final reproduction size has not been determined when you initially scan an image. Scanning it at a larger size will reduce the chances of having to rescan it again later.

Original Size

Reproduction Size

To figure out the the exact percentage at which to scale an image, divide its final reproduction size by its original size. For example, if an image's final print size is four inches and its original size is eight inches, divide four by eight to get a percentage of 50 percent. Scaling images accurately greatly increases print quality. Part of finalizing any design project is making sure that all images placed within a Quark layout are sized close to 100 percent.

PROPORTION WHEEL One handy way to determine the sizing of an image is to use a proportion wheel, long used by designers. Simply line up the two wheels and the sizing percentage appears in the window. One wheel represents the image's original size, the other its reproduction size.

DO THE MATH Calculators can also be used to figure out size proportions. Enter the reproduction size and select the slash (divide by) key. Enter the original size and select the equals key. A decimal equivalent of the percentage appears. In this sample the calculation results in .5, meaning the image should be scanned at 50 percent

display is 72 dpi. The additional resolution will only make the image slower to download to a Web site.

If your image is going to be used for print, it will need to have much higher resolution. Typically most color images require a resolution setting of 300 dpi. Choosing image resolution for print is a little more complicated than for Web output. Whereas all Web images are output at 72 dpi, print resolution is dependent on a few factors. While print resolutions are generally high, an image's exact settings will be determined by the frequency of the line screen used to output it. This line screen setting is in turn determined by the quality of the paper that the final project is being printed on.

Resolution should be set when initially scanning the image. While the image's resolution should not be increased after it has been scanned, its size and resolution can be reduced afterward.

While Photoshop will allow an image's resolution to be increased,

Scaling Images for Quark Documents

Images that are placed in Quark documents need to be sized correctly and have their links intact in order to accurately output.

SIZING IN QUARK When working on a design in QuarkXpress you can scale an image to any size you wish. When the design is finalized you will need to resize the image in Photoshop so that the image is sized at 100 percent in Quark. Quark does not actually scale the actual image file like Photoshop does. It only scales its preview.

RULE OF THUMB Images can be sized up or down slightly in Quark without having to be resized. Images that are scaled up or down by 15 percent (or less) will generally print properly. While any image sized between 85% and 115% is acceptable, the optimum setting is 100%.

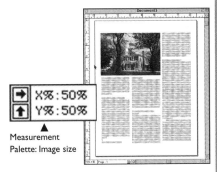

Measurement
Palette: Image size

This image is scaled at 50 percent in Quark. Before the design is finalized, this image should be scaled down by the same percentage in Photoshop and then updated in Quark.

When an image is being scaled down, Resample Image should be selected. Enter the size or percentage in Print Size.

RESIZING THE IMAGE Use the same percentage that appears in Quark's measurement palette to scale down the image in Photoshop. If the image size is larger than 115% in the Quark document, it will need to be rescanned.

UPDATING THE IMAGE Resized images need to be updated in Quark. To check the image's status, select Usage from the Utilities menu. Here the image has been modified. Select and update the image so that its status is OK.

Increasing Resolution

Low-resolution images can have their resolutions increased without losing any image quality, but their size will be decreased as a result.

Original image size is 2" by 2" and 72 dpi.

Resized image size is 1" by 1" and 144 dpi.

When the image is resized, its resolution is doubled while its print size is reduced by half.

CONSISTENT FILE SIZE The file size of both images remains the same, while the image data is reapplied to a different size. To increase resolution make sure that Resample Image is not selected when changing resolution. This will keep the file size fixed.

---

this practice is inadvisable because it will result in lower image quality. Photoshop cannot "extrapolate" or create the additional image information that is required when an image's resolution or print size is increased. Photoshop can, however, interpolate, or reduce an image's resolution and size, without any loss in image quality.

Line Screens and Resolution

When formatting images for print, the rules are not as hard and fast as they are for the Web. The color model, paper type, and film settings all have to be considered to properly set an image's resolution. The most general rule for setting resolution when scanning color images is to set them at 300 dpi. If you stick to this, you will generally be fine, but understanding the intricacies of the print process will help you to get optimum results in both image quality and output time, which can be costly.

The frequency of the line screen used to output the design will determine the resolution that the images should be set at. Line

Image Preparation: Cropping Images

Optimizing images for final output so that they print fast and accurately requires cropping away any unused sections of an image.

CROPPING PHOTOS is a common way to change the emphasis and focus of a photograph. Once the design is finalized any unused sections of the image must be cropped. Cropping away these unused areas in Photoshop reduces the file size and helps ensure faster and more reliable output. If the image is not cropped, it will take much longer to print and be subject to output problems.

Crop away unused image

Entire image

Image as used in layout ▶

The image as used in this layout represents only a small section of the entire image. Crop away the unused section.

To crop an image in Photoshop select the Crop tool and surround the image area that is used within the design. A bounding box will appear after surrounding the area. This box can be resized by adjusting its handles. You can complete cropping the image either by double-clicking in the center of the selected image area or by selecting Crop from the Image pull-down menu.

Image
Mode ▶
Adjust ▶
Duplicate...
Apply Image...
Calculations...
Image Size...
Canvas Size...
Crop

Bounding Box shows cropping area

IMAGE BLEEDS Additional image area is required if an image bleeds, or is designed to run off a page's edge. The additional bleed area provides a buffer space in case the page is not trimmed exactly. Typically an eighth of an inch extra buffer space is sufficient for images that bleed off a page.

Standard bleed allowance is 1/8 inch

This image bleeds off the bottom and right-hand side of page

The image is placed so that part of it runs off the bottom right of the page, allowing for trim

screens are measured in lpi, or lines per inch. These lines of dots compose the image. The more lines per inch, the higher the image resolution that can be accommodated. The most commonly used line screens for high-end color output are 133 lpi and 150 lpi. Once you know the line screen used to create the film separations, you can set the resolution properly. The general rule is to set the image resolution (dpi) at twice the line screen setting (lpi). For example, if film is being output at 150 lpi, the image is scanned at 300 dpi.

The quality of the paper stock that the design will be printed on ultimately determines the line screen that is used. Coated paper stocks, which are often used in magazines, use finer line screens, such as 150 or 133 lpi. Higher-quality paper stocks have finer surfaces that can handle a high level of detail. Coarser paper, like newsprint, has a much rougher and softer surface, which cannot accommodate such fine printing. The halftone dots that create the image are noticeably bigger in newspaper printing than in magazines. Typically newsprint is printed at 80 lpi, which means that the image's resolution would need to be set at 160 dpi, double the line

Getting Results: Basic Scanning Techniques

While the overall quality of an image scan is dependent on the quality of the scanner itself, there are a few things you can do to improve the quality of the scan.

FLATBED VS. DRUM SCANNING
Most images used in professional design are scanned on a drum scanner because of the high-quality scans they produce. Drum scanners are more accurate than flatbed scanners because of the way in which they scan an image. With a flatbed scanner the scanning device moves across the image. With a drum scanner the original art is attached to a cylindrical drum that turns around a stationary scanning device. With flatbeds the motion of the scanning mechanism creates less accurate scans.

ORIGINAL ART While students often design projects using images that have already appeared in print, professionals commission original art for their designs. This original work comes in the form of photographic transparencies and original pieces of artwork from illustrators.

PRINTED MATERIALS Previously printed images have copyrights and using them for profit is an infringement of those rights and an unethical and illegal practice. They should be used only for student designs that are intended to show a student's design skills.

KEEP IT CLEAN
Before you scan in an image take some time and clean the glass to remove any dust or smudges. Use glass cleaner and a soft cloth. Make sure glass is dry before placing art on scanner.

SCANNING PRINTED MATERIAL All previously printed images, whether full-color or black and white, will be composed of a dot pattern. These halftone dot patterns affect the reproduction quality of the scan.

SCANNING SOFTWARE Software may offer the ability to color-correct and adjust the image quality. Generally the proprietary software that comes bundled with scanners is limited. It is best to use it to set up image scaling, color mode, and resolution. Use Photoshop, which has much more advanced software, for any image manipulation.

STAY STRAIGHT
Make sure to place the artwork so that it is straight. If the image being scanned has been previously printed, this may help reduce the visibility of the halftone dots. Align the artwork along the edge of the glass to scan it straight.

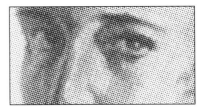

DESCREENING Removing the halftone dots from an image is a difficult task, and there are a few approaches. Some scanning software offers descreening capabilities.

---

screen. Actually, a high-resolution image (300 dpi) will not print well on newsprint, as it contains more information than the medium can accommodate. The coarseness of the newsprint would cause such an image to bleed and be blurred. So, as is the case with paper quality (and Web sites), higher resolu-

tion does not always guarantee better results.

Image File Formats
Equally integral to getting high quality output is selecting the proper file format for your images. Print images are usually saved in either the .EPS or .TIF formats.

The first of these formats, .EPS (Encapsulated PostScript), is written in Post-Script programming code, which is a page description language that the printer translates when a file is sent to print. Either format will output properly if you are printing to a PostScript printer. If you are outputting to a local

True Colors: Color-Correcting Images

Most images scanned on flatbed scanners require some image manipulation so that their colors accurately represent those of the original artwork.

COLOR-CORRECTING Adjusting the color of images accurately is a skill that requires a highly sensitive eye and a technical understanding of how color works. Production artists in imaging departments are experts in this area. While many designers depend on them to optimize image quality, all designers should be able to perform basic color correction and image sharpening.

IMAGING TOOLS Photoshop offers many ways to correct and optimize an image's color. While some of these tools and methods handle adjusting color in a more technical manner, others take a more visual and intuitive approach.

WHAT TO LOOK FOR There are three general tonal areas included in most images: midtones, highlights, and shadows. Well-balanced images are optimized to have a wide range of tones so that their shadows are dark and the highlights are bright. Midtones are the tonal variations that fall between shadow and highlight.

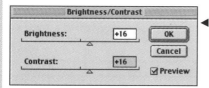

MIDTONES are the middle tonalities found within images. Images that have too much of their tonality falling into the midtone range tend to be gray and lacking in contrast.

SHADOWS are the image's darkest areas. Shadow tones should be dark but still light enough to hold some detail within the shadow. Images should not have areas of solid black tones.

BRIGHTNESS / CONTRAST is one way to quickly adjust an image's tonality, but it offers limited control. Of all the features that Photoshop offers for adjusting images, this is one of the least sophisticated.

This image is optimized so that it has contrasting values and a wide range of grays, darks, and lights.

HIGHLIGHTS are the image's lightest tones. When setting highlight values make sure that they have some gray value and are not pure white. Images that have empty white values tend to "blow out" and don't look good printed.

TOO DARK This image is overly dark because its shadow and midtone information dominates its tonal range. This gives the image a gray and tired feel.

TOO LIGHT This image is too light because its highlights are dominant, giving it a washed-out feel. Large areas around the top of the building are entirely white.

---

printer that is not PostScript-compatible, such as an Epson printer, you should use .TIF files. Make sure when you're saving a file in the .TIF format that you don't save it with LZW compression applied. Images used for print do not require any type of file compression.

The proper format for Web images is .JPG or .GIF. These are low-resolution RGB formats that are designed to load quickly and accurately on a computer monitor. Both formats take advantage of image compression, which allows an image to load up quickly to a site and then to be recompressed when the image is inactive. This helps speed up the Web site's performance. Some formats use lossy compression. Lossy compression

Optimizing Color: Using Levels and Curves

Photoshop offers numerous ways to manipulate an image. Images can be optimized by adjusting their brightness, contrast, color, or saturation. Adjusting Levels and Curves offer the most control.

The Adjust section offers a wide array of color correction tools. Levels, Auto Levels, Curves, Color Balance, Brightness/Contrast, Hue/Saturations, and Variations can all be used to adjust color information.

LEVELS adjusts the image's overall color information based on its shadow, midtone, and highlight information.

Graphic display previews the image's color profile, allowing you to see how much of its overall tonality falls into the midtone, shadow, and highlight ranges.

By moving the shadow slider to the right, the number of the dark tones within the image is reduced. This will lighten the shadows found within the image.

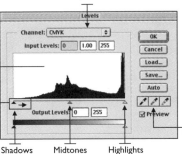

Shadows   Midtones   Highlights

Adjust the color makeup of the entire image by selecting CMYK, or select separate channels to adjust more specific color information

Adjusting separate colors can be effective, but also confusing. While reducing the cyan in an image that has a strong cyan cast seems like an obvious solution, it is sometimes better to increase the levels of the other three colors instead.

Use Eyedropper to sample image shadow, midtone, and highlights and readjust overall colors based on the sampling.

Affect the entire image by selecting CMYK, or select separate color channels to adjust.

The graphic curve display represents the image data. The vertical grayscale shows actual image (input), and the horizontal scale shows how much of that info will be output when it prints.

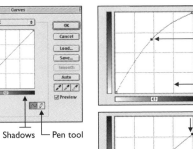

Highlights   Shadows   Pen tool

CURVES uses a graphical line to represent the image's shadow, midtone, and highlight information. The graph is divided into four sections or quarter tones. This curve can be reshaped and edited using the pen tool to adjust the tonal ranges individually.

Here the curve has a point added to it using the pen tool and the midtones are emphasized by reshaping the curve.

Gray lines represent quarter tones.

Here the section of the curve representing the shadows has been brought down, which results in a lighter image.

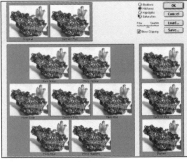

VARIATIONS is an intuitive way to adjust an image's color information, allowing you to see a range of image variations with varying amounts of color added.

results in an image's color palette being reduced each time the file is opened and closed, and consequently uncompressed and recompressed.

Once you have an understanding of how color models, image resolution, line screens, and file formats apply to different media, you can properly format your images so that they output efficiently and accurately. The proper resolution, color model, and formats for Web or print are as follows: Web images are typically 72 dpi RGB images saved in either the .JPG or .GIF format. Print images destined for high-end output are typically 266 or 300 dpi, CMYK images, saved in either the .EPS or .TIF format.

Spot Remover: The Rubber Stamp Tool

Scanned images often have spots and artifacts that can be easily removed using the Rubber Stamp tool.

Cleaning up Images

 **RUBBER STAMP** is the easiest way to clean up images. It can be used to remove spots or repair folds or tears in the original art. By sampling and cloning image areas, the Rubber Stamp allows spots to be seamlessly removed.

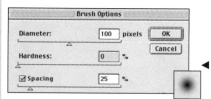

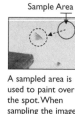

Sample Area

A sampled area is used to paint over the spot. When sampling the image, choose an area that has similar qualities to the area being repaired.

• You must select a sample area before drawing with the Rubber Stamp.

• Sample an area with the Rubber Stamp tool by holding down the Option key and clicking.

• Release the Option key and then draw over the spot. The sampled area will be applied to the area.

◀ The Rubber Stamp tool works best with a soft brush that applies the effect gradually. To soften the effect of the brush, double-click on a brush in the Brush Palette and adjust its hardness setting.

The final image shows no spots or artifacts. Beside removing dark spots from the image, keep an eye out for any unnaturally bright pixels within the image's darker areas.

Extending Images

Select and copy a similar area and position it in empty image area

Extended Area

┌─ A line is often visible where the selection is pasted over the original image.

The Rubber Stamp tool can also be used to extend an image's background. This method is best used to extend small sections of an image. It also works best when it's used to extend sections of an image that are not overly complicated.

This setting adds new space to the left of the image.

To extend an image its size must be increased. Use the Anchor feature in the Canvas Size menu to choose a direction in which to expand the image. The extended area will be filled with the current background color. Here the width is increased.

When extending an image only slightly, it's best to expand the canvas size and manually re-create the background with the Rubber Stamp tool. In this case the image extension is relatively large, so a selection is copied and placed into the expanded area. This is most effective for images with edges that are not too detailed. An unnatural line may appear on the edge of where the selection was placed. Smooth out this line using the Rubber Stamp tool.

Do It Right the First Time

Developing good work habits is essential no matter what the discipline. Designers who get in the habit of making the proper adjustments to their images immediately after they are scanned will save themselves time and avoid embarrassing and costly mistakes. Before actually scanning an image, make sure that it's resolution is set appropriately. When saving the scanned image, make sure that it is properly formatted and that its color model is correct. Once this practice has become second nature you will not have to go back and check an image's status because you will know you did it right the first time.

One word of advice to young designers is to get in the habit of using high-resolution images even when designing school projects. Eventually your designs will be realized on high-end color output devices, and it's good to get used to using high-resolution images. You may notice a slowdown in software performance. If you find that high-resolution images noticeably reduce your computer's performance, a common work-around is to design with lower-resolution versions of the images, which can be replaced with the final images when the project is ready for output.

Scanning Images Properly

Flatbed scanners can vary a great deal in the quality of the images they produce. Scanners vary greatly in price and performance. There are some high-end flatbed scanners that can produce near drum scanner quality. Most low-end scanners are capable of producing quality images. No matter what scanner is being used, initial scans usually require some additional manipulation to achieve optimal results. There are some basic procedures you can follow to increase the quality of your scanned images.

Flatbed and Drum Scanners

Images that appear in most high-quality design projects are usually scanned from a photo transparency on drum scanners. Drum scanners produce higher-quality scans than flatbed scanners because of the scanner technology used. With flatbed scanners the scanning mechanism is in motion while the art remains stationary. The scanning mechanism is what processes the image information. With drum scanners the original art is placed on a cylindrical drum that is rotated around a stationary scanning mechanism. The drum scan is much more accurate because its station-

ary scanning mechanism is not subject to the inaccuracies caused by vibrations when it scans. Drum scanners are expensive and their operators are experts in achieving color accuracy. Since very few designers actually use drum scanners firsthand and all designers use flatbed scanners, let's look at how to achieve optimum results from a flatbed scanner.

Optimizing Flatbed Scans

While there's not all that much to know about operating a flatbed scanner, there are a few common-sense approaches that will help improve scan quality. Making sure that the glass is clean before scanning will help reduce unwanted artifacts in the image. Use a clean, damp soft cloth that will not scratch the surface of the glass. Carefully aligning the artwork on the scanner will decrease the amount of manipulation that has to be done later.

Almost all scanners come with their own proprietary scanning software, and most offer the same basic functions. As a general rule, you want to use Photoshop for any color and contrast adjustments, as it offers more advanced tools and a higher level of control. Because of the limitations of the scanning soft-

Focusing In: Sharpening Images

Most flatbed scanners produce images that have slightly blurred, unclear edges that require some sharpening.

UNSHARP MASK Despite its name, Unsharp Mask is applied to sharpen images and bring them into clearer focus. Unsharp Mask uses edge detection to base its effect. Edge detection works by analyzing an image's information, looking for contrasting shades that fall next to each other. These adjacent shifts in tonality are treated by the filter as an edge. When Unsharp Mask is applied too heavily to an image it can produce a halo effect. Overapplying the filter can also result in unnatural black shapes appearing in shadow areas.

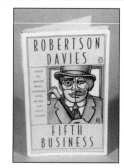

BEFORE the Unsharp Mask is applied, the type is legible but slightly blurred. Unsharp Mask is most effective when applied to images with hard, linear edges.

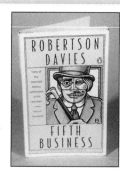

AFTER the Unsharp Mask filter has been applied, the type is much clearer and the lines found within the book cover's image are much crisper.

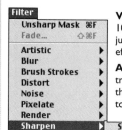

VIEW IMAGE at 100 percent to best judge the filter's effects.

AMOUNT controls how strongly the filter is applied to the image.

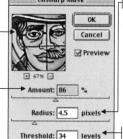

RADIUS controls how many surrounding pixels are affected. Effect can range from 1 to 100 but is usually best set low.

THRESHOLD controls which image areas are affected. Setting at zero applies effect to entire image.

OVERDOING IT When Unsharp Mask has been used too heavily, it can result in white halos appearing around the image's edges.

LESS IS MORE As a general rule, it's better to apply the filter subtly. More of the filter can always be applied later.

---

ware, it is best used for setting up basic scanning specifications such as sizing and resolution.

One thing to remember when scanning images is to make sure that the resolution is set high enough. Figure out the resolution prior to scanning by doubling the line screen that your project will eventually be output at. This is extremely important because the resolution cannot be increased after an image has been scanned without losing some image quality.

If you are planning on using an image at a size that is larger than its original size, you will need to set the scaling in the scanning software prior to scanning it. One traditional device that is still commonly used by designers is the proportional wheel. It's a simple device that is used to determine the proper percentage to scan an image at. This percentage can also be figured out using a calculator. One time-saving practice is to scan your images slightly larger than the size at which you plan to use them. This will give you some room to adjust an image's size within a layout without having to rescan the image later on.

Color-Correcting Images

All images, even those scanned on drum scanners, require some color correction after initially being scanned. Color correction demands highly technical skills and a sensitive eye. Imaging technicians are a highly skilled professionals and many have background experience with traditional production techniques. This experience gives them special insight as to how color separations work to create images. Besides color matching, imaging experts understand the intricacies of film, plates, and ink. To optimize an image's output they employ specialized techniques like undercover gray removal to reduce the amount of ink used to print without losing any image quality.

Color-correcting an image on a monitor is tricky. Any adjustment to your monitor's brightness and contrast settings and the image preview is completely changed. While there is no guaranteed way to ensure that the adjustments you

make to an image on the screen will be reflected on the printed page, you can adjust and calibrate your monitor so that it previews more accurately. One way to start

is by adjusting the screen brightness so that what it displays as white appears to be white. You could try using a print out that shows a sample of 100 percent

Dodge & Burn: Tonal Correction

Sometimes specific areas of an image will require tonal correction, and dodging and burning can be used to lighten or darken these areas.

DODGE AND BURN tools can be applied to lighten or darken specific areas within images.

 DODGING is a traditional photographic technique where part of the exposure is blocked, causing the affected area to be lighter.

 BURNING is also a standard darkroom technique that focuses additional light upon a specific image area in order to darken it.

 LARGE SOFT BRUSHES are best used when dodging or burning an image. A soft brush allows you to subtly accentuate an image's highlights or shadows. Control the size and softness of a brush by double-clicking on a brush in the Brush palette to access the brush settings. The diameter setting is used to control the brush size, and hardness controls the softness of the brush.

Original Image

The highlights have been lightened using the Dodge tool.

Shadow areas have been darkened using the Burn tool.

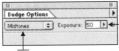

The higher the exposure setting the stronger the tool's effect.

Choose the range of tonality (midtones, highlights, or shadows) to burn or dodge.

cyan and adjust the monitor so that its display matches the printed cyan. Despite these efforts to calibrate monitors so that they accurately preview color, it's just about impossible to attain perfect monitor accuracy. Too many factors affect the way we see color. For example, the type of lighting in the room affects the image. Whereas a monitor preview is an active light source, the color you perceive on a printed page is produced by reflected light. Remember that even though an image has been converted to CMYK, as long as it is being previewed on a monitor you are seeing it as an RGB image. The printing process also plays a role in color accuracy. For instance, press gains commonly occur when printing—in particular, black inks are notorious for gaining density on press. With so many variables influencing color accuracy, it's very difficult to get perfectly accurate color. While you should never accept poor color output, slight color shifts in print are virtually unavoidable.

Most initial scans don't perfectly match the colors found in the original art. While certain scanners

Ghosting Images: Creating Textured Backgrounds

Using images as background textures is a common design approach. These background images can be ghosted back so that they don't interfere with readability or become overly dominant.

Images are often lightened so that they can be used as background textures. Using images in this manner can bring a textural quality to a design.

READABILITY When images are used as background textures they often need to be ghosted back or lightened so that they don't interfere with the readability of the type in the design.

A MATTER OF CHOICE The lightness and quality of the image should be considered before ghosting it. Images with consistent tonality work best. High-contrast images are difficult to ghost because as their dark areas become light enough to accommodate a design, their lighter areas become too light or completely blow out to white.

TEST THE TINT Finding the right lightness for the ghosted image is a matter of experimentation. Create variations of the image with different opacity settings and then print the samples to arrive at the desired effect.

FILE SIZE Because large images slow down performance and increase print time, designers often use low-res images as placeholders when designing and then place the final image when the design is finalized.

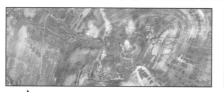

▲
ORIGINAL IMAGE This photo of petrified wood is a good example of an image that can be used as a ghosted texture. Its consistent tone makes it appropriate for a background texture.

LAYER OPACITY Select the entire image and copy and paste it. This will create a new layer and allow its opacity to be adjusted. The opacity of the background layer can't be changed.

Turn off the background layer so it is not visible. Then change the opacity of the new layer. Once the tone is good, flatten and save the image.

Place some type over your image to determine whether it will maintain its readability. Overly dark images can interfere with type.

75% opacity

Place some type over your image to determine whether it will maintain its readability. Overly dark images can interfere with type.

50% opacity

Place some type over your image to determine whether it will maintain its readability. Overly dark images can interfere with type.

30% opacity

and software achieve better color accuracy than others, with some manipulation in Photoshop you should be able to get the image to match the original art pretty closely. There are a wide range of color-correction tools available in Photoshop. Some of these tools offer more control than others, and while many designers have their own preferred techniques for color-correcting, they all basically involve similar procedures. Here's an overview of some of the available tools.

• **Curves** is probably the most accurate way to color-correct an image. The downside of using Curves is the graphical interface needed to adjust color information, which appears complicated and intimidating to first-time users. Using Curves involves some understanding of input and output ratios as well as how to manipulate color as it applies to shadow, midtones, and highlights.

• **Levels** is another method for correcting color. Like Curves, its interface is a little difficult to get used to at first. It allows adjustments to be made to an entire image or to its separate color

Tombstones: Opacity and Selections

Specific image areas can be ghosted back in order to place type above them and still maintain readability. While this technique can be effective, it can sometimes look like the last act of a desperate designer trying to find a way to get readable type. Tint boxes that are placed over images to accommodate type are referred to as tombstones.

METHOD ONE

Opacity can be applied to layers, not to the background.

Create a new layer and then make a selection on the layer and fill with white.

New layer

When the selection is filled with white, the opacity of the layer can be adjusted to give the effect of ghosting a specific area. Once you achieve the desired effect, flatten the image layers and save.

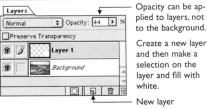

Here a ghosted tombstone is placed in the corner of the layout, allowing the image to bleed off the page while maintaining type readability.

METHOD TWO

This method is a little more involved but gives better results. Begin by making two copies of the original image.

Place a white layer behind the layer copies so that changes in opacity are easier to see. It is difficult to judge opacity settings using the checkered background.

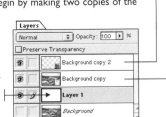

On this layer make a selection of the area to lighten. Then inverse the selection and delete the surrounding image area. Adjust the opacity setting to ghost the area.

On this layer select the same area and delete it from the image to create a hole in the layer. This area will be filled in by the above layer plates. It also allows specific tonal ranges to be adjusted separately.

• **Color Balance** provides similar controls as curves and levels with a different interface approach.

• **Brightness and Contrast** is simple to use but really not recommended for color-correcting. This technique offers limited controls, and the effects can only be applied to an image globally.

• **Variations** uses a visual approach to allowing designers to adjust an image's color. It is the most intuitive approach to color correction. Unlike Curves and Levels, which technically graph an image's color profile, Variations displays the image in a series of thumbnail variations. These thumbnail previews show the effects of incrementally changing specific color information. The color saturation of each specific plate (CMYK) can be increased or reduced.

What's the Diagnosis?

Before actually starting to color-correct an image, you need to first diagnose the overall adjustments that need to be made. Which colors in the scanned image aren't consistent with the original art? Is the image overly light or dark? Are the midtones too dominant, giving the image an overall gray cast? Most

---

Silhouetted Images: Clipping Paths

Clipping paths allow objects to be silhouetted and placed into a layout without a background. Silhouetted objects can add dimension and depth to a design.

To silhouette an image so that its background appears to be clipped away, you need to create a clipping path in Photoshop.

MASTERING THE PEN Creating clipping paths for detailed objects requires a high level of technical expertise using the pen tool.

THE PATH'S PURPOSE Clipping paths are intended to clip the object away from its background. The background imagery surrounding the object does not need to be deleted for the object to appear silhouetted in the Quark layout.

CHOOSE THE RIGHT TOOL Clipping paths are best created in Photoshop. While Quark Xpress offers the ability to create clipping paths, its low-resolution preview makes creating an accurate clipping path difficult.

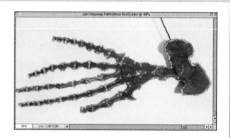

BUILDING THE PATH Start by zooming in close to the image and place points along the object's edge with the pen tool. Make sure that the path's points fall exactly on the object's edge; otherwise the silhouette will not be clean and the background will be visible in Quark.

---

scanners have their own peculiar tendencies in how they scan images. For instance, a scanner might tend to consistently produce images with magenta casts. Once you become familiar with a particular scanner's tendencies you can begin to adjust your images accordingly.

Having analyzed the scan, you can begin to optimize the image. Just as there are many color-correction tools, there are numerous ways to approach adjusting an image's color. Sometimes the most obvious way to color-correct an

image is not always the best method to use. Analyzing an image's makeup and understanding how color separations actually work will help you arrive at the best solution. For instance, the most obvious approach for correcting an image that visually appears to have too much magenta would be to reduce the amount of magenta. But depending on the overall density of an image, it can sometimes be more effective to increase the cyan, yellow, and black information and leave the magenta as it is.

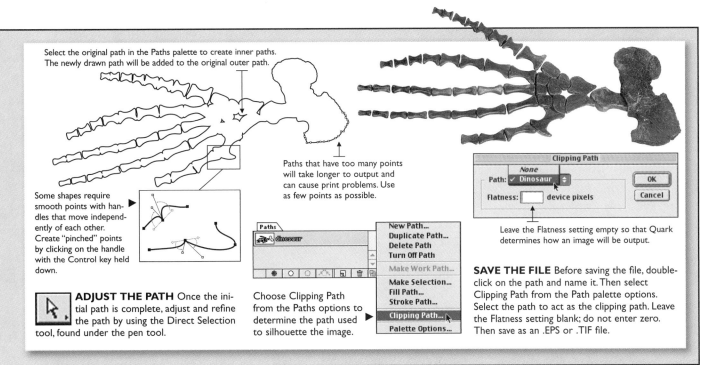

Select the original path in the Paths palette to create inner paths. The newly drawn path will be added to the original outer path.

Paths that have too many points will take longer to output and can cause print problems. Use as few points as possible.

Some shapes require smooth points with handles that move independently of each other. Create "pinched" points by clicking on the handle with the Control key held down.

ADJUST THE PATH Once the initial path is complete, adjust and refine the path by using the Direct Selection tool, found under the pen tool.

Choose Clipping Path from the Paths options to determine the path used to silhouette the image.

Leave the Flatness setting empty so that Quark determines how an image will be output.

SAVE THE FILE Before saving the file, double-click on the path and name it. Then select Clipping Path from the Path palette options. Select the path to act as the clipping path. Leave the Flatness setting blank; do not enter zero. Then save as an .EPS or .TIF file.

Light, Not White

Generally you don't want to change an image's color in an extreme fashion. For instance, when you are adjusting highlight information, make sure that no area within the image becomes pure white (0C 0M 0Y 0K). Images should never fall out to the page white, and there should always be some tone in the highlight. The same is true for adjusting an image's shadows. Shadows should not be adjusted so that large areas become solid black—you don't want the shadow information to lose its detail. Images that have some tone in their highlights and some detail in the shadows will look best when printed.

Sharpening Images

Like color correction, almost all scanned images require some sharpening. Most scanners will soften the edges found within an image to some degree. To sharpen an image you need to apply the Unsharp Mask filter. This can be confusing, as you might consider using the Sharpen filters instead. The Unsharp Mask filter is the most effective way to sharpen an image. Like most filters, it uses edge detection to determine how to adjust an image. When Unsharp Mask is applied it scans the image looking for quick shifts in tonal values, which it perceives as an edge. Based on these tonal shifts, the software sharpens the image. Before applying the filter, set the view magnification to 100 percent and preview an area that has obvious edges. This will allow you to more accurately judge the filter's effect. Overapplying the Unsharp Mask filter will produce unnatural halos, white pixellated outlines that appear around objects in the image. As with all filters, apply less than you need, as you can always add to the effect later.

Previously Printed Images

Design students often create projects using images that have already appeared in print. Previously printed images have copyright protection, and using them for profit is an infringement of those rights, as well as being an unethical and illegal practice.

Professional designers very often have the luxury of commissioning original art for their designs. This original work comes in the form of photographic transparencies and original pieces of artwork from illustrators. But even professional designers are sometimes supplied with prescreened artwork to design their projects with, and getting such images to look their best can be a difficult task.

Removing Halftones

Any image that has been previously printed, whether full color or black and white, is composed of a dot pattern. These dot patterns are referred to as halftones, and these patterns greatly affect the reproduction quality of the image scan.

Removing the halftone dots from an image is a difficult task, and while there are a few approaches to doing this, none of them is entirely successful. Some scanning software offers descreening capabilities, but these are generally ineffective. Other methods include scanning the prescreened artwork at different angles on the flatbed to reduce the obviousness of the dot pattern. You can also experiment with changing the actual screen angles used to output the image, but this approach could introduce new, more serious problems and should probably not be attempted unless you clearly understand how separations and screen angles work. The best approach for scanning in previously screened images is to use images that have been finely printed on quality paper. These images are least likely to show the dot pattern.

Dodging and Burning

So far we have discussed ways of applying color-correction techniques to an entire image. In some cases a scanned image may have specific areas that require adjustment. One method that allows you to selectively adjust the tonality of a specified area is Dodging and Burning. Photoshop's Dodge and Burn tools are designed to emulate traditional darkroom techniques, which involve controlling the amount of light that affects an area of a print while it's being exposed. Traditionally photographers would use dodging tools to block areas of light when exposing photographic paper. The area that was exposed to less light would print lighter. Traditional burn tools, often a board with a hole cut out of it, allow additional light to be applied to the exposed paper. This additional light causes the affected area to print darker. Photoshop's Dodge tool is used to lighten areas within an image, and its Burn tool is used to darken areas. The best way to use these tools is to apply them using a soft brush so that the effect is applied gradually to the image.

Increasing Resolution

Occasionally you may be supplied with images whose resolution is not high enough for print quality. This is more common as clients provide Web images for print projects, unaware of the different demands of each medium. While this is not an optimal situation, depending on the size of the supplied art, there may be a work-around to this problem. While, as a rule, resolution can never be increased in Photoshop, there is one method that will allow an image's resolution to be increased without sacrificing image quality. The downside of this method is that the image's print size will be reduced as its resolution increases.

Every image has a fixed amount of information, which can be applied to different sizings. How this fixed amount of image information is sized will result in varying levels of quality. Generally for four-color projects, you want all of your images to have a resolution of 300 dpi when sized at 100 percent. When you increase an image's print size or resolution in Photoshop (with resample selected) it increases the file size by adding new image information. The additional pixels that Photoshop adds to increase the size actually reduce the quality of the image. Photoshop does not do a good job of extrapolating, or adding the pixel information necessary to enlarge an image.

You can increase an image's resolution without actually changing the image's original file size by applying the fixed amount of information in the file to a different size. For instance, a two-by-two-inch image with a resolution

Tinted Backgrounds & Drop Shadows

Silhouetted objects with shadows that are designed to be placed over tint boxes in Quark must have matching tints created in Photoshop.

When a silhouetted object has a drop shadow that is positioned so that it falls over both a background tint and the page white, the object, its shadow, and the background tint must be merged in Photoshop.

Tint in Quark matches layer tint in Photoshop

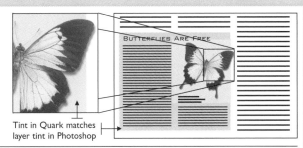
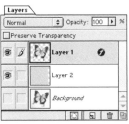

LAYER ONE Begin by creating a path around the object and then making a selection based upon the path. Then copy and paste the selected butterfly into its own layer. This will place the butterfly image on a layer that has a transparent background.

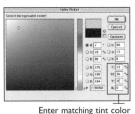

LAYER TWO Create a new empty layer and build a tint box whose color matches the background color in the Quark layout. Place the tint box so that the butterfly overlaps its edge the same way it does in the Quark layout.

Enter matching tint color

ADD DROP SHADOW Once the background tint has been created, select layer one and create a drop shadow that falls behind the butterfly. The drop shadow should be positioned so that it falls over both the background tint and the page white.

MATCHING TINTS When outputting to high-end print devices, the tints created in Photoshop and Quark will match seamlessly. These same tints may not match on lower-end color printers. This can be solved by creating the entire tint in the Photoshop file.

Soft Drop Shadows for Images

Soft drop shadows can be created and then placed behind images to give the illusion that the image is sitting above the page.

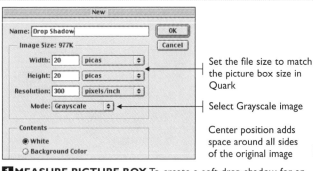

Set the file size to match the picture box size in Quark

Select Grayscale image

Center position adds space around all sides of the original image

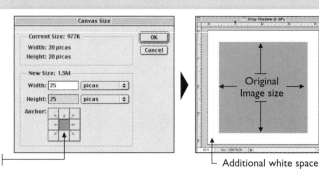

Original Image size

Additional white space

1 MEASURE PICTURE BOX To create a soft drop shadow for an image, begin by taking note of the size of your picture box in the Quark layout. The picture box size can be found on the Measurement palette. Don't build the shadow until the design is finalized and the picture box is set. Changing the picture box size requires rebuilding the shadow.

2 MATCHING IMAGE FILE Create a new Photoshop file that matches the size of the picture box in Quark. In this example the picture box in the Quark layout measures twenty picas deep by twenty picas wide.

3 FILL WITH GRAY Select all and fill the image area with 30% black.

4 CREATE BUFFER SPACE Enlarge the Canvas Size so that additional space is added around all four sides of the original gray-filled area. Canvas Size is located under the Image pull-down menu. Enlarging each side by five picas should be sufficient. The new canvas size will be 25 picas by 25 picas. The space that is added will be filled with the current background color. In this case the current background color is white, and this produces a gray rectangle surrounded by a white background.

---

of 150 dpi can be resized to become a one-by-one-inch image with a resolution of 300 dpi. The resolution is doubled while the image's print size is reduced by 50 percent. In both cases, the file size remains consistent; the information is simply reapplied to a smaller size. This can be done by changing the image size while the Resample Image button is unselected.

Before increasing the image's resolution, take note of what the file size is. Notice that the file size remains unchanged after the resolution is applied to a different file size. Once the resolution is high enough for print quality, as long as the size is not too small, the image can be used. Sometimes to accommodate the requirements of a design a balance must be reached between an image's print size and its resolution. What this means is that if an image's print size is too small at 300 dpi, its resolution could be lowered to 266

dpi without any appreciable loss in image quality. This change in resolution would result in an increase in the image's print size. In some cases images with slightly lower resolutions may output acceptably. For projects destined to be finally output on a local color inkjet or laser printer, lower-resolution settings may also work. Despite this, using lower-resolution images remains a risky practice and should be avoided whenever possible.

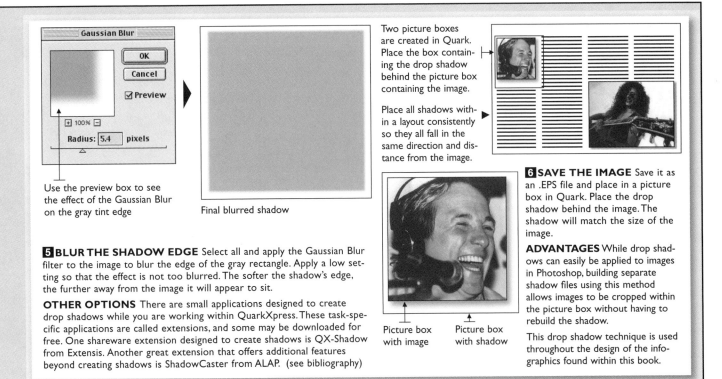

Gaussian Blur

OK

Cancel

☑ Preview

⊞ 100% ⊟

Radius: 5.4 pixels

Use the preview box to see the effect of the Gaussian Blur on the gray tint edge

Final blurred shadow

Two picture boxes are created in Quark. Place the box containing the drop shadow behind the picture box containing the image.

Place all shadows within a layout consistently so they all fall in the same direction and distance from the image.

5 BLUR THE SHADOW EDGE Select all and apply the Gaussian Blur filter to the image to blur the edge of the gray rectangle. Apply a low setting so that the effect is not too blurred. The softer the shadow's edge, the further away from the image it will appear to sit.

OTHER OPTIONS There are small applications designed to create drop shadows while you are working within QuarkXpress. These task-specific applications are called extensions, and some may be downloaded for free. One shareware extension designed to create shadows is QX-Shadow from Extensis. Another great extension that offers additional features beyond creating shadows is ShadowCaster from ALAP. (see bibliography)

Picture box with image

Picture box with shadow

6 SAVE THE IMAGE Save it as an .EPS file and place in a picture box in Quark. Place the drop shadow behind the image. The shadow will match the size of the image.

ADVANTAGES While drop shadows can easily be applied to images in Photoshop, building separate shadow files using this method allows images to be cropped within the picture box without having to rebuild the shadow.

This drop shadow technique is used throughout the design of the infographics found within this book.

Common Imaging Techniques

Once an image has been formatted and color-corrected there are any number of imaging techniques that can be applied to it. Remember that the final image is dependent upon the quality of the initial image. This means that before applying any other imaging techniques, an image should first be optimized. As the saying goes: garbage in, garbage out. Imaging techniques will not improve the overall quality of the image, so it's important to first take the time to get the scanned image looking its best.

With the introduction of digital technologies and desktop publishing to graphic design many professional photographers became interested in integrating these new digital techniques. Photographers who were experts in darkroom techniques like burning and dodging and masking were fascinated by the possibilities of digital imaging. For some photographers, the transition from traditional photography to digital techniques was smooth. Some experienced a change in their work's direction. But some photographers fell into the trap of thinking an image can be fixed in the computer. Rather than take the time to meticulously compose and light a photo, they began to take inferior images, figuring that they could be adjusted later in digital form. This led to decreased quality in their

Creating Drop Shadows for Type

Soft drop shadows can also be created for display type in Photoshop and then brought into your Quark design.

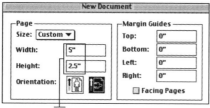

1 DESIGN DISPLAY TYPE Begin by designing a type treatment in Quark. All sizing and kerning of the type should be finalized before building the shadow. The shadow that is created will be based upon this typographic design. Fill the type with a middle-value gray.

New Document dialog:
- Page Size: Custom
- Width: 5"
- Height: 2.5"
- Orientation
- Margin Guides — Top: 0", Bottom: 0", Left: 0", Right: 0"
- Facing Pages

Create custom page size.

2 CUSTOM PAGE SIZE Create the original type design on a custom-sized page that is slightly larger than the type design requires. The type could also be designed on a larger page and then copied to a smaller custom page before going to the next step.

Specify the page to save, its color mode, and its size. Save at 100% so that the shadow created in Photoshop matches the size of the type in Quark.

3 SAVE THE PAGE Save it with the .EPS format in Quark by selecting Save Page as EPS from the File pull-down menu. Select the page to save as an .EPS file and output as a grayscale image. This will rasterize the page and make it an image file that can be opened in Photoshop.

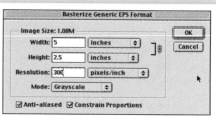

4 RASTERIZING THE EPS In order for the Quark .EPS file to be opened in Photoshop, it must first be rasterized into an image file. This will convert the page data into pixels. Rasterize the file into a grayscale format with a resolution of 300 dpi.

Once the Quark .EPS file has been rasterized and opened in Photoshop, it can be used to create a shadow for the type in Quark. The type that appears in the rasterized file is composed of pixels, not an actual font.

work. Just as it takes years to master certain darkroom techniques and to find a sense of personal style, the same holds true for mastering digital imaging techniques.

The remaining part of this chapter addresses common ways to treat your imagery once it has been color-corrected, sized, and formatted properly. It also includes suggestions as to how to adapt these techniques to meet a design's specific needs.

Avoiding Packaged Effects

Photoshop provides a diverse range of filters, many of which create showy and dramatic effects. The effects that these filters can have upon an image is always impressive to first-time users, and young designers are understandably drawn to them. While they appear to offer a fast way to a creative solution, strong original

5 BLUR THE SHADOW To give the edges of the type softness, select the entire image and then apply the Gaussian Blur filter.

6 SAVE THE FILE Once the shadow is created, it can then be saved as a Photoshop .EPS file, brought into a picture box in Quark, and placed behind the original type. Make sure to flatten the image before saving the file.

COLOR OPTIONS Shadows aren't limited to grayscale formats. Shadows with tinted colors can also be effective. To do this, specify a color in the original Quark type, save that page as .EPS, and then rasterize the page to a CMYK format.

Adjust the zoom magnification settings and pan around within the preview window to see the filter's effect on the type's edges.

Original type design

Drop shadow created in Photoshop

Drop shadow placed behind type design

design requires more than simply applying filters to achieve splashy effects. A designer's job is to find interesting ways to incorporate these filters in order to augment a design. Use effects when they are appropriate and the design project calls for it.

One general rule is to never use an effect simply for the sake of using it. Over the course of their careers, designers are continually learning and being introduced to new techniques. While it is understandable to want to find a way to use a newly discovered technique,

good designers store away this information until an appropriate project comes along where they can incorporate it.

Finding Your Own Style
While the number of filters available to designers can be tempting,

Using Quark .EPS Files to Simplify Image Placement

Using Quark .EPS files to preview a page layout in Photoshop can help accurately position images. This technique is especially useful for complex image arrangements,

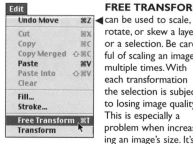

Drag out the rulers from the rulers for precise placement of images.

FREE TRANSFORM can be used to scale, rotate, or skew a layer or a selection. Be careful of scaling an image multiple times. With each transformation the selection is subject to losing image quality. This is especially a problem when increasing an image's size. It's best to figure out exactly how much scaling an image needs and transform it once.

PAGE PREVIEW Being able to view a page layout in Photoshop allows images to be more easily and accurately positioned. Save the Quark page as an .EPS file and then open it in Photoshop. Since the original page size determines the image file size, the final rasterized file in Photoshop is often large.

IMAGE PLACEMENT Once the page layout preview is opened in Photoshop, the images that are used within the page layout can be placed into the file by copying and pasting them in as layers. These image layers can then be resized, cropped, and positioned according to the layout.

COMPLEX ARRANGEMENTS Using a page preview as a positioning device is useful for designs with multiple or overlapping images or when images need to be placed in odd-shaped spaces. When the image positioning is finalized, delete the page preview layer, flatten, and save the file.

the real challenge with filters is finding original ways to use them. Filters that are applied to images in unoriginal ways produce predictable generic effects. The key is to find an original approach to manipulating images. Developing a personal style is a key challenge for young designers and is usually the result of experimentation and discipline. Having an understanding of how each tool and filter works is essential to developing a style that can be controlled.

Because of the complex ways in which filters process an image's visual information, the same filter can have very different effects depending on the type of image that it's being applied to. Some filters require images that contain linear edges for their full effect to be seen. Others filters work best with high-contrast images. One approach to experimenting with filters for the first time is to apply them to a series of images that have different qualities. These might include an image that contains type, one composed of geometric shapes, and another with organic forms. Since filter effects also vary according to an image's color information, try applying the filters to images with different types of color palettes. Applying the same filter to a range of images will lead to an enhanced understanding of how best to use a filter. Taking the time to understand how each filter setting works is essential. Once you have a clear idea of how a filter (or any tool) works, you can start considering how they can be used in tandem with each other. While arbitrary experimentation may sometimes result in a successful effect, this is more often a matter of luck than intention. It takes discipline to learn the power of each filter and creative intuition to develop a style of one's own. While experimentation can certainly lead to happy accidents, these strokes of luck are useful only when you understand how the results were achieved and are able to recreate them. While happy accidents are certainly part of the creative process, they are the exception rather than the rule.

Common Imaging Techniques

There are a series of basic imaging techniques that designers commonly use to treat their photos. These techniques, found throughout contempo-

Feathering Images

A common way to style images is to feather their edges. This will give the photograph a soft, blurred border.

Begin by selecting the entire image and copying and pasting it. A new layer will be created when the selection is pasted. Feathering can only be applied to a selection or layer.

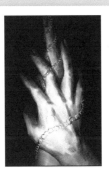

Create a new layer filled with white and place it behind the layer being feathered. This helps reveal the effects of the feathering on the image edge.

New Layer

 On the new layer select a section of the image to feather. Select the Feather function from the Select pull-down menu and adjust the feather settings. The selection marquee will have rounded corners after feathering.

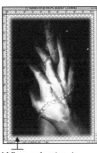

When selection is inverted, the outer area is selected.

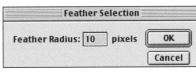

The higher the feather setting, the softer the edge will appear. For most images feathering usually works best at lower settings.

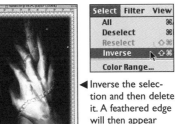

◄ Inverse the selection and then delete it. A feathered edge will then appear around the image.

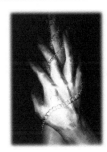

Final image has soft feathered edge.

This technique works best with images that have edges with consistent solid tones. The softness doesn't work well when the image edges are too light.

Because this technique is easy to achieve, it has become popular almost to the point of being overused in design. While it can be an effective way to style images, be careful how often you use it.

Creating Natural Shadows

Applying shadows to silhouetted objects that appear to naturally fall into the distance can be created by using paths and transforming selections.

Rather than using the shadows that are actually found in an original photograph, objects are often silhouetted with paths and then have shadows re-created based on the these paths. This method gives the designer the ability to control the shadow's direction and darkness.

1 SILHOUETTE OBJECT The original image has two shadows, which can be awkward to design with. Begin by creating a path around the object. The wire is not included in the path. Make a selection based on the path and copy and paste it to create a layer with the silhouetted lamp.

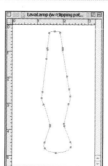

Active path

Active selection

2 Once the object is silhouetted, create another layer and fill it with white. Then make a selection based upon the path by choosing Make Selection from the Path options on the Paths palette.

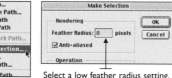

Select a low feather radius setting.

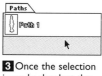

3 Once the selection is made, deselect the path by clicking below it in the Paths palette. It is important that only the selection is active when filling because paths can't be filled.

4 Feather the selection to give it a soft edge.

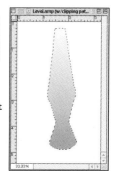

Filled selection

5 GRADIENT FILLS Use these to give the shadow the appearance of fading into the distance. The gradient tints are determined by the current background and foreground colors. Select white and gray as the current colors. Then, with the selection active, use the Gradient tool by dragging it over the selection. A guideline will appear when dragging over the selection with the Gradient tool. This line indicates the gradient's direction as well as its start and end points.

---

rary design, include ghosting, silhouetting, and vignetting images as well as creating soft drop shadows and duotones. The rest of this chapter covers how to perform these techniques and when to use them; it also suggests ways to fine-tune these effects so that they enhance your specific design.

Ghosting Images

One method that designers use to bring a sense of transparency to their images is by "ghosting" them, or lowering their opacity. Ghosting can be applied to an entire image or to specific sections of an image. Ghosting is an effective method when you want to use an image

as a background texture. Lowering an image's opacity allows an image to be lightened so that it does not dominate the layout and type maintains its readability when placed over the image. Ghosting works best with images that are textural and not overly busy.

A common tendency among

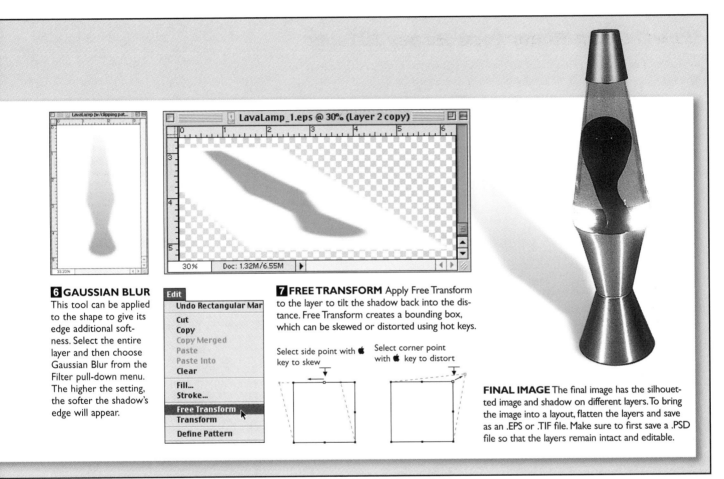

6 GAUSSIAN BLUR
This tool can be applied to the shape to give its edge additional softness. Select the entire layer and then choose Gaussian Blur from the Filter pull-down menu. The higher the setting, the softer the shadow's edge will appear.

Edit
Undo Rectangular Mar
Cut
Copy
Copy Merged
Paste
Paste Into
Clear
Fill...
Stroke...
Free Transform
Transform
Define Pattern

7 FREE TRANSFORM Apply Free Transform to the layer to tilt the shadow back into the distance. Free Transform creates a bounding box, which can be skewed or distorted using hot keys.

Select side point with ⌘ key to skew

Select corner point with ⌘ key to distort

FINAL IMAGE The final image has the silhouetted image and shadow on different layers. To bring the image into a layout, flatten the layers and save as an .EPS or .TIF file. Make sure to first save a .PSD file so that the layers remain intact and editable.

young designers is to not ghost their images back far enough. This often comes from a fear that the image will get lost if it's too light. Ghosted images don't contribute to a design the same way that standard images do. They are meant to bring a sense of tone and texture to a page. A good rule of thumb is to lighten the image more than you think you need to. This is especially true if you don't have a good proofing device and are not sure how densely the design will finally print. It's better to have the image be a little lighter (and not hinder readability) than to have it be too dark and difficult to read.

Ghosting techniques are also employed to lighten specific sections of an image. This is often done to accommodate body copy that is designed to print over an image. These ghosted sections are sometimes referred to as "tombstones." While this technique can be effective, it is often employed as a last

The Cutting Edge: Torn-Paper Effects

Sometimes images can be treated so that they appear as if they have been torn from a magazine or as if the image has been torn apart.

DON'T TEAR THE ART APART Rather than tearing the actual image, use a torn piece of white paper to create the outline shape for the art to appear in. This allows you to experiment with tearing paper into different shapes.

RIP IT UP Scan in a torn piece of white paper. Put the paper on the scanner and place a solid black piece of paper behind it. This will help with making a selection later on.

Black piece of foam core is placed behind torn paper

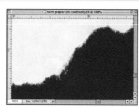

Making a selection is easier if there is high contrast between the paper and the background. Raising the contrast will reduce the background to solid black.

There are many ways to make a selection. Using Color Range to make a selection will capture the nuances of the torn paper's edge. Color Range bases its selection on color information.

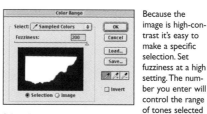

Select the color picker and then click in the white area of the torn paper. Select OK and a selection will appear around the paper.

Because the image is high-contrast it's easy to make a specific selection. Set fuzziness at a high setting. The number you enter will control the range of tones selected within the image.

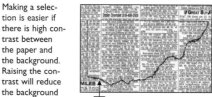

Selection dragged over image

Drag the selection marquee into the image to be cropped into the torn paper shape. Drag the selection marquee over by selecting it with the selection tool.

Once the selection is dragged over the image, inverse the selection to select the area surrounding the torn paper shape and then delete the surrounding area.

Transparent Layer background

Once the area surrounding the torn paper shape is deleted, select Inverse again to get the original selection. Then copy and paste it so it appears on its own transparent layer.

resort, when there is no other viable way to get text to read when its positioned over an image.

Making Selections
One of the keys to many of the imaging techniques covered in this chapter is how a selection is made. Photoshop offers numerous ways to make selections, and the technique you choose depends on the quality of your image. Selections can be made by using functions such as Color Range or with tools like the Magic Wand. While some selection methods are more involved than others, it is helpful to know what options are available.

In many cases the most accurate way to make a selection is to create a path using the pen tool.

DROP SHADOWS Once the image is on its own layer with a transparent background, it can have a drop shadow applied to it. Select the layer and choose the Drop Shadow effect from the Layer pull-down menu.

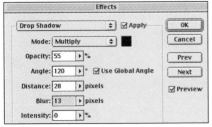

The Drop Shadow effect allows you to specifically control and style the shadow. Angle and Distance control the positioning of the shadow. Blur and Opacity control the lightness and softness of the shadow's edge.

To save the final torn paper and shadow, flatten the layers and save. Save a .PSD file first to maintain layer information in case it requires editing later on.

Similar methods can be applied to multiple torn pieces of paper. The torn sections are positioned on the scanner with a black background behind it

PASTE INTO Another way to paste the image into a selection is to use Paste Into. Create a selection and then copy the image and paste it into the selection.

Final image gives the appearance that one image has been ripped up into numerous sections

make a selection. Images with large areas of similar color information, like a sky, may be best selected by using the Magic Wand or the Color Range settings. Since Color Range bases its selection on a range of specified colors, it is probably the best tool when the image area you want to select shares a similarity of color. In a similar way the Magic Wand makes its selection based on a tolerance setting. Adjusting the range or tolerance settings for either tool expands or contracts the selection accordingly.

Another way to approach making an accurate selection is to begin by making a rough selection with the Lasso or Magic Wand and then converting it to a path so that it can be fine-tuned using the pen tool. Any selection can be converted to an editable path by selecting the Make Work Path option from the Path palette. Once the path surrounds the area that you want to select, it can be converted back into a selection by choosing Make Selection from Path in the Path palette options.

Because of their limited color palettes, there are particular advantages to selecting areas of grayscale and black-and-white images. Because bitmap images consist of

While paths are editable and can be applied to any layer, creating them can be a labor-intensive task. Selections can also be made using the Lasso or the Magic Wand. While these tools may offer quicker results than building a path,

they are more difficult to control and often don't produce accurate selections.

Image quality will directly determine which selection method to use. For some images the Magic Wand can be an effective way to

Scanning Large-Scale Artwork

Standard flatbed scanners generally have small scanning areas. This does not mean that you can't scan in larger pieces of artwork than the scanner can accommodate.

SCANNING IN SECTIONS of artwork whose size is larger than your flatbed scanner will accommodate is the easiest method of getting large images. Begin by scanning in part of the artwork and then scan in a second section. These two images will then be seamlessly integrated to create one larger image file. When scanning in the image make sure that both sections are placed perfectly straight on the flatbed and that both sections are scanned at the same resolution.

Here the size of the original art is larger than the flatbed scanner bed.

Align artwork to the flatbed's edge to scan the artwork straight.

OVERLAPPING SECTIONS Scan the artwork into as many sections as necessary. This image is scanned into two sections. Make sure to scan the image so that both sections of the image have some common overlapping areas. This will help seamlessly align them later.

---

only black or white pixels, selecting specific areas is a quick and simple process. This reduced palette greatly simplifies the selection process. Because a bitmap image's data is either black or white, any tool that makes a selection based upon a color range can be easily used to create an accurate selection.

Vignetting Images

Another technique that is similar to ghosting is vignetting. Vignetting is a process in which images are manipulated so that they gradually fade to white. One example of a vignetted image might be a rectan-

gular image that has one or more of its edges fade out to white. This technique is most effective when used with images which have inactive background areas. It is more difficult to softly vignette an image with busy areas and the effect is often unnatural. Vignetting works best with images that already fade naturally into lighter inactive areas. Vignetting effects require some expertise in manipulating color channels.

Feathering Edges

Feathering images involves softening the border edges of an image. It

is a simple and commonly used technique that involves making a layer selection and then feathering that selection's edges. Feathering is usually most effective when the image edges remain relatively sharp and not overly blurred.

Drop Shadows

Drop shadows are an effective way of bringing depth to a page design. They can be applied to silhouetted or hard-edged images, tint boxes, or type. Like vignetting and feathering, creating drop shadows also involves blurring and softening imagery, and similar rules apply.

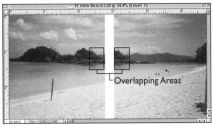

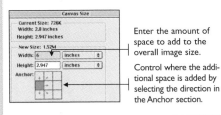

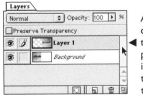

EXPAND CANVAS SIZE to create space for the second section of the image to be placed into. The current background color will fill the new space.

Enter the amount of space to add to the overall image size.

Control where the additional space is added by selecting the direction in the Anchor section.

TWO HALVES Select the second half of the image and copy and paste it into the empty canvas area. The second half is placed on its own layer.

A new layer is created when the section is pasted into the image. Select the new layer to position it.

POSITION THE LAYER Using the Selection tool, move the new layer over the other half until they align accurately. Zoom in close to ensure that the integration of the two images is seamless. When finished, flatten the layers and save the image.

USING VISUAL MARKERS Images can be aligned seamlessly by finding a shared visual marker within the two sections to base their alignment upon. Here the treeline on the edge of the horizon is used to align the sections.

Like feathered edges, drop shadows look most natural when their edges remain relatively sharp. The softer the shadow is, the further away from the page they will make the image appear.

Drop shadows can be applied to numerous design elements, and treating them in a consistent manner will give a design an integrated feel. Since drop shadows imply a light source, all of the drop shadows found within a design should be placed so that they fall in the same direction and to the same relative distance from the element they are placed behind. Drop shadows should also be created using the same settings so that the softness of their edges matches. The best way to do this is to take note of the drop shadow settings when you are originally creating them.

Drop Shadows and Type

Drop shadows can also be applied to display type. While drop shadows can be used simply as a design element to bring depth to a design, they also can be used as a means to increase a type design's readability. This is especially true when type is positioned over an image. Very often a busy background image can compete with the type. Placing a drop shadow between the type and the image can help separate the two elements and push the type to the foreground.

While Photoshop offers many ways to stylize type and its type functionality has been greatly improved in recent versions, it is still preferable to use Quark to design type treatments. A good rule of thumb is that if a type design can be created in Quark, it should be. Illustrator and Photoshop should be used only when a type design requires an effect or feature that can't be achieved in Quark.

While creating soft drop shadows for type is a slightly more involved process than building drop shadows for images, the way in which these shadows are used is similar. While it is generally advisable not to soften the shadows too much, this is especially true for shadows designed to be placed behind type. Overly soft shadows can have a negative effect and actually make type less legible. The typeface you select to apply a drop shadow to is very important. In general, sans serif faces work very well with drop shadows because their stroke widths don't vary as much as is the case with many serif faces. It is more difficult to place a drop shadow behind type that has thick and thin stroke weights.

Accurately Composing Images

Creating .EPS files from your QuarkXpress files is a handy technique that can make placing photos so that they fit accurately into a page's composition a much easier task. Quark .EPS files can be opened in Photoshop to provide a visual page reference so that you don't have to go back and forth between Quark and Photoshop measuring and comparing the image's placement within the page layout. This technique is most useful for layouts

Using 3D Objects: The Scanner as Camera

One way to create original imagery is to use the flatbed scanner to directly scan in three-dimensional objects.

A wide range of objects can be scanned on a flatbed scanner and incorporated into a design. The shape and depth as well as the surface quality of the object will pose different challenges. In some cases the object may need to be scanned with a black or white background cover to improve the scan quality and make its selection easier later on.

DROP SHADOWS can be added to scanned 3D objects once a clipping path is created in Photoshop.

PROTECT THE GLASS from heavy objects by placing a piece of clear acetate over the glass so that the object does not scratch it.

NATURAL OR TECHNICAL objects can be be easily found and scanned in on a flatbed scanner. Larger and deeper objects will not work as well as flatter ones, as they are subject to having sections fall out of focus.

that require images to be placed in odd positions or when multiple images need to be composed in the same file.

Creating Clipping Paths

Silhouetting images is a common and powerful way to handle photographs. They can bring interesting shapes to page layouts, help break up the page grid, and be placed so

that body copy wraps around them. Silhouetted images are created by "clipping" an object away from its background image by building paths in Photoshop. Creating clipping paths is an essential skill for all designers, as paths must be built accurately to work successfully.

Creating clipping paths involves tracing the edges of the object that you want to silhouette with the pen

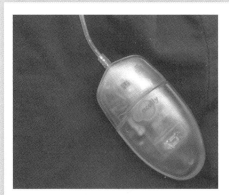

UNDER COVER For some 3D objects it's best to place a black background over the image. This will help to define the object's edges and make creating an accurate path easier.

By the dawn of the twentieth century industrialism had swept its way across the country, leaving nothing untouched in its wake. Seemingly overnight industrialization profoundly changed the face of the nation, influencing every aspect of life. The events that took place between 1885 and 1910 represent the metamorphosis of the country from a society relatively untouched by industrialism to one almost transformed by it. Emphasizing the speed and intensity of industrial advance

Samuel Hays states that "seldom, if ever, in American history had so much been altered within the lifetime of a single man." The accelerated rate of technological progress quickly rendered obsolete everything that had provided meaning for members of preindustrial America. These sudden and unprecedented changes left people disoriented and unable to call on previous experience to help understand their changing surroundings. Religious beliefs were funda-

▲

3D SCANS can be integrated into a layout in many ways. Here a clipping path is created in Photoshop and the mouse is rotated and placed so that it straddles two columns of text.

While a black board can be placed behind flat objects, for objects that have depth a black cloth can be used. Black felt works best.

By the dawn of the twentieth century industrialism had swept its way across the country, leaving nothing untouched in its wake. Seemingly overnight industrialization profoundly changed the face of the nation, influencing every aspect of life. The events

that took place between 1885 and 1910 represent the metamorphosis of the country from a society relatively untouched by industrialism to one almost transformed by it. Emphasizing the speed and intensity of industrial advance Samuel Hays states that "seldom,

IN THEIR OWN WRITE

Urbanization redefined community standards and the rise of the industrial city in the 1880s resulted in the consequential decline of long-standing agrarian ideals. Mass production, which had become a significant characteristic of the American industrial economy by the 1880s, determined how and where Americans worked, as well as redefined .

▲

A SENSE OF DEPTH is achieved by placing a silhouetted three-dimensional object over the edge of the background tint. This positioning makes the object appear as if it is moving back into the distance, and this brings a sense of depth to the layout.

tool. Mastering the pen tool and being able to manipulate paths accurately is essential for both silhouetting and rendering shapes. Quark, Illustrator, and Photoshop all include pen tools, and they generally work in the same way. So once you learn to how to use it in one software package you have essentially learned how to use it in the others.

Many designers find using the pen tool for the first time to be frustrating and awkward. Since its mastery is an essential skill for all designers, it is worth taking the time to learn how to use it properly. The worst thing to do is to avoid using it. For example, in attempting to attain the look of silhouetting an image, many young designer will choose the paint-

brush and try to white out the background so that the image appears clipped. This technique, while it avoids using the pen tool, will not produce good results and the image edge will not look smooth and natural.

There are a few things to keep in mind when creating clipping paths. A path's points should be placed so that they fall slightly

Using the Scanner to Create Custom Textures

Just as any number of three-dimensional objects can be scanned and integrated into a layout, a wide range of actual objects can be scanned for their surface textures.

SCANNING FOR TEXTURE Just about any-thing that can be placed on a scanner bed can be scanned and used as a background texture to augment your designs. While some objects such as wood or cloth are obvious sources for textures, there are many objects that will yield successful and surprising effects.

When scanning in small, fine objects place a piece of glass or acetate over the scanner glass so that the glass doesn't get scratched and the scanner doesn't get damaged.

ABSTRACT TEXTURES There are a wide range of objects that will yield surprising results. The best way to do this is to experiment with textural objects. Try scanning objects at high scale percentages and then cropping into sections to get abstract textures.

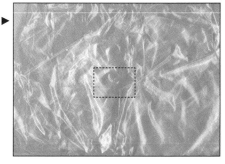

Using glass will allow you to experiment with fine granular textures like sand, salt, spices, or seeds. Even water droplets or cut fruit can be used. Placement of grains can be positioned and controlled to work within your design's layout.

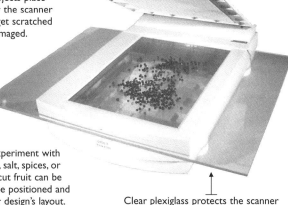

Clear plexiglass protects the scanner

INCOGNITO
Here a plastic bag is scanned and then cropped into. Because only a small section of the original scan is used, the original object is not recog-nizable. Here a soft, flowing texture is the final result.

within the object's area and don't allow any of the background to show through. This will produce cleanly silhouetted objects. The path should move smoothly around the image and use as few points as is possible. Paths with fewer points output more quickly, while those composed of too many points are

subject to output problems.

Once you've learned how to create intricate clipping paths you can begin to use these paths in numerous creative ways. Paths can be applied to any layer and used interchangeably between Illustrator and Photoshop. Selections can be made based on these paths.

From Illustrator to Photoshop

Another great advantage to using paths is that they can be shared between software applications. This means that any path created in Photoshop can be copied into and manipulated in Illustrator and vice versa. This ability to copy and paste paths between applications intro-

Trial & Error: A Textural Sampler

Coming up with original custom textures is often a matter of experimentation. Some objects will yield obvious results while other less obvious objects can produce surprising results.

Denim

Aluminum foil

Flannel

Crushed photocopy

Leather

Spaghetti

Handmade paper

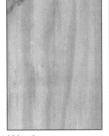
Wood

duces many options and allows designers to take advantage of each application's strengths. By using paths to trace complex images in Photoshop, you can avoid tracing in Illustrator, which in some versions offers a low-resolution preview and has limited autotracing functions. Paths also allow you to take advantage of Illustrator's complex illustration tools and features and create objects and technical renderings that would be difficult to do in Photoshop. Creating elaborate geometric shapes is a much easier task in Illustrator because of its advanced illustration tools. These shapes can then be copied into Photoshop. Building such an involved shape is difficult in Photoshop because of its limited illustration capabilities.

When copying paths between these two programs, there are a few things to consider. When copying from Illustrator to Photoshop, you will choose whether you want to paste the shape into Photoshop as pixels or as a path. If you paste the shape as pixels it will be pasted into its own layer as a raster object. You may want to do this occasionally, but generally the most powerful way to make use of the technique is to paste the shape into the file as a path. Once you do this, you can apply the path to any layer in the file, or make selections based upon the path.

Shadows & Silhouetted Objects

Silhouetted objects can have natural-looking shadows added to them in Photoshop. These shadows can be simple flat shadows or can be manipulated so that they fall into the distance, giving the object the appearance of sitting on a surface. These complex shadows recede into the distance and give the object a sense of lighting. While creating receding shadows can be a more involved process than building flat shadows, either shadow type begins

Layering Type & Silhouetted Images

Placing silhouetted objects so that they sit in front of display type is a technique that is commonly used on magazine cover designs.

Placing type so that it appears to sit between an object and its background involves silhouetting images using paths, working with and positioning separate layers, and creating the display type treatment in Illustrator and then pasting it into Photoshop.

This method is most commonly used on magazine covers, where portraits are positioned so that they overlap the magazine's masthead. This often requires very complex clipping paths to be created so that the type falls naturally behind the portrait's hair.

The key to this technique is the positioning of each layer on the Layers list. Each element within the design should be placed on its own layer and then positioned so that it gives the proper effect.

ORIGINAL IMAGE A path is drawn around the head of the man using the pen tool. Then make a selection based on the path by choosing Make Selection from the Path palette options.

SILHOUETTED IMAGE Deselect the path before copying the selection. Copy and paste the selection of the man's head. A new layer with a transparent background is created when the image is pasted.

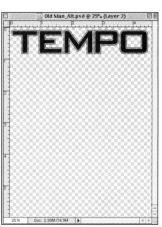

DISPLAY TYPE Create the display type in Illustrator and then copy and paste it into Photoshop. Paste the type as pixels so that it appears on its own transparent layer. Size the type design in Illustrator before copying.

with building accurate paths.

Very often designers will re-create shadows using the methods covered in this text rather than using the actual shadows found in the original photograph. Re-creating shadows, rather than using the shadows found in an image, provides the designer with more layout options. Since objects are commonly photographed using multiple light sources, they often have multiple shadows. These complex shadows can sometimes be hard to design with, whereas custom-made shadows can be shortened or extended to fit within the spaces dictated by the layout. The density and color of the shadows can also be specifically controlled. One thing to keep in mind when building shadows is to place them so that they accurately reflect the original light source and direction used to photograph the image.

Torn Paper Effects

Another technique that takes advantage of paths and path selections is creating the effect of torn paper, in which a piece of previously printed material is made to look as if it has been torn directly from a magazine or newspaper. While you could actu-

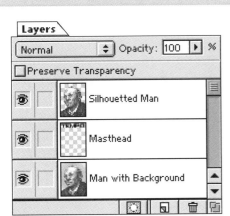

POSITION LAYERS The three layers should be positioned on the Layers palette in the appropriate order. The lower a layer falls on the Layers list, the further back it will appear. Place the original image in the back. Then place the type layer in front of the original image and the silhouetted layer on top to give the impression that the type sits between the man's head and the background.

FINAL IMAGE is flattened and then saved.

The Scanner as Camera

Besides being used to scan in photographs and produce sharp color images, scanners can be used in many diverse ways. Try thinking of the scanner more in terms of a camera than as a standard input device. Too often the creative possibilities offered by a scanner are overlooked. Just as you don't want the computer or the software to limit you as a designer, the way you use a scanner doesn't have to limit you. Designers have long known about the powerful creative results that can be produced using machines that are not typically thought of as design tools, such as photocopy machines. Scanners can be approached in the same manner.

Thinking Different

We rarely consider alternative ways of employing the machines and devices that we use on a day-to-day basis. This unquestioning approach and blind acceptance of how to use standard tools is limiting. Often students designing on a computer tend to limit their projects to standard-sized formats like letter and tabloid sizes and rarely consider odd-shaped or larger formats. The similar tendency also applies to how designers approach

ally tear the artwork from the page it was originally printed upon, you risk not tearing the paper properly and ruining the artwork. This is especially dangerous if you only have one copy of the original artwork. One method that is less risky and offers much more control is to tear pieces of blank paper into interesting shapes, scan them, and then paste a scan of the original art into

the torn paper shape. This allows you to try different torn shapes without affecting the original art. Once you have a torn shape that you like, place it on the scanner with a black sheet of paper behind it. This helps clearly define the torn paper's edge and makes the selection process easier. You can also experiment using different paper stocks, like newsprint, which has a grain.

Fade Away: Creating Vignetted Images

Vignetting images so that part of an image gradually fades out to white is an easy task when using layer masks.

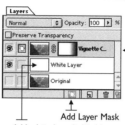

When layer masks are created they appear linked to the layer. Either the layer or the layer mask can be selected. To create the vignette make sure to select the layer mask.

Add Layer Mask

Add white layer behind image to see vignette's effect

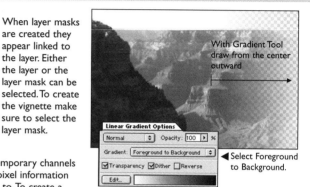

With Gradient Tool draw from the center outward

Select Foreground to Background.

ORIGINAL IMAGE Vignetting works best with images that are not too busy or high-contrast. This image of the Grand Canyon naturally fades out to the right. Begin by copying and pasting the entire image into a new layer. This will allow a layer mask to be built.

LAYER MASKS These are temporary channels that can be used to mask out pixel information from the image they are linked to. To create a layer mask, select the Add Layer Mask button at the bottom of the Layers menu and the mask will appear on the Layers palette.

APPLY GRADIENT Select the layer mask and draw a line with the Gradient tool that extends from the image center outward to its edge. The beginning and end points as well as the length of the line determine the gradient.

using a scanner. There is a tendency is to accept the scanner as a limited input device rather than considering alternative ways to use it. Understandably, scanner use is generally limited to scanning in flat artwork, but scanners can also be used in much more creative ways.

Thinking Big
Scanners can be used to scan pieces of art that are larger than their flat bed. Conversely, scanners can be used to enlarge tiny sections of an image to create abstract patterns and textures.

Working with a piece of art whose size is larger than the bed requires scanning the art in separate sections and then piecing them together in Photoshop. While this is relatively easy to do, the process can require a lot of memory because of the size of the images being worked with. Closing out images once you no longer need them can help speed up performance. Purging the clipboard will also help free up memory.

Thinking in 3D
A great way to create original imagery is to use the scanner to scan in three-dimensional objects. A little experimentation can yield very creative results. While many types of objects can be used, flat objects generally work best, for obvious reasons. You can take a point-and-click approach to scanning in 3D objects or a much more controlled approach. Either way can produce quality results.

There are a few things you can do to enhance your scans and make

FINAL IMAGE Vignettes can be applied to images that are placed within picture boxes or to silhouetted objects. They can be an effective way to give depth to a layout as well as place emphasis on particular areas within an image. Here the vignette directs the eye across the page and helps the type maintain its readability.

working with them easier. For some objects, try placing a piece of black material, preferably felt, over the object on the flatbed. This reduces the amount of light that bounces off the object being scanned. The black background also helps to define the object's edge, which is especially helpful when clipping paths need to be created.

Placing objects on a flatbed scanner can scratch the glass. One way to protect the glass is to place a sheet of clear acetate over it. For heavier objects you might try using a piece of plexiglass. Plexiglass can also be used to scan in wet or granular substances.

Because of their depth, rounded objects are more subject to having their edges fall out of focus when scanned. This creates a depth of field, which, depending on the desired image quality, can also be beneficial. This depth of field can be further enhanced by propping up or holding objects in place while being scanned.

There are so many ways to build upon these scanning techniques. Try introducing secondary light sources to backlight your object. This is sometimes used when scanning in objects that are transparent. Another technique involves building an exterior box out of foam core that allows you to more specifically control the lighting. Experiment moving flat art or objects across the scanner as the scan light moves across it. This will result in a blurring effect.

These are just a few alternative approaches to using flatbed scanners. Once you start thinking in these terms, you'll find that there are countless ways to use a scanner, or any machine, to perform tasks it normally wouldn't be asked to do, and achieve interesting and original results.

Scanning for Texture

Scanning in actual materials is an effective way to create background textures and patterns. Any number of things can used, including fabrics, leather, burlap, marble, aluminum foil, leaves, or wood. Fabrics and soft materials can be scanned flat or draped over themselves to add variety to their surface texture. Using scans of handmade paper can give a design the appearance of being printed on a custom paper stock. Materials with reflective and translucent surfaces, such as glass, aluminum foil or plastic bags, reflect light in random ways and can produce abstract effects.

Summary

Image preparation is an important part of any project. Images that are sized, formatted, and color-corrected properly help to maximize the impact a design has as well as ensure that the image will output properly. The imaging techniques covered in this chapter represent many of the basic ways to stylize images, but there are an endless number of possibilities. Take the time to master the tools and develop a sensitive touch to the way you treat photography, and before you know it you'll be developing your own techniques.

Chapter Six
Illustrating Effectively

Another of the basic skills that is required in graphic design is being able to illustrate simple graphics using Illustrator. While designers are rarely required to have full-fledged illustrator skills, they all need the ability to create basic graphics for use in their designs. The same applies to designers and type. While all designers are required to cre-

ate type treatments and designs, very few design actual fonts or logotypes. While there are many areas of design that require specialized skills, all designers require a basic skill set, and illustrating effectively is one of them. Many of the tools and techniques used for designing typographic treatments also apply to creating technical illustrations.

Many young designers who are interested in doing layouts often resist creating their own illustrations. Perhaps this arises from the fact that the need for good hand skills has diminished with the advent of the computer in design. However, being able to create technical illustrations, tables, and charts can make you a more versatile designer. For young designers with a fear of drawing, this chapter will introduce you to basic tech-

niques that will simplify the illustration process and enable you to create attractive graphics, in many cases without having to draw them in a traditional sense.

Many of the techniques here provide a foundation for how to create a wide range of objects. One of the things stressed throughout the chapter is thinking in terms of building shapes rather than drawing or painting them. One of the most important parts of illustration is understanding how to approach particular illustration tasks. Since there is almost always more than one way to illustrate a particular object, taking some time to think through your approach before you begin will save you time and eliminate the frustration that comes with having to redo the illustration later. Sometimes what may initial-

ly seem to be the most obvious and direct method is not the best approach. Short cuts are fine as long as they yield the results you are looking for, but if they require substantial tweaking, it may be better to use another method. This is often the case with seemingly complex shapes. Whereas drawing the shape from scratch using the pen tool is certainly the most obvious and direct approach, it often takes less time to create the object by building it using simple shapes and applying Pathfinder filters. It will save you a lot of time and effort if you first understand how you are going reach a desired end before you begin.

Using Your Head
Anyone can draw accurately as long as he or she is willing to focus on the subject. You may never become a master draftsman, but you will be able to accurately represent the objects you need to. Using some common sense and a few basic rules in your approach to drawing will help immensely.

Common Sense
The first rule to remember is that objects get smaller when they appear in the distance. This means if you are creating a three-quarter

view of an object with wheels, the size of the wheels in the back will be smaller than those in the front. Another basic thing to remember is that an object's color becomes grayer and less brilliant as it falls further back into the distance. Another technique that you can use when creating complex shapes is to break the object down into its basic underlying shapes. This is very much in line with the technique that the painter Paul Cézanne used. He saw complex forms in terms of cubes, spheres, and cylinders. Reducing a complex shape in this manner helps you to visualize a way of building it.

Visual Reference

The last of these commonsense approaches, and perhaps the most important, is to use visual reference materials when creating recognizable objects. Unless you are intimately familiar with the object you are illustrating, you will need something to refer to. Reference material provides the visual details that make an illustration appear accurate. Of course, there are some simple objects whose shapes require no reference material to create them. For example, a football has a familiar shape that could be rendered accurately without visual reference

so long as it is being drawn in profile and without a high level of detail.

Once you have reference material, tracing also becomes an option. While tracing objects can be effec-

tive, it is a technique that should be used with some discretion. In some ways tracing can be construed as copying. It depends on how the tracing is used. If you are tracing a generic image of a landscape and

Simple Illustration Approaches

Here are a few commonsense guidelines that will help you realistically illustrate objects that have volume and sit in proper perspective to one another.

You don't have to be a master draftsman to illustrate successfully. Even with limited drawing skills you can render objects accurately if you follow a few simple rules.

INTO THE DISTANCE A few things happen to objects as they are placed in the distance. Most obvious is that the further into the distance an object falls, the smaller it becomes, but color and detail are also affected. The brilliance of color tends to become grayer as it moves into the background, and the amount of detail is also reduced.

DETAILS, DETAILS Here the glass in the foreground has highlights along its edges. Notice that the further back the glass is placed, the less detailed the illustration becomes. The object's line weights also get thinner accordingly.

SHADES OF GRAY You can get a real sense of distance by controlling the amount of gray in the glasses as they fall into the distance. Notice how the glass in the background becomes grayer as it falls into the distance. Gradients can also be used to create a sense of space. The background gradient shifts in shade to give a sense of depth.

BUILD, DON'T DRAW Drawing complex shapes from scratch using the pen tool can be a daunting task if you have limited drawing skills. Building shapes by breaking the object into its component shapes and combining them is often quicker and easier.

As the glasses fall further into the distance they lose detail and become grayer.

then filling the traced shapes with flat color to create an illustration, there is really no problem. In this case, the original image that is being traced is used as reference material. You are not directly copy-ing an original piece of art and then calling it your own, which is con-sidered illegal use. An example of this would be tracing over an exist-ing illustration found in a magazine and using it as if it were your own. The best way to use tracing is to create the basic shapes and then to reshape and change these shapes so that your illustration takes on an original look.

If you are going to trace an

KEEP IT SIMPLE Drawing people can be a difficult task. One way to handle this is to render them graph-ically. Here simple primary shapes are used to simu-late a crowd. Both size and color are used to create the sense of distance. The original row of people was created using a blend and then copied and resized.

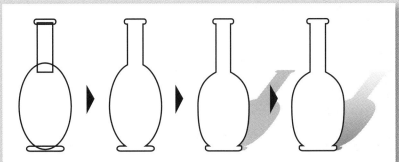

SIMPLE TO COMPLEX Complex shapes can be built by breaking down the object into its primary shapes and then combining them using the Pathfinder Unite filter. Here the bottle is started by combining an oval with rectangles, some which have rounded corners. Once the shape is united it can be refined by manipulating its individual points. The shadow is created by copying the final shape, applying a gradient to it, and then skewing it so that it appears to fall naturally into the distance.

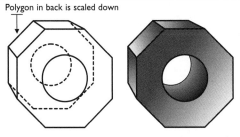

Polygon in back is scaled down

SIZE MATTERS When creating three-dimensional objects the shape placed in the background to form the back plane of the object should be sized smaller than the front shape. The larger the difference between the two shapes, the greater the sense of perspective will be.

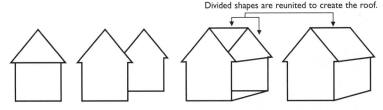

Divided shapes are reunited to create the roof.

BUILDING OBJECTS The Pathfinder filters offer powerful ways to build shapes with-out having to draw them from scratch with the pen tool. Here the side of the house is built by creating its primary shapes and then combining them by applying the Pathfinder Unite filter. Because the back of the house falls further into the distance, its shape is resized so that it is slightly smaller. Connecting lines are then drawn between the two shapes. The roof and the front of the house are created by selecting the lines and shapes and then applying the Pathfinder Divide filter. This will divide all intersecting lines into separate shapes, which then are reselected and united to form proper shapes.

Using Visual Reference Materials: Tracing & Autotracing

Using reference materials is integral to accurately illustrating objects. While Illustrator offers an Auto Trace tool, you may get quicker and better results tracing an object with the pen tool.

TO TRACE OR AUTOTRACE The quality of an image helps determine whether to autotrace an image or manually trace it with the pen tool. Illustrator's Auto Trace tool is most effective with images that have clearly defined edges and are not too busy.

 AUTO TRACE TOOL Illustrator offers an Auto Trace tool with a limited range of tolerance settings. This limited amount of control can make it difficult to get accurate results.

BETTER RESULTS are often achieved by simply drawing over a scanned image with the pen tool and then adjusting the points along the paths individually.

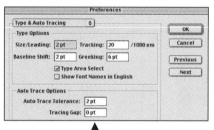

TOLERANCE SETTINGS are adjusted by editing the Type & Auto Tracing Preferences. The Tolerance setting controls how precisely a path is drawn and how many points are used to create it. Higher settings trace less precisely. Tracing Gap controls the smallest width that will be traced.

TOO MANY POINTS The paths created by autotracing often contain extraneous points. These points make the file overly complex and subject to output problems.

AUTOTRACING Here the Auto Trace tool is used to select an image area. Image complexity and the limitations of the Auto Trace tool result in a selection that is rough and contains extraneous points that must later be removed.

MANUALLY TRACING is often the best way to trace an image. Manually drawn shapes created using the pen tool produce more accurate shapes that use fewer points. Too many points can result in complex files and output problems.

FINAL PRODUCT Here the final image is consistent with the original image. While using the pen tool may produce slower results than the Auto Trace tool, the end result is more accurate shapes built with fewer points.

Using Photoshop Paths in Illustrator

Creating paths in Photoshop to use in Illustrator is sometimes the best way to trace an image. Taking advantage of Photoshop's high-quality preview can make tracing an easier task. Once the path is created it can be copied and pasted directly into Illustrator.

LOW-RESOLUTION PREVIEW Until recently images in Illustrator were displayed using a low-resolution preview, making it difficult to trace detailed images very accurately.

COPYING PATHS To copy a path from Photoshop to Illustrator, simply select all of the path's points by selecting the path with the Direct Selection tool and then copy it. Then open the Illustrator file and paste the path in. You can also paste paths from Illustrator into Photoshop.

IDENTICAL PEN TOOLS The pen tools in Illustrator and Photoshop work in exactly the same way.

Use the pen tool to trace over the image shapes. These shapes can be edited and reshaped using pen tool variations.

◀ As you trace the image a path will appear on the Path palette.

Use the Direct Selection tool included in the pen tools to select points or reshape the path.

Paths can be applied to any layer. They can be resized by selecting the points with the Direct Selection tool and using Free Transform from the Edit pull-down menu.

Path pasted into Illustrator

Tracing Bitmap Images

Scanning images in the bitmap format reduces an image's palette to black or white pixels. Don't confuse this format with grayscale images, which have tonal variation. The reduced palette makes it very easy to make accurate selections using the Magic Wand tool.

 To create a path from a bitmap image, select the white area of background with the Magic Wand. Then choose Select Similar to select the image's inner paths. Then apply Inverse Selection so that black pixels are selected.

Once the selection is complete it can be converted into a path by selecting Make Work Path from the Path menu options. This creates a path that can then be copied and pasted directly into Illustrator.

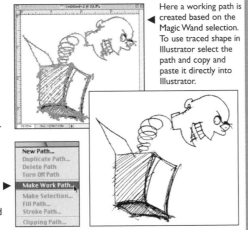

Here a working path is created based on the Magic Wand selection. To use traced shape in Illustrator select the path and copy and paste it directly into Illustrator.

image, the best method is to manually trace over the image using the Bézier pen tool rather than using Illustrator's Auto Trace feature. This feature can be difficult to control and creates objects that usually have too many points. The autotraced shape usually has to be refined and simplified, which requires meticulously deleting any extraneous points. In the end it's often quicker to simply trace it with the pen tool. The most accurate way to trace a complicated shape is to re-create it by using the pen tool in Photoshop. Tracing the image with the pen tool creates a path that can be copied back into Illustrator. Photoshop provides a high-quality preview of the image, which makes tracing it an easier task.

Another option for tracing is to use a software program dedicated to autotracing, like Adobe Streamline. These programs are dedicated to one specific task, autotracing, and so provide a high level of control. Because they offer detailed tolerance settings and the ability to control the number of points applied, they can produce accurately traced shapes with a minimum of points.

The Pathfinder and the Pen

Many of the same techniques used to create the typographic treatments covered in Chapter 4 can be adapted to illustrating objects. Two of the tools that are called upon most often in illustration are the pen tool and the Pathfinder filters. A common approach to illustration involves simplifying complex shapes by breaking them down into their component shapes. These basic shapes can then be combined to form a more complex shape by applying the Pathfinder Unite filter. This illustration approach of uniting and cropping shapes takes advantage of the full range of Pathfinder filters. Because of the uniqueness and detail found in many objects, this method of combining component shapes is often limited to roughly approximating a complex shape. Usually a

Combining Primary Shapes

Breaking down a complex object into its primary component shapes and then combining them is a common illustration approach.

BUILDING BLOCKS Combining shapes to build more complex forms is a method that is effective and easy to understand. Some shapes are easier to create this way than by using the pen tool. While often used in technical illustration, it can also serve as a building block for stylized and looser illustration styles.

PATHFINDER FILTERS The use of filters is integral to this method, offering powerful ways to build shapes. Always use Align to ensure exact placement of shapes.

▲
Place the rectangle so it overlaps the circle and apply the Pathfinder Minus Front filter. This will delete the shape in front from the shape behind it.

Shape after Minus Front applied.

Copy the shape and rotate.

Select shapes and apply Unite filter. The shape's edges must touch to be united properly.

• Place unfilled circles above shape.
• Convert strokes to shapes using Outline Path before applying Pathfinder filters, which work best applied to shapes rather than lines.

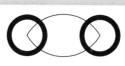

Select all three shapes and apply the Divide filter to divide all overlapping shapes into separate shapes. Then ungroup the shapes and delete any unnecessary shapes. Change the colors of the shapes to get the stripes on the football.

Use Align to equally space circles.

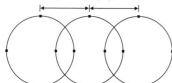

Create overlapping circles that are equally spaced. To copy a circle, select and drag with the Option and Shift keys held down. Option copies the shape and Shift constrains its position.

Delete these shapes after dividing shapes.

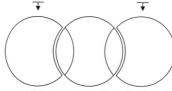

Select all three circles and apply the Pathfinder Divide filter to separate the overlapping areas into individual shapes. Ungroup shapes and delete any unnecessary shapes.

When resizing with the scale tool, hold down Opt + Shift. Option resizes from the center outward and Shift constrains the shape's proportions.

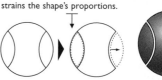

Resize the side shapes to create space between the shapes. Select the side shapes and reduce their size proportionately. Use the Scale tool or Offset Path to resize. Then delete the outer shape and move the smaller shape outward.

shape needs to be refined to some degree to accurately reflect the object. Sometimes a higher level of detail needs to be added to give the object a unique character. The pen and Direct Selection tools are called in at this point to fine-tune the object—a process that often involves a combination of moving, adding, or deleting specific points and manipulating the handles to reshape and refine the shape. This illustration approach is both effective and attractive because it offers an understandable way of creating objects that are seemingly difficult to illustrate.

Combining Simple Shapes

There are many techniques used in combining simple component

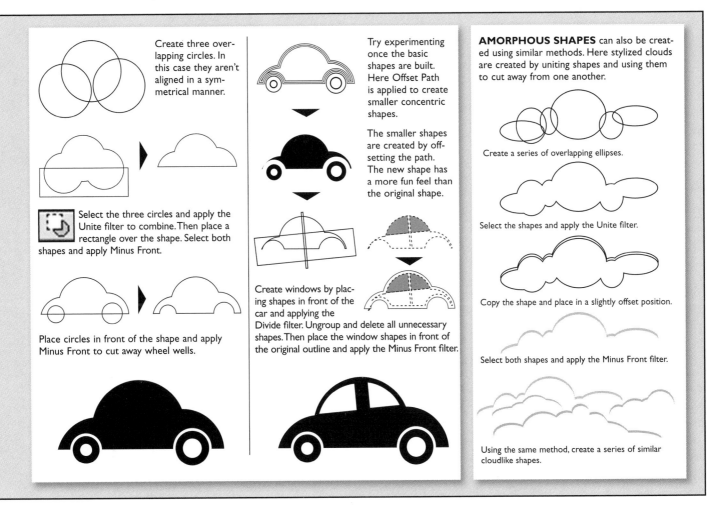

Create three overlapping circles. In this case they aren't aligned in a symmetrical manner.

Select the three circles and apply the Unite filter to combine. Then place a rectangle over the shape. Select both shapes and apply Minus Front.

Place circles in front of the shape and apply Minus Front to cut away wheel wells.

Try experimenting once the basic shapes are built. Here Offset Path is applied to create smaller concentric shapes.

The smaller shapes are created by offsetting the path. The new shape has a more fun feel than the original shape.

Create windows by placing shapes in front of the car and applying the Divide filter. Ungroup and delete all unnecessary shapes. Then place the window shapes in front of the original outline and apply the Minus Front filter.

AMORPHOUS SHAPES can also be created using similar methods. Here stylized clouds are created by uniting shapes and using them to cut away from one another.

Create a series of overlapping ellipses.

Select the shapes and apply the Unite filter.

Copy the shape and place in a slightly offset position.

Select both shapes and apply the Minus Front filter.

Using the same method, create a series of similar cloudlike shapes.

Mirror, Mirror: Creating Symmetrical Shapes

Another approach to building symmetrical shapes involves drawing half a shape and then using the Reflect tool to create a mirror image to complete the shape.

Certain complex symmetrical shapes are best built by drawing half of the shape's outline using the pen tool. The shape is completed by mirroring a copy of the line. The two open paths can then be connected to create a closed shape.

GRID SYSTEM Using a system of guidelines will help place the points specifically. Create a series of guidelines that intersect where the object's points should be positioned.

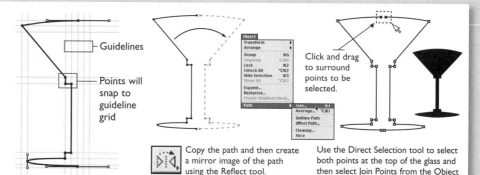

Guidelines

Points will snap to guideline grid

Click and drag to surround points to be selected.

Copy the path and then create a mirror image of the path using the Reflect tool.

Use the Direct Selection tool to select both points at the top of the glass and then select Join Points from the Object pull-down menu to close the shape.

Here a grid of evenly spaced guidelines is created so that the path's points can be positioned at specific intervals.

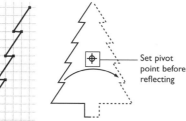

Set pivot point before reflecting

Reflect tool is used to mirror shape. Here the pivot point is placed on the right edge of the original and the Reflect tool is used while holding down Shift (to constrain).

Select corresponding endpoints on each line and join the top and bottom to create a filled shape.

A bounding box affects overall shape in KPT Warp Frame. Select multiple points and use the Shift key when adjusting the shape.

The closed shape is manipulated using KPT Warp Frame to give the angular shape a more curvilinear form.

shapes to create more complex ones. Some involve an additive process of uniting smaller shapes to create more complex ones; others employ a reductive method of using shapes to cut away or divide other shapes. Sometimes the

creation of a shape involves both approaches.

A football is an example of a shape whose creation involves both the additive and subtractive methods. It is not an overly complicated shape, and so it would be

understandable to consider drawing it manually with the pen tool. Creating a symmetrical shape like a football with the pen tool usually requires creating a grid of guidelines and manually manipulating and pinching the shape's points. Because of the nature of the shape, an easier approach would be the additive and subtractive methods.

Symmetrical objects are often best created by combining basic shapes. While rounded, asymmetrical, amorphous shapes are often best created from scratch with the pen tool, there are many natural forms that can be created by combining shapes.

Additive and Subtractive Methods

The first step in creating the football employs a subtractive method. A rectangle is placed over a circle so that only part of the circle is visible. The rectangle is positioned so that the visible area of the circle reflects half a football's shape. The rectangle is then used to cut away from the circle, leaving half a football shape.

The additive method is used to finish the football shape. The half football is copied, rotated, and positioned so that together the two shapes form the object. They are then combined to make one shape.

Both the additive and subtractive methods require applying different Pathfinder filters to build the shapes. The first step used the Minus Front filter to cut the rec-

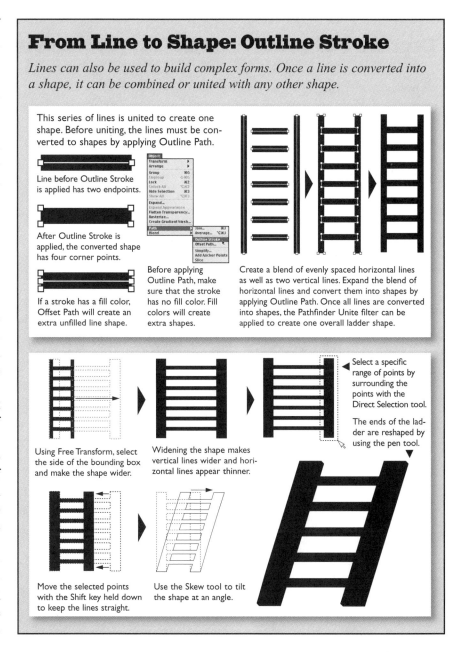

From Line to Shape: Outline Stroke

Lines can also be used to build complex forms. Once a line is converted into a shape, it can be combined or united with any other shape.

This series of lines is united to create one shape. Before uniting, the lines must be converted to shapes by applying Outline Path.

Line before Outline Stroke is applied has two endpoints.

After Outline Stroke is applied, the converted shape has four corner points.

If a stroke has a fill color, Offset Path will create an extra unfilled line shape.

Before applying Outline Path, make sure that the stroke has no fill color. Fill colors will create extra shapes.

Create a blend of evenly spaced horizontal lines as well as two vertical lines. Expand the blend of horizontal lines and convert them into shapes by applying Outline Path. Once all lines are converted into shapes, the Pathfinder Unite filter can be applied to create one overall ladder shape.

Using Free Transform, select the side of the bounding box and make the shape wider.

Widening the shape makes vertical lines wider and horizontal lines appear thinner.

Select a specific range of points by surrounding the points with the Direct Selection tool.

The ends of the ladder are reshaped by using the pen tool.

Move the selected points with the Shift key held down to keep the lines straight.

Use the Skew tool to tilt the shape at an angle.

Stylizing Illustrations: Linear Techniques

Once you've built an object, lines can be used to create a sense of volume and light as well as to give your illustration a more personalized style.

BASIC SHAPES As with all cylindrical shapes, begin with the basic shapes that make up the more complex form. Here two ellipses and a rectangle are aligned.

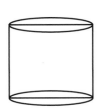

UNITE SHAPES Basic shapes are combined using the Unite filter to create the cylindrical shape. Be sure to make a copy of the ellipses and rectangle before Unite is applied.

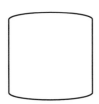

LAMP SHADE Create the shade by selecting the points along the top of the shape with the Direct Selection tool and then scaling the points with the Shift key held down to constrain the proportions.

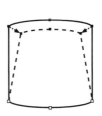

LAMP BASE This shape is based on the original cylinder. Select the points along the top of the shape with the Direct Selection tool and move them down to build a shallow cylinder shape.

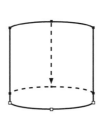

ONE SHAPE Each of the lamp parts, the base, stem, and shade, are based on the same original cylinder shape.

The stem of the lamp is an extended cylinder made using the same technique employed to create the lamp base. Once the cylinder is lengthened, it is then scaled down proportionately.

REFLECTED SHAPES are a simple way to create a sense of dimension and volume. This cube began with a single square that was reshaped so that it appears to move back into the distance. The shape was then reflected and positioned so that it reflects the original shape.

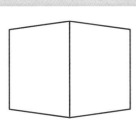

WRAPPING PAPER was created by taking a series of lines and applying the Zig Zag filter to create wavy lines. To get variance in line widths, each line width is adjusted. The lines are then rotated to match the angle of the cube by using the KPT 3D Transform filter. The lines are cropped into the box using the Pathfinder Crop filter.

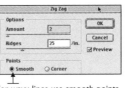

For wavy lines use smooth points.

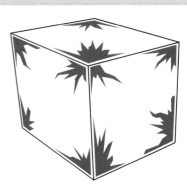

HAND-DRAWN SHAPES are another way to get a more illustrative feel. Here simple gray shapes are added to the box corners using the pen tool to give the shape a sense of surface.

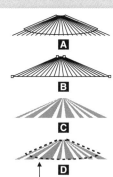

A Make a copy of shapes that make up the lamp base.

B Using the Scissor tool, cut the shape to get separate lines.

C Create a blend between lines by selecting corresponding endpoints.

D Add a point to the blend path line with the pen tool and then move the point down.

E Expand the blend and then place the lines within the base of the lamp shape.

The same blend technique (A-E) is used to create the lines in the lamp shade, the stem, and along the edge of the lamp base. ▶

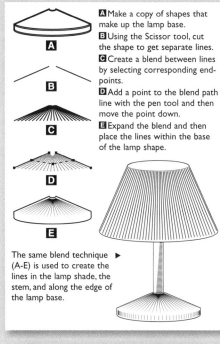

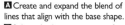

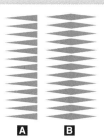

The shape used to crop the lines is slightly smaller than the object so that the lines fit within the shape. The smaller shape is created using Offset Path.

The white gap along the base edge separates the gray shapes and creates a highlight.

A Create and expand the blend of lines that align with the base shape.

B Select the bottom points of the outside lines and connect using Join. Repeat for the top points. A closed shape appears around the series of lines. Select shape and lines and apply Divide.

C Ungroup and delete shapes to create white areas. Unite others for larger shapes.

D Place the base shape over the united shapes and apply Crop.

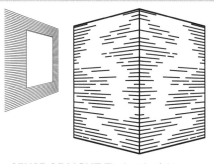

A Create a blend of triangles and expand.

B Diamond shapes are created by copying and rotating triangles. Place the second set of triangles so that they overlap the original set and then apply the Unite filter.

Triangles are reshaped to give the lamp shade a round appearance by applying KPT Warp Frame.

The blend of triangles can be applied to many shapes to give a stylized feel.

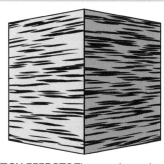

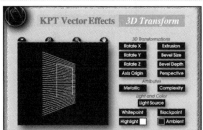

CONTOUR LINES These follow the planes of a shape and give it volume. Here a series of lines is rotated to match the sides of the cube using KPT 3D Transform. The lines are then fitted to the box by placing the shape over the lines and applying the Pathfinder Crop filter. Watch out for extra white or unfilled shapes that the Crop filter may create that need to be deleted.

SENSE OF LIGHT The length of the contour lines is adjusted by using the Direct Selection tool. A second set of lines is placed above the original by using Paste in Front. One line is shortened to the left, the other to the right

HATCH EFFECTS These can be used to create realistic textures. Here a wood grain is applied to a square, which is then rotated using KPT 3D Transform so that the angle of the texture matches the side of the cube. The texture is then simplified and cropped into the cube.

Creating Linear Patterns

Linear geometric patterns can be created using Transform Each, which allows shapes to be rotated, scaled, and moved to create stepped sequences of shapes.

TRANSFORM EACH allows you to apply numerous transformations to a shape simultaneously. A shape can be resized, rotated, and moved in one operation. One of the most useful aspects of Transform Each is that it allows a copy of the transformed shape to be made.

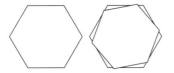

Shape on right has been rotated, resized, and copied.

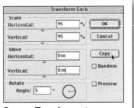

Repeat Transformation repeats the previous transformation and can be used to quickly create a series of stepped shapes. Use ⌘ + D to repeat the transformation without using the pull-down menu.

NATURAL FORMS are often based on symmetrical geometric patterns. These patterns are emulated using Transform Each and converted into natural, less mechanical forms by applying filters that introduce randomness and anomaly to the form. The pattern on the left is created by scaling and rotating a polygon using Transform Each. The Scribble and Tweak filter is then applied to create a more curvilinear form.

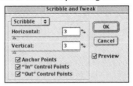

STAR TOOL Select the Star tool and click in the document to access its settings. Radius 1 controls the outer length of the star points. Radius 2 controls inner depth. The greater the difference in radius settings, the longer the star's points will be.

Transform Each applied to a star that is scaled down, rotated, and copied. Pattern is created using ⌘ + D.

Transform Each applied to an ellipse. Here the ellipse is rotated and copied.

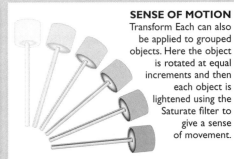

SENSE OF MOTION Transform Each can also be applied to grouped objects. Here the object is rotated at equal increments and then each object is lightened using the Saturate filter to give a sense of movement.

tangle away from the shape. The second used the Unite filter to combine the shapes. These are two of the most commonly used Pathfinder filters, but the Divide, Crop, and Minus Back filters are also used frequently.

There are numerous ways to use basic shapes to build objects. Experiment with breaking down complex forms into their primary components. Consider how different shapes can be used to refine and add detail to larger ones.

Building Shape from Lines

Another method for building complex shapes involves using lines as a primary component. Lines, like shapes, can be used to build more complex forms or to add detail to them. This is a method that requires

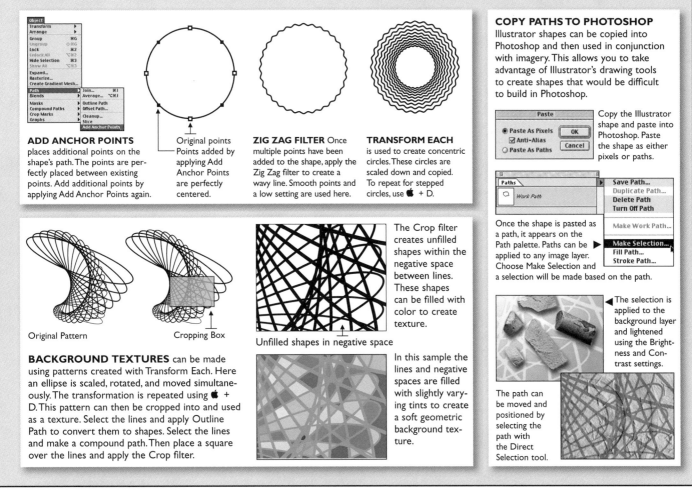

ADD ANCHOR POINTS places additional points on the shape's path. The points are perfectly placed between existing points. Add additional points by applying Add Anchor Points again.

Original points Points added by applying Add Anchor Points are perfectly centered.

ZIG ZAG FILTER Once multiple points have been added to the shape, apply the Zig Zag filter to create a wavy line. Smooth points and a low setting are used here.

TRANSFORM EACH is used to create concentric circles. These circles are scaled down and copied. To repeat for stepped circles, use ⌘ + D.

COPY PATHS TO PHOTOSHOP
Illustrator shapes can be copied into Photoshop and then used in conjunction with imagery. This allows you to take advantage of Illustrator's drawing tools to create shapes that would be difficult to build in Photoshop.

Copy the Illustrator shape and paste into Photoshop. Paste the shape as either pixels or paths.

Once the shape is pasted as a path, it appears on the Path palette. Paths can be applied to any image layer. Choose Make Selection and a selection will be made based on the path.

The Crop filter creates unfilled shapes within the negative space between lines. These shapes can be filled with color to create texture.

Unfilled shapes in negative space

In this sample the lines and negative spaces are filled with slightly varying tints to create a soft geometric background texture.

Original Pattern   Cropping Box

BACKGROUND TEXTURES can be made using patterns created with Transform Each. Here an ellipse is scaled, rotated, and moved simultaneously. The transformation is repeated using ⌘ + D. This pattern can then be cropped into and used as a texture. Select the lines and apply Outline Path to convert them to shapes. Select the lines and make a compound path. Then place a square over the lines and apply the Crop filter.

The selection is applied to the background layer and lightened using the Brightness and Contrast settings.

The path can be moved and positioned by selecting the path with the Direct Selection tool.

lines to be seen in terms of their shape. To combine a series of lines into a larger form, the lines must first be converted into shapes.

Converting Lines to Shapes
Converting any line into a shape requires Outline Path to be applied. In essence it converts a thick line into a rectangle. Once a line has been converted, the line's two endpoints are replaced by the rectangle's four corner points. Outline Path, along with Offset Path, are two commonly used Path functions. Young designers often overlook these powerful tools.

One of the benefits of converting lines to shapes is that they can now be united to form larger, complex shapes. Once a line has been

Keeping Perspective: Cylindrical Shapes

Creating illustrations with objects that sit in proper perspective can be challenging. Here are some ways of building cylindrical shapes that sit in space naturally.

Basic Transformations

Building objects that are proportionately accurate is done by following a few basic guidelines.

CONSISTENT SHAPES The ellipse used to form the cylinder must be shared by all elements within an illustration to give the appearance that they all sit on the same place.

CONSTRAIN SHAPES While the ellipse can be resized, it must maintain its proportion. This is done by always holding down the Shift key while transforming the object.

MASTER SHAPES The original shapes that make up the cylinder are integral to maintaining consistency between objects. Be sure to make a copy of them before uniting the shapes.

Begin building the cylinder by creating two ellipses and a rectangle with the same widths. Use Align for accurate vertical placement. Make a copy of the group for later use. Then select the shapes and apply the Unite filter.

The cylinder shape is reshaped by transforming specific points. To shorten, select the top points with the Direct Selection tool and move down. A shape can be fluted by selecting the same points and using the Scale tool. Hold down the Shift key when scaling.

To center the shapes accurately over each other, align their centers horizontally.

Horizontal Align Center

Viewing the file in Artwork mode provides a wire-frame preview of objects. This helps accurately place shapes and points.

Building on the Process

Complex shapes can be made by using variations of the transformation techniques shown above. Here the same original cylinder shape forms the basis for all the elements that make up a jar. These elements include the cap of the jar, its base, and its label.

These basic shapes make up the entire object. Always keep a copy of original shapes.

To create a cap for the jar, copy the cylinder and shorten its length, then place it above the original cylinder to form the cap.

All three shapes that make up the jar are created from the original cylindrical shape.

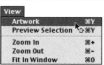

The base of the jar is the same as the cap shape at a reduced size and placed behind the jar.

To add detail to the cap, the cap top and rim need to be separate shapes. Begin by placing a copy of the original ellipse over the cylinder.

Select both shapes and align the tops of the objects using Align. Then apply the Divide filter.

Create the inner shape using Outline Path.

Create a blend of lines and expand. Place the shape over the lines and apply the Crop filter.

The Crop filter will create unfilled shapes between lines. Delete these extra shapes.

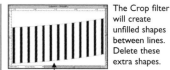

Unfilled shapes are created in negative space between line segments

This is how lines should appear after the Crop filter has been applied and the extra unfilled shapes have been deleted.

Place the lines inside the jar rim to give the cap edge a grooved, textured appearance.

Creating Pushpins: Blends & Gradients

Similar shapes are used to create the pushpin. Here gradients and blends give the object volume and provide a sense of light source.

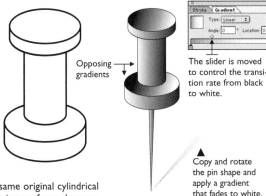

Opposing gradients

The slider is moved to control the transition rate from black to white.

Make an inside path using Offset Path. Fill the inside shape with white, the outer shape with gray. Neither shape should have a stroke color. Then apply Blend.

Copy and rotate the pin shape and apply a gradient that fades to white.

The same original cylindrical shape is transformed proportionately to form each section of the pushpin.

Opposing gradients give a sense of shadow and of an active light source.

Blends are used to give the shape's edges a rounded feel and a highlight.

Fluted Shapes

Other variations on the cylinder include fluted shapes, in which the top ellipse is larger than the bottom one.

Select the points on the bottom of the cylinder and scale them inward. Hold down the Shift key to constrain proportions.

Inside shapes give the glass a sense of thickness. They are created by applying Offset Path to the original master shapes.

The fluted shape is rotated to create other variations. When rotating, hold down the Shift key to rotate exactly 90 degrees.

A doorknob shape incorporates both the rotated fluted shape and the cylinder.

A series of fluted shapes creates a telescope-like form. The shapes are scaled and aligned on center.

Here the repeated cylinder shape is altered to give a more natural channeled form.

Placing the ellipse off center vertically gives the shape a rounded feel.

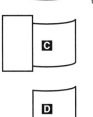

A To create a label for the jar, begin by placing the original ellipse in front of the cylinder shape. **B** Select both shapes and then apply the Pathfinder Minus Front filter to delete the ellipse from the cylinder shape. **C** Place a rectangle above the shape and use it to crop the shape by applying the Minus Front filter. **D** Place the label shape above the jar.

• Place the text and rules above the label shape and convert type to shape using Create Outlines.
• Select the type and apply KPT Warp Frame to reshape the type so it appears to wrap around the jar.
• Place a rectangle over the type. Then select the type and the rectangle and apply Minus Front to crop the type and give the appearance that it ends at the edge of the jar.

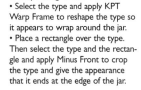

KPT WARP FRAME
Select multiple handles and use the Shift key so that the type strokes stay straight. Use Show Unselected Art to view the jar outline.

converted, the Pathfinder filters can be applied as they would be to any shape. Converting a line into a shape also allows the designer to add, delete, or move points. Using converted lines to build complex shapes is best used for creating objects whose general shape is a linear one, like a ladder or a fence.

Symmetrical Shapes

While creating the football did not require any actual manipulation of the shape's points, there are many symmetrical shapes that require more specific fine-tuning. While combining shapes can be an effective way of building symmetrical shapes, in some cases you may want to employ other approaches. One of these involves using the pen tool to create half the shape. This is similar to the method used to create the football in that it starts by creating half of the shape and then uses a copy of that shape to complete the form. Instead of using shapes to produce the object, the pen tool is used. The benefit of drawing a shape in this way is that it can produce objects that are elaborate and detailed. This technique uses the Reflect tool to mirror the pen-drawn path. Once these mirrored paths are positioned properly to form the overall shape, their

Building Interlaced Shapes

Building shapes that appear to have interweaving sections is useful in designing logos and symbols.

  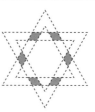 

Create an unfilled triangle with a thick stroke by double-clicking the Polygon tool in the document and specifying three sides. Use Outline Stroke to create the shape.

Copy and rotate the triangle and then use Align to center the triangles over each other horizontally.

Select both the triangles and divide them into separate shapes by applying the Pathfinder Divide filter.

Select the separate shapes and reunite using the Unite filter. Then fill with colors that will emulate interlocking shapes.

Equal spacing between circles

Distribute circles evenly

Arrange five unfilled circles with thick strokes. Align the top and bottom rows of circles separately. Then use Align to distribute the circles evenly. The distribution functions are found on the second row of features in the Align palette.

DIVIDE AND CONQUER Using the same technique as shown above, convert the lines to shapes using Outline Stroke, and then select all shapes. Apply the Divide filter and reunite the separate shapes to get interlaced shapes.

endpoints can be joined by applying Join Path. This will combine the two paths into one closed shape. This technique is especially useful in cases where basic primary shapes cannot be easily used as building blocks. Common sym-

metrical shapes that might be built using this method include wineglasses, chess pieces, or hearts.

Creating Stylized Shapes

There are many ways of applying the Pathfinder filters to shapes.

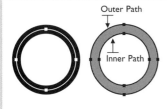

Outer Path

Inner Path

OUTLINE STROKE Converting a stroke into a shape is integral to building interweaving shapes. The circle on the left is a standard unfilled shape with a thick stroke. The circle on the right has had its stroke converted to a shape by applying Outline Stroke. The converted shape on the right is a compound shape that has both inner and outer paths.

ARRANGE SHAPES Use Align to accurately position the circles over one another. Start with two circles that are vertically aligned and then copy and rotate them to get the second pair of circles.

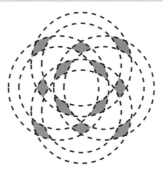

DIVIDE & REUNITE Select all overlapping circles and apply the Divide filter. Ungroup the shapes and then select specific shapes and reunite. Position the reunited shapes in front or behind accordingly.

WHITE OUTLINES These help to enhance the appearance that the circles are actually interwoven. Because strokes have been converted to shapes, they can have an outline stroke.

BEVELING SHAPES The circles are beveled using the same methods for beveling type. Begin by offsetting paths and drawing bevel lines between the shapes. Then select all and apply the Divide filter.

DROP SHADOWS Make a copy of the Olympic symbol and apply the Unite filter to form one shape. Fill this shape with gray. Then draw an unfilled box around the symbol. This creates a buffer space around the shape. Select the box and symbol and rasterize the objects. Once the objects are rasterized, apply the Gaussian Blur filter to soften the image's edges. If you rasterize the symbol without the unfilled box, the blur will be clipped off.

Place the drop shadow behind the Olympic symbol and offset it slightly to create depth. The more the drop shadow is offset, the further away the symbol will appear from the page surface,

Besides using them to build symmetrical shapes, they can be used to ornament and bring a sense of style to an illustration. Becoming familiar with the functions of all the filters will help you develop your own original techniques for

using them. So far we have used them to create generally technical shapes, but the Pathfinder filters can also be used to create more organic and stylized shapes.

One example of this is illustration technique is shown on page 195 of this chapter, which demonstrates how to create stylized clouds using only a series of simple ellipses and circles. This technique uses a set of overlapping ellipses that have been united. A copy of this combined shape is

Creating Coiled Objects: Chain Links & Slinkys

While coiled objects are similar to interlaced shapes in that they also have sections that appear to interlock, building them requires a much different technique.

Building Chain Links

Create an unfilled oval with a thick black stroke. Copy the oval and paste it over the original by selecting the original oval and then selecting Edit:Paste in Front. This will paste the copy directly over the original oval.

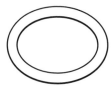

Select the top oval and give it a thinner white stroke. Overlapping ovals have different stroke weights, so they appear to be one white oval with a black stroke.

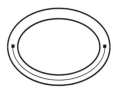

Select the white oval. Using the knife tool, cut the left and right points, so that the oval's path is cut in half. Select half of the oval and send it to the back.

Once half of the white oval is in back, the black oval comes to the front. Using the knife tool, cut the left and right points of the black oval. Then send the black oval to the back.

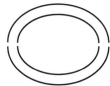

The oval is now split into two halves. Group the two arcs on the bottom and then group the two arcs on the top.

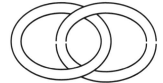

Copy both halves of the oval and place them over each other, as shown above. Then select the bottom half of the oval on the right and send it to the back. Make sure to select both halves of the oval on the bottom, not just the top white oval.

Continue to copy and place the individual links over each other. Make sure that they are spaced accurately by grouping each individual chain link and then using Align to distribute the chain links evenly.

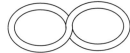

This technique can be used to create many type of symbols that have interlocking shapes.

placed over itself so that it slightly offsets it, just like a drop shadow would sit behind type. The front shape is used to cut away from the shape behind it, leaving a fine cloudlike shape. This technique of building complex forms by crop-ping into other shapes has many applications.

Developing Personal Style

Building complex shapes to use as a cropping device is a technique that can be adapted and applied in many different ways. Accurately building an object's shape really represents only half the job. An equally difficult task is giving the objects that you've created a fin-ished quality. Developing a person-al sense of illustration style is in

Building Coiled Shapes

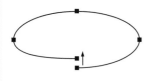

Create an oval with a black stroke and no fill. Then use the knife tool to cut the oval by selecting the bottom point. Use the Direct Selection tool to select the bottom point and move it up. Hold down the Shift key when moving the point up to constrain its horizontal positioning.

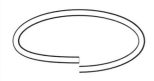

Select and make the stroke thicker. Then copy the line and paste directly in front of the original shape using Paste in Front. This places a copy directly over the original line. Select the top shape and make the stroke white and thinner than the original stroke behind it.

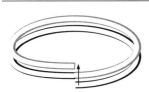

Select the overlapping strokes and group them. Then copy them by clicking and dragging with both the Option key (to copy) and the Shift key (to constrain) held down. Move the copy up until it aligns properly with the original shape.

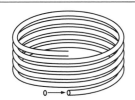

Finish off both ends of the coil by placing an ellipse over wire's end. This will make the coiled wire appear to be round.

Slinkys & Other Variations

In this sample each successive coil in the stepped series has been scaled.

Here the original ellipse is wider to give a looser coil.

Pivot point

To create this Slinky-like object, the coil is rotated at specific increments. The rotation pivot point must be set prior to rotation. The series can be repeated by using Transform Each or by using + D to repeat the transformation.

some ways more difficult in that it requires you to give the illustration an original look, one that is consistent with your personal aesthetic as an artist. Your personal sense of style will be determined by your preferences of color, line, shape, pattern, and other elements of design. Personal style takes a long time to develop and is usually the result of working on numerous projects over a long period of time. Personal style also tends to change slowly over time. It is probably the most difficult aspect of design for young designers who don't have the benefit of years of experience developing creative solutions to a multitude of design projects. Young designers are in the process of being introduced to

Nuts & Bolts: Building & Styling Technical Shapes

Illustrating technical objects that appear three-dimensional is a less difficult task if you think in terms of building shapes rather than drawing them.

Building the Basic Shapes

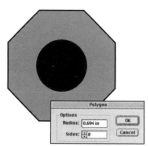

Click in the document with the Polygon tool to specify an eight-sided shape. Place a circle over the polygon and use Align to perfectly center the shapes over each other.

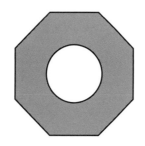

Select both shapes and create a compound shape by going to Compound Paths:Make to put a hole in the shape. Make sure to save a copy of this master shape for later use.

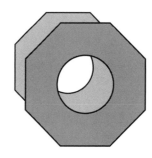

Copy the shape and place it behind the original. Reduce the size of the shape in back. Remember that objects in the distance appear smaller than objects in the foreground.

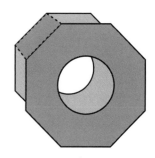

Using the pen tool, draw lines between the front and back shapes. Zoom in close and view in Outline mode to accurately place the points.

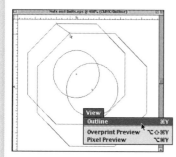

Outline preview shows objects in wire-frame mode and helps specifically place the line's endpoints. Draw all the lines and apply the Divide filter. Then ungroup the shapes and reunite to get side shapes.

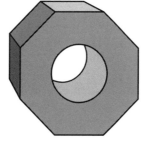

Adjusting the color of each of the object's sides will give the illusion of light falling upon the object.

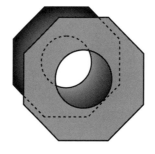

Place a copy of the master shape in the background and fill with a radial gradient to give a sense of light to the inside of the hole.

Gradients can also be applied to the object's individual shapes to give a sense of lighting to the illustration. Control the direction of each gradient by using the Gradient tool.

Styling Objects: Smooth Blends

Once the object shapes are built, there are numerous ways to stylize the illustration.

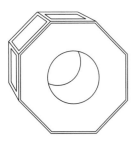

BLENDED SHAPES give the edges a roundness and highlight. Apply Offset Path to each shape to create a slightly smaller inner shape.

All shapes should have no stroke. Fill the inner shapes with gray, the outer shapes with white. Create a blend between each pair of shapes.

Styling Objects: Linear Blends

◄ Select and copy the side shape and use the scissor tool to divide the lines. Then delete the side lines.

◄ Create a blend between the two lines. The line on the right has a heavier weight than the line on the left, which creates a linear gradation.

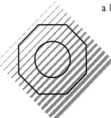

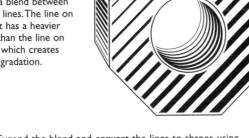

◄ Expand the blend and convert the lines to shapes using Outline Stroke. Select the lines and make a compound path. Place the nut shape in front of the lines and apply the Crop filter.

new aspects of design constantly. The examples found throughout this book are meant to serve only as an introduction to some of the ways designs can be stylized, as well as to provide some insight into how new techniques can be developed on their own.

Styling Illustrations: Woodcuts

One common way of styling an illustration is to give it a woodcut feel. Woodcut styling emulates the look of block printing. It has a hand-rendered feel, which gives the object a less slick and technical finish. As with the previous examples, you can build a complex series of shapes to use as a cropping device, rather than drawing it out manually using the pen tool.

The first step is to create a pattern whose shapes emulate the line quality and shape commonly associated with woodcut blocks. A series of elongated triangles will simulate the cutaway shapes that are common to this style. The triangles' edges could be hard and pointed or soft and rounded, depending on what type of look you want to attain. Probably the simplest way to create a series of equally spaced triangles is to build a blend. The series of shapes will serve as a pattern to be applied to

Vanishing Points & Two-Point Perspective

Traditional methods for creating perspective can also be applied to technical illustration. Setting up a vanishing point helps achieve true perspective.

Creating Mechanical Gears

There are several approaches to creating shapes like gears. Here's one unique method that uses type to build shapes.

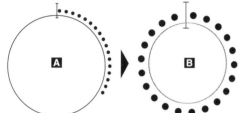

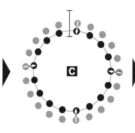

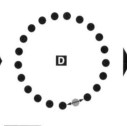

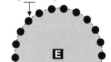

Larger circle placed in back

TYPE ON A PATH is used to create the teeth of the gear. Draw a circle and then select it with the Type on a Path tool. This will convert the circle into a text path.

A Fill the circular text path with round bullets by typing in Opt + 8. Place a character space between each bullet.

B Increase the size of the bullets in the Character palette so that they approximate the size of the gear's teeth.

C Adjust the baseline shift of the bullets so that they intersect the circular path. The baseline shift settings are found at the bottom of the Character palette. A negative setting will shift the bullets below the baseline.

Baseline shift   Tracking

D Use Tracking to adjust the spacing between bullets. When the spacing is correct, convert the text to shapes using Create Outlines. Select the circles and make a compound path.

E Place a large circle in back and apply Minus Front filter.

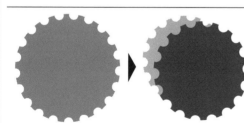

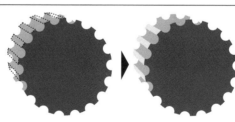

Fill the gear shape in the back with a radial gradient

The Minus Front filter crops away the smaller circles from the larger circle to create the gear shape. Select the gear shape and copy it. Place the copy behind the original and reduce its size. Objects in the distance are always smaller than those in the foreground.

Use the pen tool to draw in the sides of the teeth on the top left. Zoom in close and use View Outline to see objects in wire-frame mode. This will help ensure accurate placement of the shape's points.

Give the space between the gears a roundness by selecting the background gear shape and filling it with a radial gradient.

True Perspective & Vanishing Points

Using vanishing points is a traditional method of creating shapes that appear in the proper perspective.

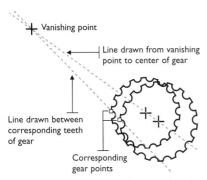

Vanishing point

Line drawn from vanishing point to center of gear

Line drawn between corresponding teeth of gear

Corresponding gear points

Place rotation pivot point over vanishing point

Rotate with Option key to copy line

Lines drawn through corresponding gear points on bottom

Establish a vanishing point by drawing a line that crosses through the centers of both gears, and extend it out to the left. Draw a second line that crosses through corresponding points on the teeth of the cog. Extend this line out to the right until it intersects the other line. The point where the lines intersect is your vanishing point.

Draw lines that extend from the vanishing point through each corresponding pair of gear teeth shapes. To ensure accurate placement of points, view in Outline mode so that you can see the objects as wire frames. Select the shapes and perspective lines and apply the Divide filter to divide the gear into multiple pieces.

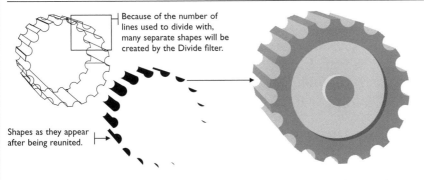

Because of the number of lines used to divide with, many separate shapes will be created by the Divide filter.

Shapes as they appear after being reunited.

Ungroup and delete any unneeded shapes. Reselect the divided shapes and form proper shapes by applying Unite. Some shapes will need fine-tuning with the Direct Selection tool.

Drag the new shapes over the original gear. Having separate rounded shapes between the gear teeth gives more control in creating volume and a three-dimensional feel.

the different shapes that make up an object. While a blend gives you a series of triangles, because the shapes are perfectly spaced and identical the overall feel is somewhat technical and not really conducive to emulating a woodcut. Once the blend has been expanded, the triangles can then be manually reshaped to give the pattern a more hand-drawn feel. Once the pattern is created, it can be applied to separate parts of the illustration to give it a stylized feel.

There are a few ways that you can start to apply the pattern to an illustration. One method is to place the pattern within the sides of an object. By resizing and reshaping the pattern, it can be used to give different tonality to different sides of an object so that the illustration has a sense of light source and the relief created by the woodcut pattern appears real. The woodcut pattern can also be resized so that more detail is given to certain areas of an illustration.

The pattern can also be used to crop away from the shapes of an illustration using the Minus Front (or Minus Back) filters. Because the woodcut pattern is composed of multiple objects, this method will require you to make it a compound path before applying it to the illustration's shapes.

Linear Stylings

The same process of using the woodcut pattern to crop into or away from an illustration's shapes can be adapted to create more technical linear stylings. Instead of creating a series of elongated triangles, a blend of straight lines can be used. The lines can then be cropped into the illustration's shapes to provide shading. One way to achieve a sense of tonal shading is to create a range of different linear patterns. These patterns might be composed of tighter lines or heavier line widths. They might also have lines that graduate from heavy to light line widths. The types of lines used to make up a pattern can also be varied in many ways, from wavy lines to dotted or dashed lines.

There are a few basic steps that must be applied to enable you to crop a series of shapes into another shape. If you are using a blend to create the basic pattern, the blend must be expanded before any of the Pathfinder filters are applied. If you are cropping a line pattern into a shape, all of the lines must first be selected and converted into a compound path. The

compound path enables Pathfinder to treat the lines as one shape. Remember that any number of patterns can be used to crop into your illustration's shapes. Experiment using this method with other types of patterns such as circle and cube patterns.

Geometric to Organic

Since many natural forms like trees, seashells, and flowers are somewhat symmetrical in form, they can be created using a series of geometric shapes, such as circles or squares. By applying specific filters, these shapes, which are technical in nature, can be given a more rounded and organic feel. These filters will also give a very ordered stepped series of shapes a sense of randomness often found in nature.

One way to create geometric patterns is to use the Transform Each function. Transform Each is different from the other basic transformation tools (Scale, Size, Skew, and Rotate) in that it allows the simultaneous application of multiple transformations to shapes. One of the most useful aspects of Transform Each is that it lets you create a copy of the transformed shape.

Try creating a basic primary

shape, like a square, which has a black stroke and no fill, and then select the square and apply Transform Each. As with any new tool that you are using for the first time, start by applying small, incremental settings that are easy to understand. Transform Each has many settings, which can become confusing when they are all used in conjunction with each other.

With this in mind, begin by applying a transformation that is easy to visualize. For instance, try rotating the square by 5 degrees and simultaneously increasing the size by 5 percent. Select Copy so that a second transformed square is created. You will now see two squares, the original and the resized and rotated square.

If you continue to apply Transform Each to the newly created square, you will begin to get geometric patterns. To quickly see the pattern take shape, use the Repeat Transformation hot key, ⌘ + D, which applies the current transformation settings to the new copy. If you continue to enter ⌘ + D, you will see transformed copies begin to form a geometric pattern. Experiment using different settings in conjunction with each other. Using the Move settings with the Rotate or Scale settings will create a pattern that has a sense of motion.

Cropping Geometric Patterns

Geometric patterns that are created this way can be used to crop into other shapes. They can be used to give objects texture as well as for background textures. As with any line that you want to apply the Pathfinder filters to, they must first be converted from lines to shapes by applying Outline Path. Before cropping these converted outlines into a shape, you must first apply the Pathfinder Unite filter to combine them into one shape. Once this is done you can simply crop the linear geometric pattern into another shape by applying the Crop filter.

From Technical to Natural

Certain filters can be applied to these linear geometric patterns to soften up their hard edges and corners, create a sense of randomness, and give a more organic feel to the shape. For instance, if you start with a square and use Transform Each to rotate and reduce its size slightly, you will get a pattern that roughly resembles a flower. To give it a more realistic feel, you can apply the Scribble and Tweak filter.

Technical Illustration

While most graphic designers use Illustrator to create simple graphic illustrations and icons to augment their design projects, some graphic designers make a living as technical illustrators, creating informative graphic illustrations. Most art departments have someone on staff whose main responsibility is creating informative graphics as well as tables and charts. If you find yourself more interested in this area of design, rather than page layout, this may be a career path for you.

Complex technical illustrations that emulate a three-dimensional space can be created by using combinations of the techniques previously covered. How involved and lengthy the process is depends on the complexity of the shape.

Using Master Shapes

One thing to remember when creating complicated shapes is to save and copy master shapes as you build the object. It also doesn't hurt to save copies of many of the shapes that will be created during the process of building complex shapes. Saving master shapes, especially those that may be needed often and are hard to re-create,

is common practice. You will see that ellipses are used as the basis for creating cylindrical shapes throughout this chapter. If you are using circles or squares as master building components, it is not the end of the world if you don't save a copy. But trying to accurately re-create a particular ellipse can be more difficult than you might expect. The ellipse as master shape is also integral to maintaining consistent perspective. Getting into the habit of saving master shapes will save you much time and frustration, as many of the processes discussed here are involved and exacting. It is not uncommon that in the process of figuring out how to properly and most efficiently build technical shapes you will have to start over or repeat parts of the process, and in this case a master shape will be invaluable.

Creating Cylindrical Shapes

Creating cylindrical shapes like bottles, pencils, or pushpins in which the elements all sit in proper perspective and relation to each other can at first seem to be a daunting task. Rectangular and square shapes such as boxes are generally easier to build. There is one simple technique that will make creating any shape that has a

Using Blends to Build Shapes & Create Volume

Blends are a powerful tool that can be used to make a series of evenly spaced shapes, morph one shape into another, or create shapes that have rounded surfaces.

Corresponding points

 To create a blend, draw two circles. Then select the Blend tool and select corresponding points on each shape.

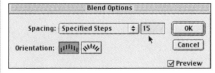

The blend appears after selecting corresponding points on each shape. The number of blend steps is set by double-clicking on the Blend tool.

The blend line can be altered by adding points to it using the pen tool. Here a corner point is added and moved up using the Direct Selection tool.

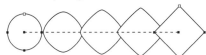

Blends can be applied to different shapes. Here a blend is created between a circle and square. The shapes created by the blend morph from one shape to the other.

EXPAND BLENDS The shapes created by a the blend are not separate shapes until they have been expanded. Expand blends by selecting Blend:Expand from the Object pull-down menu.

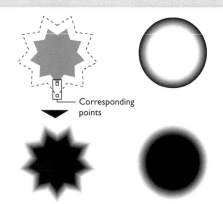
Corresponding points

USE BLENDS TO SHADE Blends may be used to create soft shifts of color that follow a shape's contours. The star blend is made by creating two stars that both have no stroke. Fill the outside star with white and the inside star with black. Then create a blend between the shapes.

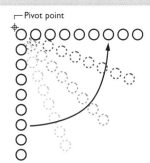
Pivot point

Create and expand a blend of circles. Rotate and copy the circles by holding down the Shift and Option keys. Place the pivot point before rotating.

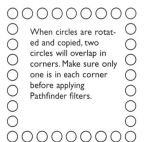

Continue to copy and rotate circles to create a square. Ungroup and delete any overlapping corner circles.

When circles are rotated and copied, two circles will overlap in corners. Make sure only one is in each corner before applying Pathfinder filters.

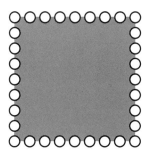

Group the circles and convert into a compound path. Then place a square behind the circles. Select all and apply the Minus Front filter.

Minus Front uses the smaller circles to crop away from the square placed behind it, producing a perforated stamplike shape.

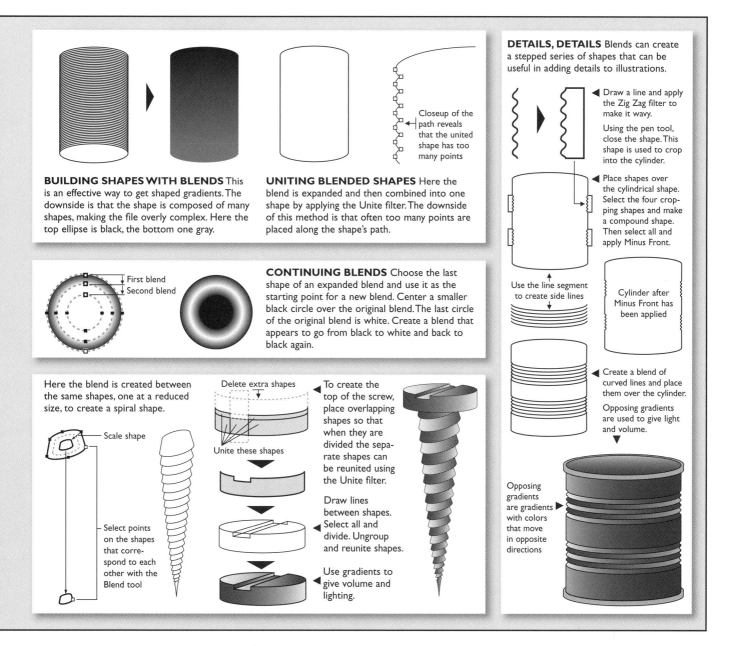

BUILDING SHAPES WITH BLENDS This is an effective way to get shaped gradients. The downside is that the shape is composed of many shapes, making the file overly complex. Here the top ellipse is black, the bottom one gray.

UNITING BLENDED SHAPES Here the blend is expanded and then combined into one shape by applying the Unite filter. The downside of this method is that often too many points are placed along the shape's path.

Closeup of the path reveals that the united shape has too many points

DETAILS, DETAILS Blends can create a stepped series of shapes that can be useful in adding details to illustrations.

Draw a line and apply the Zig Zag filter to make it wavy.

Using the pen tool, close the shape. This shape is used to crop into the cylinder.

Place shapes over the cylindrical shape. Select the four cropping shapes and make a compound shape. Then select all and apply Minus Front.

Use the line segment to create side lines

Cylinder after Minus Front has been applied

First blend
Second blend

CONTINUING BLENDS Choose the last shape of an expanded blend and use it as the starting point for a new blend. Center a smaller black circle over the original blend. The last circle of the original blend is white. Create a blend that appears to go from black to white and back to black again.

Create a blend of curved lines and place them over the cylinder.

Opposing gradients are used to give light and volume.

Here the blend is created between the same shapes, one at a reduced size, to create a spiral shape.

Scale shape

Select points on the shapes that correspond to each other with the Blend tool

Delete extra shapes

Unite these shapes

To create the top of the screw, place overlapping shapes so that when they are divided the separate shapes can be reunited using the Unite filter.

Draw lines between shapes. Select all and divide. Ungroup and reunite shapes.

Use gradients to give volume and lighting.

Opposing gradients are gradients with colors that move in opposite directions cylinder as its basic shape a much easier task. The key to this technique is the use of master shapes and constraining the proportions of the shapes when resizing. Like some of the other samples included in this chapter, it combines primary shapes to build more complex ones. In this case two ellipses and a rectangle are used to create the master cylinder shape that forms the basis for all of the forms.

The cylinder is created by combining an ellipse and a rectangle that are the same width. You can ensure that both shapes have identical widths by clicking with each tool in the document and specifying an exact width. The shape of the ellipse is integral to the illustration because it determines how the cylinder sits on a surface. (Save a copy of the ellipse as a master shape, or write down the specific dimensions of the ellipse when you create it originally.) Once the ellipse and rectangle are created, copy the ellipse and place two ellipses at the top and bottom edges of the rectangle so that they begin to form a cylindrical shape. Select all three shapes and use Align to line them up horizontally. Select the three shapes and combine by applying the Pathfinder Unite filter.

Creating Banners

Banners are commonly used in editorial and package design. Here are a few ways to style banner treatments.

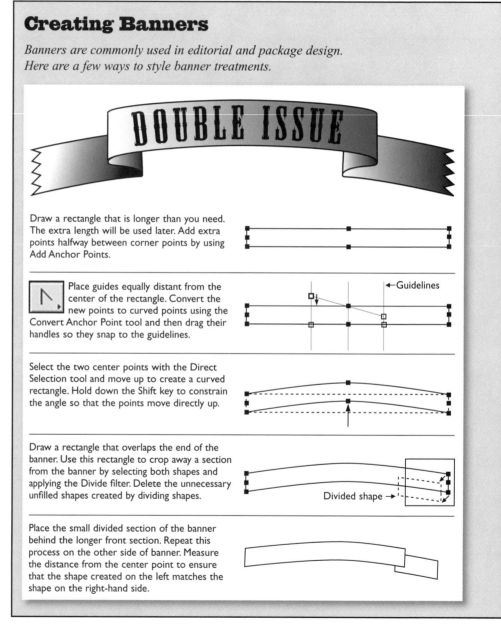

Draw a rectangle that is longer than you need. The extra length will be used later. Add extra points halfway between corner points by using Add Anchor Points.

Place guides equally distant from the center of the rectangle. Convert the new points to curved points using the Convert Anchor Point tool and then drag their handles so they snap to the guidelines.

Select the two center points with the Direct Selection tool and move up to create a curved rectangle. Hold down the Shift key to constrain the angle so that the points move directly up.

Draw a rectangle that overlaps the end of the banner. Use this rectangle to crop away a section from the banner by selecting both shapes and applying the Divide filter. Delete the unnecessary unfilled shapes created by dividing shapes.

Place the small divided section of the banner behind the longer front section. Repeat this process on the other side of banner. Measure the distance from the center point to ensure that the shape created on the left matches the shape on the right-hand side.

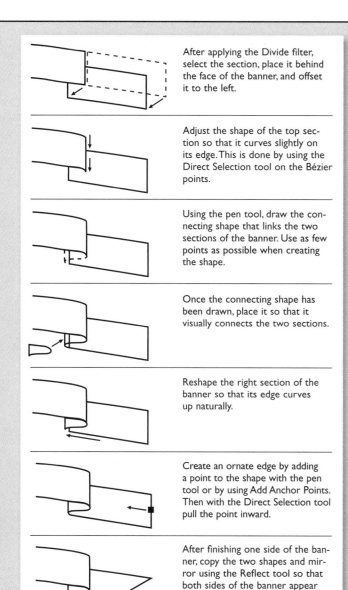

After applying the Divide filter, select the section, place it behind the face of the banner, and offset it to the left.

Adjust the shape of the top section so that it curves slightly on its edge. This is done by using the Direct Selection tool on the Bézier points.

Using the pen tool, draw the connecting shape that links the two sections of the banner. Use as few points as possible when creating the shape.

Once the connecting shape has been drawn, place it so that it visually connects the two sections.

Reshape the right section of the banner so that its edge curves up naturally.

Create an ornate edge by adding a point to the shape with the pen tool or by using Add Anchor Points. Then with the Direct Selection tool pull the point inward.

After finishing one side of the banner, copy the two shapes and mirror using the Reflect tool so that both sides of the banner appear symmetrical.

Corner Banners

Banners are commonly designed to fit over page and label corners. This banner design is composed of straight lines.

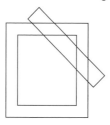

Delete extra shapes

Begin by drawing three overlapping shapes: two rectangles centered over each other and a longer rotated rectangle.

Select all the shapes and apply the Divide filter. Then ungroup shapes and delete any unnecessary shapes created in the Divide process.

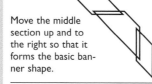

Move the middle section up and to the right so that it forms the basic banner shape.

Using the pen tool, draw small shapes and position so that they connect the sections of the banner.

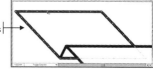

Delete any extra points

Give the edges an ornate quality by using Add Anchor Points. This evenly spaces the points but also adds more points than are needed. Then select specific points with the Direct Selection tool and move them inward to create a zig zag edge.

Develop the design by adding new shapes. Here rotated ellipses are positioned above the shape and then united.

Offset Path is used to create smaller versions of shapes so that they can be fitted within a specific shape.

Once the master cylinder shape is created, it can be used to create any number of objects that share a cylindrical shape. As long as you don't distort the cylinder shape when resizing it or extending its height, any object that uses this shape as a foundation element will appear to sit in perfect perspective and on the same plane.

The master cylindrical shape can also be resized and reshaped to form other parts of an elaborate shape. For instance, the same cylinder that is used to create a jar can be manipulated to create a lid, base, or label. The shape can also be used as a base form for fluted cylinder shapes in which the top of the cylinder is wider than the bottom, like a drinking glass. This is done by scaling specific points of the master shape while constraining proportions.

Interlaced Shapes

Creating shapes that appear to be linked and have sections that interweave uses a technique in which overlapping shapes are divided and then reunited. This technique gives the shape a contiguous appearance in which some of its parts appear to be in the front while other sections appear in the background. An example of an interlaced shape is

Creating Rounded Edges with Blends

Besides being used for a stepped series of shapes, blends can also be used to give object edges a rounded feel.

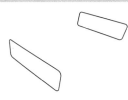

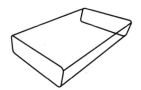

Create two rectangles with rounded corners. Place in relative position and scale down the one in the background. Then rotate the rectangles into the distance using the KPT 3D Transform filter.

Draw lines between the two shapes. View objects in Outline mode so the endpoints of the lines are positioned accurately. Select the shapes and apply the Divide filter. Ungroup and reunite divided shapes to get individual sections of the object.

Create the highlight shape using a thin rounded rectangle. A line segment with rounded corners could also be used. If using lines, convert them to shapes using Outline Stroke. Select both the highlight shapes and then apply Unite.

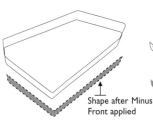

Shape after Minus Front applied

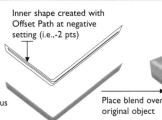

Inner shape created with Offset Path at negative setting (i.e.,-2 pts)

Place blend over original object

To give the bottom edge of the shape a soft shadow, place overlapping copies of the overall shape and apply the Minus Front filter.

Apply Offset Path to the shape to create an inner shape. Create a blend between the two. The outer shape matches object color; the inner shape has darker tone.

Expand the blend and place it along the bottom of the object to get a soft, dark shadow along the bottom of the object.

the Star of David, in which two triangles make up an interwoven six-pointed star.

Since Illustrator is not a true three-dimensional program, there is no way to actually create shapes that have interlacing parts. This means you must create the illusion of interlacing. The key to this technique is the Pathfinder Divide filter, which divides overlapping areas into separate shapes. This allows for

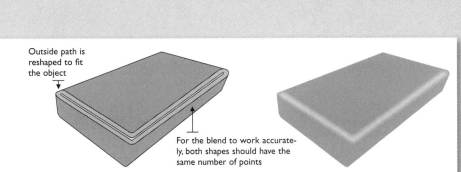

Outside path is reshaped to fit the object

For the blend to work accurately, both shapes should have the same number of points

Apply Offset Path to the shape to create a larger path. Reshape the corners of the outside path to fit the object's shape. Fill the inner shape with white and the outer shape with the same color as the object. Create a blend between the two shapes.

Once the blend is applied, a highlight appears to define the edge of the object. This happens because the color of the outside shape matches the background object.

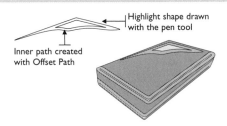

Highlight shape drawn with the pen tool

Inner path created with Offset Path

Use the same technique to create highlighted shapes on top of the object. Here a hand-drawn shape that follows the contour of the shape is created with the pen tool. The inner path is created with Offset Path.

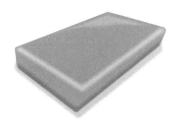

The final object has natural rounded edges with highlights. The shadow has been added by copying the object's shape and filling it with a light gray tone. It is then rasterized and blurred to give it a soft edge.

you are going to use the outside stroke of the triangle to create the form, the strokes must be converted to shapes using Outline Path. Once the Pathfinder Divide filter is applied you can select and reunite the pieces so that they appear to fall in front or behind each other accordingly.

Nuts & Bolts

Creating technical objects like gears and bolts can be relatively simple or complex depending upon how much detail and what kind of perspective you want to give the object. Building a simple hexagonal nut begins by clicking with the Polygon tool in the document and specifying the appropriate number of sides. The hole in the middle of the nut is created by centering a circle over the hexagon and then making a compound path of the two shapes or by applying the Minus Front filter. Once the master shape is created, copy it and place on the side for later use.

To give the nut a sense of volume, you need to make it three-dimensional. This can be done by placing a copy of the master shape behind the original shape so that it is offset. Remember that as objects fall further into the distance, they appear smaller. With this in mind,

separated shapes to be reunited and repositioned in front or back to give the appearance of interlacing.

The Star of David is created by placing two triangles, one of which has been rotated, over each

other. The easiest way to create the triangle is to select the polygon tool and click within the document to specify the number of sides of shape. Use Align to center the triangles horizontally. Because

The Final Touch: Backgrounds & Shadows

Once you've built and styled your objects, create a setting to place them in to give your illustration a finished feel.

Creating Drop Shadows

Soft drop shadows help give objects the appearance of sitting on a surface. Raster images or blends can be used to create a drop shadow.

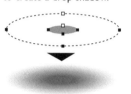

Create a blend between the two ovals. The inner oval is gray and the outer oval is white.

Place the shadow behind the object. Make sure that the blend doesn't contain too many steps.

To make a drop shadow using a rasterized image, make a copy of the object (page shape) and fill it with gray. Draw a box with no stroke or fill around the shape.

Select the page shape and box and select Rasterize Image from the Object pull-down menu. The empty box serves as a buffer space so that the blurred edge isn't cropped.

Apply a Gaussian Blur to the rasterized drop shadow to give the image soft edges. Then place the original image in front of the rasterized drop shadow,

Skewing Shadows

Shadows that fall naturally into the distance give an illustration a sense of real space. Skew the shadow by applying the Shear tool. You can also skew an object with the Free Transform tool by selecting the side points of its bounding box and pressing down the ⌘ key.

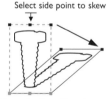

Select side point to skew

Here the Free Transform tool is used to skew the shape into the distance.

Gradient applied to shape

Last color in the gradient matches background

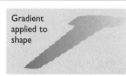

Wood grain is made by applying the Hatch Effects filter to a square and then rotating the square using KPT 3D Transform.

Here the shadow gradient fades to the background color. Select the rotated background and the shadow and divide. Adjust the colors of the separate shapes so that the wood grain is darker in the shadow area.

---

the hexagon in back should be scaled down. To create the sides of the nut, draw lines between the two shapes and then apply the Pathfinder Divide filter. This technique is basically the same as used for manually extruding type.

Dividing Accurately

You can save yourself a lot of time if you make sure to perfectly position the lines that you are using to divide the shapes accurately over the shapes. If the line's endpoints are not precisely placed over an object's

corner points, it will not divide properly. There are a few methods that you can use to more accurately place your points. One way is to zoom in on the area in which you are positioning points and to view the illustration in Preview mode, which

The vertical shadow makes the object appear to be sitting on a highly reflective surface

Here the same shadow is skewed and lengthened using the Free Transform tool.

The shadow shape is used to crop a linear blend. Expand the blend before cropping.

Shadow lines are converted to shapes with Outline Stroke and then filled with a gradient.

Using Transparency

Illustrator now includes transparency settings, which allow an object placed in front of another to be transparent. This feature works in generally the same way as Photoshop's Transparency settings.

◄ Place the shadow shape over the background and change the opacity setting on the Transparency palette.

Blending modes determine the transparency effect and how the underlying image is affected.

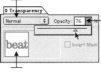

The Opacity setting controls the transparency of the selected object.

The preview window shows a thumbnail preview of the effect.

Merging Shadows & Surface

Creating shadows that merge naturally with a surface's texture gives the illustration a finished, complete feel.

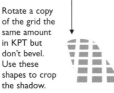

◄ Make squares a Compound Path before cropping.

Rotate a copy of the grid the same amount in KPT but don't bevel. Use these shapes to crop the shadow.

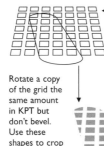

Create a grid of squares and apply KPT 3D Transform to rotate and bevel the squares, giving the appearance of tiles.

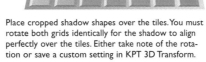

Place cropped shadow shapes over the tiles. You must rotate both grids identically for the shadow to align perfectly over the tiles. Either take note of the rotation or save a custom setting in KPT 3D Transform.

Transparency is applied to a rasterized and blurred shadow. The background texture is created using the Hatch Effects and then rotated into the distance using KPT 3D Transform.

will display the objects in wireframe mode. This makes it much easier to see the point positioning. Another method you can try is to use the Snap to Point option, which will snap the point you are placing to an object's points.

Applying Tonality & Surface

Once you've got the basic shapes created, you can then begin to think about how you want to treat the shapes tonally to give a sense of surface and light. The simplest method is to apply different shades

to each shape. Another way is to apply a gradient to all of the shapes and then use the Gradient tool to control the direction of each shape's gradients. You could also try cropping in linear patterns to get a technical illustration feel.

Gears & Two-Point Perspective

Generally as shapes become more complex, so does the process of making them appear three-dimensional. While creating the sides of a nut was relatively easy, doing the same for a shape like a gear is more involved. This is in part due to the shape's more detailed outline, which makes using the Divide and Unite technique a much lengthier procedure. The nature of the shape, which includes rounded concave shapes, also plays a role in how the shapes are built. As with most design problems, there are a few ways to make the shape appear three-dimensional. One traditional method that can be applied to computer illustration is using a vanishing point to determine perspective.

The first step is to create the actual gear shape. Different designers prefer different ways to do this. Some prefer repeatedly applying Add Anchor Points to a circle to add equally placed points along the circle's path, then manually centering smaller circles over each of the points along the circle. Once the smaller circles are placed on a circular path, they can be used to crop into the larger circle to create the teeth of the gear.

Another possible method takes

Using Custom Brushes

Customized brushes allow original artwork to be applied to a path or shape. There are numerous ways to take advantage of this unique feature.

Brush Basics

There are four types of custom brush: Calligraphic, Scatter, Art, and Pattern. Calligraphic brushes produce smooth, varying stroke widths. The Scatter brush places one or more objects along a path. The Art brush applies artwork to a path or shape. Pattern brushes allow different objects or tiles to be placed on a shape's corners or sides.

Rather than using Illustrator's sample brushes, create your own original custom brushes. Sample brushes are intended for demonstration.

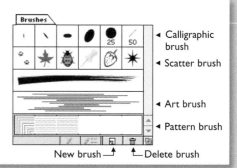

◄ Calligraphic brush
◄ Scatter brush
◄ Art brush
◄ Pattern brush

New brush ⬑   ⬐ Delete brush

Creating Art Brushes

Art brushes allow you to apply original artwork to a line or shape. To build an Art brush, create a piece of artwork to apply to a shape. Then either select New from the Brush menu or drag the artwork into the Brush palette.

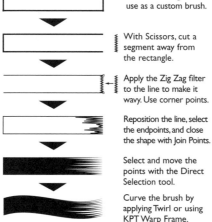

Draw a rectangle to use as a custom brush.

With Scissors, cut a segment away from the rectangle.

Apply the Zig Zag filter to the line to make it wavy. Use corner points.

Reposition the line, select the endpoints, and close the shape with Join Points.

Select and move the points with the Direct Selection tool.

Curve the brush by applying Twirl or using KPT Warp Frame.

Once the artwork is created, drag it into the Brush palette. The New brush dialogue box will appear. Select Art brush and the brush will appear in the Brush palette. To apply the brush, select a line or shape and then choose the brush from the Brush palette.

Art brush applied to circle

As long as the brush remains applied to a shape, its objects can't be manipulated until it is converted back into a shape by selecting Expand from the Object pull-down menu.

Art brush applied to type. Convert the type to outlines before applying the brush.

Building Pattern Brushes

The Pattern brush differs from other brushes in that it assigns different tiles or objects to parts of a shape. Objects can be specifically applied to corners or sides.

Begin by creating side and corner pattern tiles. Then drag the objects into the Swatch palette. Objects must be swatches before they can be used as a Pattern brush.

Select New Pattern Brush.

In Pattern brush menu choose pattern tiles from the list below for sides and corners. The original objects will appear in the list only if they are dragged into the Swatch palette first.

Pattern Brush positions control what part of the shape the object is applied to.

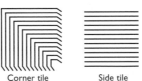

After selecting a position at top, choose an object (swatch) from list.

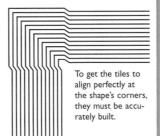

Corner tile   Side tile

To get the tiles to align perfectly at the shape's corners, they must be accurately built.

Type as Brush

Convert the type to outlines before making it an Art brush.

Art brush applied to small circle

◀ Create a blend of lines and expand the blend. Then vary the lengths of the lines by using the Direct Selection tool.

◀ Art brush is made by creating a blend of rounded rectangles and then expanding the blend into separate shapes.

The Art brush is applied to a curved path to create a segmented line. Change the brush size by adjusting the proportion settings. Click on the brush in the Brush palette to access these settings.

Art brush applied to spiral

Art brush applied to circle

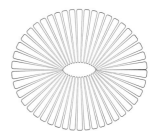

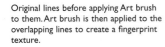

Original lines before applying Art brush to them. Art brush is then applied to the overlapping lines to create a fingerprint texture.

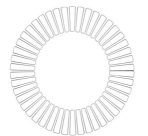

Art brush applied to circle

Art brush applied to ellipse shape

a more mathematical approach to the problem. It solves the problem of placing small circles equidistant along a circular path by rotating a smaller circle by 18 degrees. This process is repeated twenty times, completing a full circle. Each rotation of the smaller circle shares a common central pivot point.

Yet another technique involves placing typographic bullets along a circular type path and then converting the bullets to outlines. The way in which this technique makes use of type on a path as well as thinking of typographic symbols in terms of shapes is an interesting and unique way to solve the problem. This technique also allows any number of circles to be placed along the path. All that has to be done to create more circles is type them in. The spacing and sizing of the circular bullets can be easily changed by adjusting the tracking and type size settings in the character menu.

Despite the differences in approaches to placing smaller circles along a circular path, all of the approaches involve placing a larger circle behind the smaller ones and applying the Pathfinder Minus Front filter to create a gear shape.

Just as there are numerous ways to build the gear's outline,

Applying KPT Filters to Custom Brushes

Learning how to combine the wide range of tools available in Illustrator takes time. Here's an example of using custom brushes with KPT Vector Effects.

Getting the stitching to wrap naturally around a baseball, poses a challenge. Here the stitching is created and saved as a custom Art brush and then wrapped around the baseball by applying KPT Vector Distort.

1 The stitching is created by drawing one complete stitch. Then select all of the object's elements and group before creating a blend.

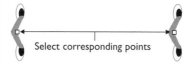

Select corresponding points

2 Copy and paste the stitch. Create a blend to get an evenly spaced series of stitches. Blends can be created between complex objects as long as they are grouped first.

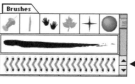

Brushes

3 Expand the blend of stitches and place a line behind the stitches.

4 Select and drag the stitching into the Brush palette. Select New Art Brush.

5 The Options menu sets brush controls like sizing and brush direction. Art brushes can't be made from objects that contain a gradient, gradient mesh, or mask.

6 A preview of the brush appears in the Brush palette and can now be applied to a shape.

there are also a few ways to give the shape three-dimensionality. Two of these approaches are covered here. One involves creating a vanishing point and then drawing lines from the vanishing point to the points along the edge of

the gear. The second method is simpler and doesn't involve creating a vanishing point and perspective lines.

Whatever method you end up using, you should be familiar with at least one way to set up true per-

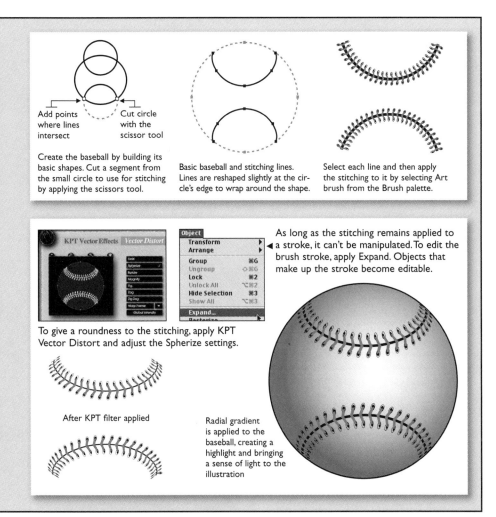

Add points where lines intersect

Cut circle with the scissor tool

Create the baseball by building its basic shapes. Cut a segment from the small circle to use for stitching by applying the scissors tool.

Basic baseball and stitching lines. Lines are reshaped slightly at the circle's edge to wrap around the shape.

Select each line and then apply the stitching to it by selecting Art brush from the Brush palette.

To give a roundness to the stitching, apply KPT Vector Distort and adjust the Spherize settings.

As long as the stitching remains applied to a stroke, it can't be manipulated. To edit the brush stroke, apply Expand. Objects that make up the stroke become editable.

After KPT filter applied

Radial gradient is applied to the baseball, creating a highlight and bringing a sense of light to the illustration

two ways to create 3D type. One method involved manually creating the pieces by using the pen tool in conjunction with the Divide and Unite filters. The second involved extruding type by using the KPT 3D Transform Filter.

While applying the KPT filter is certainly quicker, it is important to understand how to create such effects manually. Keep in mind that the KPT filters tend to create overly complex files that could cause output problems. Three-dimensional shapes produced by KPT often have to be simplified because of this. Sometimes it takes more time to simplify these shapes than to create the shape with more traditional methods.

Chain Links and Coils
Similar to objects that have interlacing sections, chain links and coils also appear to have sections that fall in front and behind other shapes. Despite this similarity in appearance, creating coils and chain links involves a much different approach. This unique method requires placing identical unfilled shapes with different stroke widths directly above one another using the Paste in Front feature.

Creating chain links that appear to be interlaced essentially

spective. For those designers who are really interested in technical illustration, Illustrator offers two- and three-dimensional templates that have built-in perspective grids. You might also explore building your own custom per-

spective templates by converting lines to guides.

KPT Filters and 3D Shapes
KPT filters are perhaps the easiest way to create three-dimensional shapes. In Chapter 3 we looked at

Designing Charts & Graphs

Getting technical data to be readable and attractive is a challenge. Here's a look at the basic chart types, when to use them, and how to approach designing them.

GRAPHING TOOLS Illustrator can be used to create a wide range of chart and graph types, but its design controls are limited. It is best to use it to simply plot the data and and get a basic chart. Then you can dress up the chart by using more standard illustration tools.

CHART TYPES While there are many types of charts, the most commonly used are line charts, bar charts, and pie charts. The technical data will determine which chart type you should use.

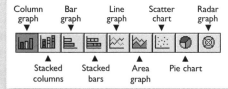

Column graph · Bar graph · Line graph · Scatter chart · Radar graph

Stacked columns · Stacked bars · Area graph · Pie chart

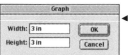

Click in the document with the Graph tool to specify the chart size.

PIE CHARTS Because pie charts are used to show comparative percentages of a whole, the data that is entered into the spreadsheet must combine to equal 100 percent.

Enter numerical data here and then hit Enter so that the data appears in the table.

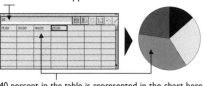

40 percent in the table is represented in the chart here.

Restyled pie chart · Generic bar chart

BAR CHARTS These are used to show comparative values within a scale. The scale along the bottom of the chart is based on the numerical data.

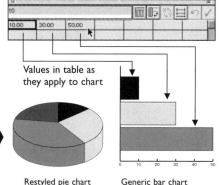

Values in table as they apply to chart

BAR CHARTS Use the Graph tool to plot the chart. This ensures that the bars accurately reflect the data. Then exit the Graph menu and style the graph to give it a less generic appearance.

Keep type small and easy to read · Broken bar is used when one bar is much longer than others

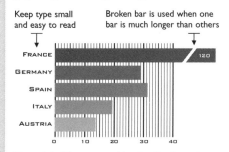

The original bars created by the Graph tool remain the same, but the type and scale lines have been redesigned.

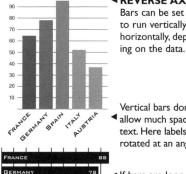

◄ REVERSE AXIS Bars can be set to run vertically or horizontally, depending on the data.

◄ Vertical bars don't allow much space for text. Here labels are rotated at an angle.

◄ If bars are long enough, the text and values can be placed within the bar to save space

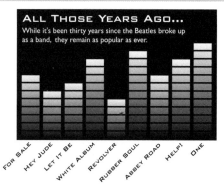

FUN CHARTS Depending on the nature of the chart's information, you may try creating more illustrative charts that convey the information while being visually attractive.

LINE CHARTS are also easy to adapt for conveying casual information. If the information that is being plotted is simple and not highly specific, you may choose to build the chart from scratch without using the Graph tools to create the original chart.

ROCKY MOUNTAIN HIGH

With new surveying procedures in place, the height of the tallest peaks in the Rocky Mountain range are being reassessed.

14,250
14,000
13,750
13,500

PIZZA HUT — DOMINO'S

FRANK'S — TONY'S

PIE CHARTS are commonly adapted to convey information in a fun way. There are so many shapes that are based on an ellipse, making it easy to come up with objects that are related in some manner to the data being shown.

Use ellipse to build column

To create column pedestals, create a series of circles centered within squares. Use Align to accurately center pairs of shapes and to distribute the space between them evenly. Then apply KPT 3D Transform to rotate the pairs of shapes back into space.

A **B** **C**

140
120
100
80
60
40
20

GREECE ROME EGYPT PERSIA

A The rounded base is created using two offset ellipses. For the inner ellipse at the top, apply Offset Path to the original ellipse.
B A series of lines with rounded ends are converted to shapes using Outline Path so that a gradient can be applied to the shape.
C The inner ellipse at top is manually reshaped.

involves dividing the chain link in half and then positioning these sections in front or behind one another to give the appearance of interlacing shapes.

Like chain links, coils are built using a similar method of placing unfilled shapes that have varying stroke widths directly above each other. Coils require the original oval to be reshaped. Once the master coil shape is created, you can create interesting variations of the coil that result in Slinky-like shapes and telephone cables.

Round Edges & Soft Highlights
Another approach to creating 3D shapes that involves less manual drawing is to use blends. Blends can be used to create original shapes or for giving shapes rounded edges and natural highlights. Like the KPT filters, blends are also subject to creating overly complex shapes, which often have to be simplified.

Blends can be used to create cubes, spheres, and cylinders. The Blend tool produces a series of repeating shapes that give the illusion of being connected. To reduce this group of shapes to one overall shape, the blend must first be expanded and then united to create one shape. The one problem with this approach is that the shape's path will often have more points than is necessary. Like the KPT filters, this method may initially seem quicker, but it can end up taking as much time as it would to create manually.

While using blends to create shapes yields varying results, blends can be used to give hard-edged shapes softly rounded, highlighted edges. Blends are an effective way to give shapes a sense of volume and light. While linear gradients are ideally suited to render the flat surfaces found in hard-edged geometric forms, and radial gradients are appropriate for giving perfect spheres tonality, both are limited in their ability to give more amorphous shapes form. Because of the amount of control and the subtlety they offer, blends are much better suited to the task of creating complex highlights that give the object detail.

Keep It Simple

While using blends gives the sense that a complex gradient, or air-brushed technique, has been applied to one large shape, in actuality the way the Blend tool achieves this soft shift of color is through the repetition of shapes. The number of steps used in the blend affects the size and complexity of the file, sometimes needlessly making the file larger than it has to be. Make sure to always check the number of steps a blend uses by double-clicking on the Blend tool. Try to keep the number of steps used as low as possible without being able to see the actual stepped pattern that is creating the appearance of the gradient.

The Gradient Mesh tool offers another approach to giving form and texture to rounded and uneven surfaces. While this is not the easiest tool to use, it does provide the ability to apply and control asymmetrical gradients to single objects. This tool can be used to achieve effects similar to that of the blend without creating overly complex files.

Using Blends to Add Detail

Besides being used to create objects or give them a sense of volume, blends can also be used to add detail to shapes. Blends can be used to create arrays of equally spaced shapes that can then be used to cut away from larger shapes. An example of this is shown in the "Using Blends" graphic, in which a series of blended shapes is used to create a series of indentations along the outline of a can. Remember that before using any blend with a Pathfinder filter, the blend must first be expanded and its separate shapes must be converted into a compound path.

Creating Realistic Shadows

If an object has the appearance that light is falling upon it from a consistent direction, then it will also need a shadow to give it a sense of sitting on a plane. We sometimes get so involved in rendering an object accurately that we overlook the background space it is sitting within. Creating a sense of background and shadow gives an illustration a finished feel.

There are a few ways to create shadows, and they can be designed so that they are appear flat or as though they are receding into the distance. One method involves creating a rasterized image of the object's outline and then applying a Gaussian Blur to give a soft edge to the shadow. The shadow can be skewed to give it the appearance of receding into the distance.

Besides positioning a shadow behind an object and receding, shadows can also be placed so that they fall directly below the object and appear to reflect the shape. This will give the sense that the object is sitting on a highly reflective surface.

Creating Graphics for Type

Banners are one common graphic element that most designers will use in their designs. Banners have a long history in design and are commonly used to draw attention to a separate piece of information. Banners are usually decorative graphic flags in which type is placed. They can be elaborately rendered with complex waves or simple and flat.

Custom Brushes

Another method to explore is creating custom art brushes, which allow you to apply an original piece of art to a path or object. The Brush menu comes with several default brushes already created. These brushes are intended to demonstrate how they may be used, not to be used as original art. The more you experiment with this tool, the more uses you'll find for it.

One effective way to build a custom brush is to use a blend that has a repeating pattern of shapes. Using blends for brushes produces a wide range of results, depending upon whether they are applied to a line, shape, or type.

Creating Graphs and Charts

Another design task that most designers are faced with is designing charts and graphs. The nature of the tabular or numerical information contained in these informational graphics will greatly determine how the design should be approached. Some charts and graphs involve highly technical data that needs to be presented clearly so that it can be analyzed by the reader easily. There are other types of charts that serve more as visual elements, providing information of a lighter nature. Creating successful, easy-to-read charts and graphs involves having a basic understanding of the technical information being shown. This applies whether you are designing a large, detailed infographic or a small, illustrative pie chart. There is a wide range of graph and chart types, and you need to have a basic understanding of when each of these chart types is appropriate. These chart types include the commonly used pie, bar, and line charts as well as more technical forms such as bubble and scatter charts.

While Illustrator offers basic graphing and chart tools, they are usually best used to plot the basic information. Because these tools produce accurate but generic-looking charts, the best approach is to use the software to plot the points and then fine-tune the look of the chart later.

In some cases, charts may be created from scratch without using the graphing tools. This usually occurs when the chart doesn't include heavy amounts of specific information. This type of casual chart is commonly found in *USA Today* and their purpose is usually more visual than informative.

If you look back over the two chapters in this book that address using Illustrator to design type and technically illustrate, you will see that there are certain tools that are consistently used in conjunction with each other. Despite the countless tools that Illustrator offers, you can see how often certain tools and techniques are called upon. The pen and selection tools, Pathfinder filters, blends, and compound paths are consistently used for numerous tasks. Once you understand how to use these tools in conjunction with each other, you're on your way. Before you know it, you will be developing new ways to use and combine these same tools to produce your own custom look.

Chapter Seven
Putting It All Together

The preceding chapters introduced many of the basic principles for reaching successful graphic design solutions. They included approaching and planning a design, composing pages in a consistent manner, and creating interesting typographic and photographic treatments. While being able to create designs that successfully fulfill

the purpose of a project is a prominent concern, getting that project to output properly is equally important. There is nothing more frustrating than having a well-designed project fall short of your expectations because of poor final output. While you do not want production concerns to dictate how you design a project, production issues certainly need to be given consideration, especially when the file is ready to go to print.

While some designers have the luxury of working with production departments whose primary concern is making sure that projects output correctly, many designers working on their own or in smaller graphic design firms play a much larger role in the production process. Whether you work for a large or small design company, you need to be aware of the basic production issues.

An Array of Concerns
When it comes preparing your files for final output, there are numerous things that need to be considered before sending the file out. These include font management, image formatting and linking, accurate mechanicals, path complexities, and embedded images.

Fonts
Any fonts used within a design need to be submitted to the printer. Fonts are a tricky and confusing business. Most fonts are composed of a screen font file and a printer font file. The screen font allows the font to be displayed on screen, while the printer font enables the font to print accurately. This is why sometimes you may find that a font displays properly on-screen but prints inaccurately. Both screen and printer

fonts need to be submitted to the printer. To check which fonts are being used within a QuarkXpress document, you can use the Usage utility. This will list all the fonts that are currently being used within the layout. You may notice that Usage sometimes lists a font that you are sure is not being used within your design. The reason for this is most often that somewhere in your document a space or paragraph return is styled with that font. This usually does not cause any output problems.

Unless you are using a preflight program designed to collect fonts and images for output, you will need to collect the fonts manually. The best way to do this is to write down the fonts that are listed in the Usage utility and collect these fonts from the Fonts folder. Since fonts can be confusing, a good practice is to simply collect any font file that has the same name as the fonts you're using. This means if you are using a Garamond face in your layout, collect all the fonts in the folder that have Garamond in their names. It's better to submit too many fonts to your printer than be missing one.

Quark Attributes
If you have styled any of your type using the bold or italic attrib-

The Final Touch: Preparing Your Files for Final Output

Before finally outputting a design project, it needs to be prepared so that it will print properly.
By following this checklist, you should be able to output your files without any surprises.

 IMAGE LINKS All images must be linked to the Quark document. To check the status of the images, use the Usage utility. The status of all the images should be listed as OK. If an image's status is Missing or Modified, it needs to be updated.

 IMAGE RESOLUTION All images must be set at the proper resolution. Four-color printing typically requires a resolution of 266 or 300 dpi, depending on the line screen used. Black-and-white projects may require lower resolutions. To figure out the required resolution, double the line screen frequency.

 COLOR MODEL All print images should be converted to either CMYK or grayscale. Images that are formatted as RGB color will not print properly on high-end image setters.

 CHECK IMAGE INFO Selecting More Info from the Usage dialogue box will provide specific information about the selected image's color model, resolution, file size, and format. This is easier than opening and checking each image in Photoshop.

 IMAGE SCALING All images should optimally be sized at 100 percent in the Quark document. Check the image sizing settings on the Measurement palette. Generally you can increase or reduce an image's size by 15 percent either way in the Quark document and still get quality results.

 COLLECT FOR OUTPUT This allows you to set a destination for all of the images being used within a design. It also places a copy of the document file in the destination folder. Collect for Output does not collect fonts.

 COLLECT FONTS All fonts that are used within a design need to be collected and provided to the printer. To get a listing of the fonts used in a document, use the Usage utility. Select all of the required fonts and copy them to a disk with the images and the document file. Make sure to select both the typeface's printer and screen fonts.

 IMAGE ROTATION Final images should not be rotated in QuarkXpress. Rotate the images in Photoshop and then update them. This will speed up the file's output time and make the document less complex.

 UNUSED COLORS AND STYLE SHEETS Delete these from the QuarkXpress document before final output. Any RGB or Pantone colors being used should be converted to CMYK values if the file is being printed in four-color.

 AVOID EMBEDDED GRAPHICS Illustrator files that have image files placed within them make the document more complex and are sometimes subject to output errors.

 CLIPPING PATHS Paths with too many points are subject to output problems. Paths should be simplified so that they do not include any extraneous points.

 FINAL SUBMISSION Include the document file and all associated images and fonts. A good practice is to provide the printer with a printout of how the final design should look. If the project's final format is three-dimensional, like a brochure, provide the printer with a 3D prototype.

---

utes found in Quark's Measurement palette, these fonts will not print as you expect them to. High-end image setters do not recognize these attributes, and the font will print as if the attribute was never applied. Go through your document and make sure that these attributes are not being used before sending the file out. If they have been used, you will need to restyle your text so that it uses an italic or bold font instead.

Prepping Images
Getting your images ready for final output is much more complex than collecting and checking your fonts. Like type, the images used within your design must also be collected and submitted to the printer. Images must also be linked to the Quark document, and their status can be checked in the Usage utility. Besides being linked, the images need to be formatted and sized properly in order to print quickly and accurately.

Other Things to Consider
While type and images are the primary concerns when sending out a file for final output, there are an array of other things that could

cause potential output problems.

• **Clipping Paths.** If your design includes silhouetted images created using clipping paths, you will need to check to make sure that these paths do not contain too many points. The simpler the paths are, the more likely they are to output properly.

• **Embedded Images.** Designs that include Illustrator files that have raster images placed within them can also cause output problems. Images that are placed within Illustrator files are referred to as embedded images. While embedded images do not always cause printing problems, it's best to try to avoid them. One way to work around this potential problem is to try to re-create the illustration without embedding the image into the Illustrator file. While this is not always possible, you should be aware of the problems they can pose and notify your printer that you are using them when you submit the files.

The File Prints Locally
Just because a design prints properly when its sent to a local low-end printer, this is not a guarantee that it will output accurately on a high-end printing device. High-end printers are outputting at a much higher resolution and process the document's information differently.

Mechanicals
In order for a printer to properly produce your design project, the layout's mechanical must be built accurately. The mechanical represents the blueprint for your design, and the instructions that you build into it, such as bleed, trim, and fold marks, tell the printer how to produce the project.

Talk to Your Printer
The best way to ensure that your design is printed and produced the way you intended is to discuss the project at length with your printer or production artist. Building a four-color prototype for three-dimensional projects like brochures is a good way to make sure that the mechanical is working. Bring the prototype and a printout of the mechanical to the printer so they clearly understand how you expect the final design to be produced.

Collect for Output
QuarkXpress has a Collect for Output function that will collect all of the images being used within the document and copy them into a separate file folder. It will also create a copy of the document as well as a report file. This method is much easier and more accurate than collecting images manually. Unfortunately, this feature does not collect the fonts used in the design.

Preflight Packages
There are a number of useful software packages designed to prepare files for print production. Some software applications like Collect Pro will collect a document's images and its fonts. Other applications like Flight Check will check the images' file formats, resolution, and color model to ensure that the document will output properly when it goes to print. Many design firms use these programs, and if you're doing a lot of design work, they are well worth the investment.

A Word About InDesign
A few years ago Adobe introduced a page layout application, InDesign, which was intended to compete with QuarkXpress. In- Design offers many attractive features including transparency capability and refined control of hyphenation and justification settings. Because Adobe also produces Photoshop and Illustrator, InDesign is able to seemlessly integrate native files from these applications. For example, this means that a Photoshop file could be imported into a page layout with its layers intact. While there are many advantages to InDesign, it has taken a while for it to be embraced by designers. Designers were initially reluctant to abandoning QuarkXpress to learn a new program.

Only recently have large design firms seriously begun to consider shifting to InDesign and printers have recently begun to accept InDesign files for final output. While change is always slow, I believe that InDesign may eventually challenge Quark as the standard page layout program.

Color Proofing

There are many ways of proofing a design before it actually goes to final output. Proofs are high-end four-color prints that are produced by the printer before going to press. While they are generally used to judge color quality, they also provide an opportunity for last-minute adjustments. Color proofs offer varying degrees of color accuracy and range greatly in price. Different proofing systems can be selected depending on what is being proofed. Match prints, color keys, and Iris prints are some of the more common types of color proofs. All three are accurate ways to proof color output. Printers offer different types of color proofing, and it's a good idea to ask what type of color proof you will receive before your project goes to print.

Fifth Colors

Some design projects require colors that cannot be reproduced by the CMYK color model. For example,

gold or silver can only be produced by using a Pantone metallic ink. This additional color is referred to as a fifth color because it is being added to the four-color process. With five-color projects, the design is printed first in CMYK and then the fifth color is printed over the four-color design. Pantone inks are not transparent, so they must be printed on top. Adding a fifth color to a design project is expensive, and for this reason their use is usually reserved for a design's high-profile sections. Fifth colors are commonly seen used on the covers of magazines, books, and CDs.

Paper Stocks

One consideration for designers is the paper stock that the design will be printed upon. There is a wide range of paper colors, weights, and surface types to select from. For young designers, selecting paper stocks is often not an option. One way to achieve the look of being printed on a custom paper stock is to scan in the paper stock and use it as a background image.

There are a few ways to become familiar with different paper stocks. Try going to your local printer and ask to see what standard stocks they use. Most printers don't mind providing samples. Likewise, most paper companies are happy to send

out samples. Their advertisements in design-related magazines often offer free sample selections.

PDF Formats

One recent development that has made file preparation easier for designers and production personnel is the use of .PDF files. These portable document files allow another user to open a document without having the software that it was originally created in. Because .PDF files have the document's images and fonts embedded into them, they can be used to preview or output a document.

Printers have been accepting .PDF files for final output for a few years, and some actually prefer receiving them. The big advantage of this file format is that it includes the fonts and images within the file. This is in many ways easier than having to collect for output and then providing your printer with a document file and its related images and fonts. The downside of .PDF files is that should any adjustments need to be made to the design after you've submitted them to the printer, a new PDF file needs to be created.

Creating .PDF files

The native format of Adobe Acrobat is .PDF. Acrobat is actually a suite of three software applications that includes Distiller and Reader. Each of these applications is designed for a certain task. Acrobat is used to view, notate, or output the .PDF file. Reader is used to simply view the file. Distiller is designed to generate the .PDF format. Distiller is a freeware application and can be downloaded from the Web.

All .PDF files are generated by exporting a document to the .PDF format. These files can be created directly from Illustrator or Photoshop. To export a .PDF file from a Quark document, a .PDF export filter needs to be loaded. Before generating a .PDF file from any software program, Distiller must first be loaded onto the computer.

Building a Design Vocabulary

The design process is a diverse one, and it requires conceptual skills, technical expertise, discipline, and a developed sense of design. One thing that often surprises young designers is how many facets there are to design. There are numerous ways to enhance both your design skills and knowledge. There are many design-related organizations and user groups that are worth joining. These clubs will introduce you to other members of the design community. They provide a chance to meet and discuss design with other working designers. More technically oriented user groups are also common and can be useful in enhancing your technical skills.

One way to enhance your design vocabulary is to subscribe to design-related magazines. These publications can help provide a sense of current design trends as well as serve as visual reference for your projects. There is nothing more important to any artist than looking.

It is common for designers to draw inspiration from other sources. This is part of the process of defining your own style. Being exposed to a wide range of design helps shape your design sensibilities. Developing personal style begins by defining what you like.

Another benefit to subscribing to design magazines is that you can get numerous free samples through them. By taking advantage of the mailers and reader service cards found in these magazines, you can be sent font catalogs, paper samples, stock photography collections, and other various information. All these materials will add to your knowledge of design.

There are also a wealth of design-related books available that cover many different aspects of design. There are wonderful collections of award-winning designs to draw inspiration from. There are many design books that focus on particular periods and can be used as visual reference.

Software-related texts can also be helpful in fine-tuning your technical expertise. It's advisable to have reference books for any software that you use on a regular basis. There are also books that cover more advanced ways to use design software. These books are geared toward advanced users who are familiar with standard design tools and techniques.

Be a Working Designer

The only way to become a designer is through experience. This means taking on design work whenever you can. Your design skills will be further enhanced with each project you take on. It is especially helpful for young designers to go through the design process on their own from start to finish. In the beginning any type of design work will broaden your skills and knowledge, whether it's a black and white flyer or a four-color menu. Sometimes even working free of charge can be worth the experience you receive. Seeing something that you designed in print for the first time never loses its excitement. Perhaps the best part of designing is the sense of personal satisfaction and accomplishment you receive from designing something well.

Photography Credits

The author would like acknowledge the following people for their contributions to this book and for the permission to reproduce their illustrations and photographs:

Yaritsa Arenas, Shannon Beadle, Andrea T. Capalongo, Dina Castro, Sohee K. Conover, Fran Dulaski, Aghogho Emenike, Mike Falco, David Foster, Jesse Gottesman, Alex Jepes, Ryan Kasal, Diana Lobosco, Dean Markadakis, Jackie Martling, Nora McElroy, Catherine Murray, Genta Nakahara, Thomas Nicotra, Thom O'Connor, Diane Marie Portigiano, Chris Ramirez, Charles Roth, Alli Rufrano, Zach Samuel, Ji-Yeon Shin, Juwen Sin, Nancy Sirianni, Matthew Starr, Russell Starr, Atsuko Tanaka, Rachel Weiss,

Elvis Presley images used by permission, Elvis Presley Enterprises, Inc.

Photograph of Nancy Sirianni by Doug Gorenstein

Bibliography

• Dover Publications, Inc. 31 East 2nd Street, Mineola, New York 11501

• Designing with Type, James Craig Watson Guptil Publications, New York

• Shadowcaster, A Lowly Apprentice Production, Inc.
  5963 La Place Court, Suite 206, Carlsbad, California 92008 www.alap.com

Index